# Violence

This series of publications on Africa, Latin America, Southeast Asia, and Global and Comparative Studies is designed to present significant research, translation, and opinion to area specialists and to a wide community of persons interested in world affairs. The editor seeks manuscripts of quality on any subject and can usually make a decision regarding publication within three months of receipt of the original work. Production methods generally permit a work to appear within one year of acceptance. The editor works closely with authors to produce a high-quality book. The series appears in a paperback format and is distributed worldwide. For more information, contact the executive editor at Ohio University Press, 19 Circle Drive, The Ridges, Athens, Ohio 45701.

Executive editor: Gillian Berchowitz
AREA CONSULTANTS
Africa: Diane M. Ciekawy
Latin America: Brad Jokisch, Patrick Barr-Melej, and Rafael Obregon
Southeast Asia: William H. Frederick

The Ohio University Research in International Studies series is published for the Center for International Studies by Ohio University Press. The views expressed in individual volumes are those of the authors and should not be considered to represent the policies or beliefs of the Center for International Studies, Ohio University Press, or Ohio University.

# Violence

ANALYSIS, INTERVENTION,
AND PREVENTION

Sean Byrne and Jessica Senehi

Ohio University Research in International Studies
Global and Comparative Studies Series No. 13
Ohio University Press
Athens

To obtain permission to quote, reprint, or otherwise reproduce or distribute material
from Ohio University Press publications, please contact our rights and permissions
department at (740) 593-1154 or (740) 593-4536 (fax).

www.ohioswallow.com

Printed in the United States of America
The books in the Ohio University Research in International Studies Series
are printed on acid-free paper. ∞

20 19 18 17 16 15 14 13 12    5 4 3 2 1

Cover media collage courtesy istockphoto.com

Library of Congress Cataloging-in-Publication Data

Byrne, Sean, 1962–
Violence : analysis, intervention, and prevention / Sean Byrne and Jessica Senehi.
    p. cm. — (Ohio ris global series)
Includes bibliographical references and index.
ISBN 978-0-89680-285-8 (pbk.) — ISBN 978-0-89680-481-4 (electronic)
1. Violence. 2. Violence—Prevention. I. Senehi, Jessica, 1959– II. Title.
HM886.B97 2012
303.6—dc23                                          2011036032

*This book is dedicated to the memory of our grandparents Hanom and Morteza Senehi, Jane and John Alex, Mary and John Reilly, Annie and Jim Byrne, and Jessica's father David Senehi Sr., people of wisdom, peace, and integrity. We also honor Sean's uncles Bernard Reilly and Jim Byrne, and aunts Ann Clear, Kathleen Reilly and Anna-Rose McGurn; Jessica's uncles Alex, Simon, and Manoutchehr Senehi and mother Rose Senehi; and Dr. John Stapleton, Rector Emeritus, St. Paul's College, and Dean Emeritus in Education, University of Manitoba. Finally, we remember our friend, colleague, and former doctoral student Dr. Karen Jenkins. Karen Jenkins was a professor of conflict analysis and resolution at Metro Community College in South Omaha, Nebraska. On October 17, 2010, Dr. Jenkins was abducted and brutally murdered. We remember Karen Jenkins as a loving, bright, and caring person.*

# Contents

# Illustrations

# Preface and Acknowledgments

We hope that the topics treated in this book will provide guidance for students interested in the analysis and resolution of violent conflicts. The recent election of President Barack Obama and the increased popularity of Peace and Conflict Studies (PACS)—conflict analysis and resolution, conflict transformation, human rights, social justice, and peace studies—in undergraduate and graduate schools around the globe makes this an auspicious time for a book of this kind.

The book is written for students interested in the nature of violence and how to intervene to prevent it and is also targeted toward students in social science programs that emphasize the micro (interpersonal) to macro (international) dimensions of conflict and violence. Conflict analysis and resolution most often uses a local-level problem-solving approach that is inclusive of multiple narratives whereby a third-party intermediary intervenes to transform relationships in a balanced and neutral process that advocates for all parties (Sandole, Byrne, Sandole-Staroste, and Senehi 2009). Peace studies more often focus on specific issues such as disarmament, human rights, and social justice at the international level to nonviolently transform structures by advocating for and empowering the disempowered (Webel and Galtung 2007). Analyzing the multiple social, economic, cultural, historical, political, and psychological features is important if we are to address conflict situations and behavior constructively (Jeong 2008). Using the language of PACS in this book signifies that we seek to encompass and synthesize both theoretical and practice-oriented approaches.

We wish to thank Dr. Arthur V. Mauro, OC, OM, QC, KSG, who has made it possible for us to work at such a wonderful and important center as a result of his generous gifts and farsightedness. Dr. Mauro's generosity, wisdom, and vision made possible the creation of the Arthur V. Mauro Centre for Peace and Justice and the Storytelling for Peacebuilding and Renewing Community (SPARC) institute and led to the establishment of Canada's first PhD Program in Peace and Conflict Studies and a joint MA program with the University of Winnipeg within the Faculty of Graduate Studies, University of Manitoba, both housed at the Mauro Centre. Dr. Mauro is truly an outstanding person; his passion to create a more peaceful world is truly engaging and inspiring.

We want to thank Christine Retz for copyediting the manuscript and Ariann Kehler, Pauline Tennent, Gayle Roncin, Mavis Matenge, Olga Skarlato, Peter Karari, and Chuck Thiessen, research assistants in the Arthur V. Mauro Centre of Peace and Justice, for proofreading the manuscript and for assisting us in compiling the references. We also wish to thank Niall Byrne, Jennifer Ruiz-Byrne, David Senehi Jr., Alan Conlan, Dan Lenoski, Tom Boudreau, Hamdesa Tuso, Maureen Flaherty, David Creamer, Anna Snyder, Vincent O'Brien, Brian Rice, and John Perry for reading various drafts of this book. We are forever grateful to the love and dedication of our parents Michael and Patricia Byrne and David and Rose Senehi. Our nine-year-old precocious daughter, Katie Byrne, has a big heart and a beautiful smile for such a wee wane; she gives us inspiration for the future. We are grateful to our former student, Heather Tanksley, for granting us permission to use figures 3.1, 4.1, 4.2, and 5.1; to the Anti-Defamation League for the use of table 5.1; and to U.S. Department of Justice for the use of tables 6.1 and 6.2. We thank the Mauro Centre for giving us a small research grant to make this study and our book possible.

Sean Byrne and Jessica Senehi
The Cottage, VB
August 20, 2011

# 1

## The Confluence of Violence

### From Analysis to Resolution

Two young children play with a pile of toys on their porch. Kaitlynne pulls a G.I. Jane from the toys. Her young brother Andrew shouts, "No, my toy." He grabs it and pushes her away. Kaitlynne is now very interested in the toy and tries to pull it back. A fight ensues, with Kaitlynne and Andrew busy pushing each other. As the conflict escalates, Tommy, a young child from the neighborhood, wanders onto their porch wanting to play. At that point both siblings stop fighting, and Kaitlynne says meanly, "Oh, there's Tommy!" "Yeah," shouts Andrew, "Tommy!" Kaitlynne and Andrew, having forgotten the G.I. Jane doll, now ignore their conflict and run Tommy back home. Harmony is restored between the two siblings, while their young neighbor is now indoors crying (Girard 1979).

As professionals in Peace and Conflict Studies (PACS), we seek to understand the dynamics of violence and some of its major themes as well as violence intervention and prevention approaches prevalent in the PACS field. PACS training often focuses on settling nonviolent disputes through mediation, arbitration, negotiation, problem solving, etc., since these are considered more tractable. Yet there is great need for a comprehensive analysis of nonviolent approaches to violent conflicts, which are highly destructive in a more immediate sense. The primary objective of this book is to become familiar with the theories and facts concerning violence and how violence against people, animals, and the biosphere can be prevented. We also seek genuine reasons for hope, despite the destruction of our global milieu.

Violence is such a pervasive part of our world that the underlying complexities of violence are problematic (Christie, Wagner, and DuNann Winter 2001). We deplore violence but condone the use of the death penalty and war (Christie, Wagner, and DuNann Winter 2001). We read or watch the media, and every day we hear about youths dying on our streets from drive-by shootings or militia bullets, people blown up in terrorist bombings, women raped or forced into prostitution, impoverished elderly people dying of hunger, corporations dumping toxic chemicals in our waterways, and children wasting away from preventable diseases (Christie, Wagner, and DuNann Winter 2001). All of these images are destructive.

Simultaneously, signs of hope are evident in the changes taking place in our communities. Protestant Unionists and Catholic Nationalists are coexisting, albeit uneasily, in Northern Ireland; apartheid has ended in South Africa; Bono from the Irish rock band U2 launched a nonprofit organization to reduce African debt; Sven Erickson, the former English football coach, and Rabbi Michael Melchior are part of a peace-through-soccer program that in 2005 brought a mixed team of Israeli and Palestinian youths to Sweden to compete in a local tournament; and President Jimmy Carter's brainchild, Habitat for Humanity, builds homes for low-income families in our inner cities.

William Ury (2000) persuasively argues that one critical move to create positive social change is to de-legitimize violence. In 1986 during the International Year of Peace, twenty renowned scientists issued the Seville Statement on Violence, declaring that violence and aggression are not a law of nature and hence that science should not be used to justify violence and war (Fry 2006). While human beings have a capacity for aggression, they also possess an ability to prevent and resolve conflict without resorting to violence (Fry 2006; Carnegie Commission On Preventing Deadly Conflict 1997). Some scholars believe that there is a universal desire to solve basic human needs such as security, identity, and recognition (Burton 1990a, 1990b, 1997) and that individuals are fully capable of "alleviating sexism" and slavery, celebrating multiculturalism, "reclaiming neighborhoods," demanding social and economic justice for youths and the elderly alike, and "finding nonmilitaristic solutions to global problems" in order to build lasting peace (DuNann Winter and Leighton 2001, 101).

## Violence, Systems, and Structures

A plethora of questions surrounds the study of violence. What exactly is violence? How do we define it, and how can we prevent violence from occurring? What is the difference between legitimate and illegitimate violence? When does structural or cultural violence lead to direct violence, and when does it not? Or vice versa, when does physical violence worsen the other types? Why does violence seem to be spreading throughout our society—in our homes, our workplaces, our schools, the media—as well as throughout the world in places such as Afghanistan, Libya, Syria, Egypt, Somalia, Iraq, Sudan, and Colombia? What is the attraction of violence? Why do so many men and an increasing number of women participate in violence? In what ways can a hierarchical social structure generate violence? What kinds of structural conditions are needed to transform violence that stems from socioeconomic inequity and emerges in the global economy? And finally, when we discuss violence, are we discussing the same phenomenon as we move from the interpersonal level to the intergroup to the international level?

By their very nature, systems and structures involve parties with different interests, goals, power bases, and worldviews (Jeong 2009). Nazi death camps, the use of rape as a weapon of war, and the horrors of the machine gun and mustard gas during the trench warfare of World War I illustrate the fact that violence, and especially political violence (armed struggle over the allocation of goods and values in a society), can be both organized and efficient. Parties with conflicting goals and perspectives may come to blows, and fight with fists and weapons about their priorities, depending on factors present in themselves or their environment (Jeong 2008). However, identifying the sources of conflict and violence may not be a simple task when the causes are embedded in a structure (Reiss and Roth 1993). If social and political roles, rules, and expectations (norms) are structured to produce conflict and/or violence, then resolving these conflicts often requires some structural or systemic change (Senehi, Ryan, and Byrne 2010). Giving women the vote and banning slavery in the United States created the space for Senator Hillary Clinton and Senator Barack Obama to compete for the Democratic Party's nomination in the 2008 U.S. presidential election. In any intervention, it would appear that "do no harm" should be a cardinal principle (M. Anderson 2001).

This book adopts an interdisciplinary approach to analysis intervention, and prevention, or what Johan Galtung (2009) calls a transdisciplinary approach is clearly needed, that draws from the social sciences and PACS fields to review violence in many different yet interrelated environmental settings, such as home, workplace, and community, and the dimensions of social life, including interpersonal, group, community, and society to transform relationships and structures. Human agency is always "embedded in an ontological site" consisting of unique ecologies, geographies, cultures, and epistemologies (Boudreau 2009, 131). Children's cognitive growth occurs in a sociocultural context that influences the form that this growth takes since their cognitive and emotional skills also evolve from interactions with parents, peers, and teachers in their environment (Vygotsky 1978). Children acquire moral knowledge as a result of the influence of cultural experiences that shape their values and behavior through modeling and reinforcement (Bandura 1977). Children are also firmly enclosed in multiple ecological microsystems and influences such as family, school, neighborhood, and media in which they exert reciprocal interaction and influence on the environment simultaneously (Bandura 1977; Bronfenbrenner 1979; Erikson 1950).

Conflict and violence exist in society at the intrapersonal, interpersonal, group, organizational, national, and international levels (Bartos and Wehr 2002). Since the interconnected parts or levels of the system fit together and in some cases influence each other, we must be aware of the various means, methods, types, functions, and forms of violence as well as culturally sanctioned behavior. How do different forms and types of violence related to family, youth, and the workplace operate as conflict built into their structure and system, and how can we proceed to redesign aspects of the system to produce more effective and peaceful relations? Turpin and Kurtz (1997) make the point that there is a dialectic among different forms of violence that occurs at the interpersonal, collective, and global levels. This book explores the causes of violence and intervention from multiple levels and also examines a range of prevention and intervention approaches.

## The PACS Paradigm

Some scholars have argued for the need to apply a PACS paradigm so that sources of the dominant structure that generate conflict and violence within a war culture (usually patriarchal; see Cheldelin, Druckman, and Fast 2003; Webel and Galtung 2007) can be identified.

This book uses a PACS lens to examine and analyze violence in different dimensions of society and at various levels. Violence may simply be seen as a problem that needs to be eradicated. While that ultimately may be the case, in this book violence is seen less as an entity and more as a product of social divisions based on the intersection of race, power, ethnicity, class, culture, gender, sexual orientation, religion, and other identities or competing ideologies. Underlying these identity-based issues may be Burton's (1997) unresolved human needs, including needs such as security and welfare, since fear and loathing directed at a stranger or at an enemy seems so often to characterize the resort to force and brutality (Dunn 2004). Using the interdisciplinary lens of PACS, we gain a profound means of analyzing and addressing violence in all dimensions of world society and at all levels.

PACS brings an interdisciplinary and multilevel approach encompassing structural, cultural, and direct notions of violence (Webel and Galtung 2007). These notions will be defined more fully in this book, and their implications will be noted. In addition, PACS looks at power relationships, especially the valuing of what might be termed deep democracy and the grassroots that also explores identity and the need for mutual recognition (Pearson and Olson-Lounsberry 2009). On the more active side, the field of PACS develops social knowledge and action through consciousness raising, storytelling opportunities (many conflicting parties indeed want or need to be heard and taken seriously), and empowerment (affording voice) with an emphasis on theory, practice, and social change linkages (Senehi 2009a). Also included is an introduction to a range of violence intervention and prevention approaches developed for use at the interpersonal, intergroup, and societal levels.

Philosophies and means of nonviolence are central to the PACS field, and nonviolence is seen to encompass not only the absence of direct physical violence but also the presence of positive peace, which includes the elimination of systems of exploitation and the presence of social justice (Galtung 1996). Critics of the positive peace approach cite the difficulties of defining justice as well as factors of human nature and existing power structures to argue that expanding the definition of peace to include social justice is unrealistic (Dunn 2004 DuNann Winter and Leighton 2001). In order to treat this debate, this book offers a broad context for understanding the role of the individual in fostering peace and promoting nonviolent conflict resolution in everyday life.

We specifically focus attention on various ecologies, ethnographies, or case studies on the nature of youth violence, violence against women, hate violence, corporate violence, and violence in the workplace as well as an organic multilevel intervention system to tackle the deep roots of the violence. Furthermore, we unearth and explore the deep roots that cause ethnic conflict and war and how to intervene to prevent or halt violence at these levels. Of particular importance is the realization that gang fights among unemployed youths, genocidal rape, workplace strife, riots and uprisings, hate crimes, interethnic fighting, war, and even some examples of family violence can be explained within Galtung's (1990, 1996) frame of structural violence that erodes human dignity through poverty, hunger, repression, misery, and alienation. There are also cases of violence perpetrated by unscrupulous and vindictive leaders intent on aggrandizing their power.

Protracted conflicts are often rooted in value differences and the oppression of the less powerful (Deutsch, Coleman, and Marcus 2006). Since fighting can be a rational calculation (see Schelling 1981) when peaceful means to resolve the underlying causes of conflict are absent, violence is often the result. On the psychological and cultural side, symbols such as parades, flags, and national anthems can instigate hatred and trigger violent responses (Ross 2007). When do structural and cultural violence (racism, sectarianism, ethnocentrism, sexism, and heterosexism) lead to direct violence (i.e., the employment of physical force), and when do they not? When does physical violence worsen the other types? What qualifies as a source of cultural violence, and are the criteria by which we gauge the negative potential held by all?

Hierarchical power-over structures are deeply entrenched in our day-to-day relationships (Jeong 2000a, 16; Jeong 2008, 25). Replacing the existing power politics paradigms with their hierarchical structures, economic exploitation, and political manipulation entails a change in relations, or what Jeong idealistically calls a "new social epistemology," so that a "horizontal social structure with values of inclusion, equity, and rights" provides a greater opportunity for peace (Jeong 2000b, 14). Building a culture of peace is a long-term process that creates equality and prevents oppression by restructuring society's institutions (DuNann Winter and Leighton 2001).

This book examines these forms of violence to see what they would look like if a problem-solving approach was used rather than an adversarial power-over approach at micro and macro levels of negotiation and interaction and in interpersonal and structural relationships. By exploring the connections among nonviolence, justice, social change, research, and practice, we illustrate the analysis and resolution of conflicts as well as introduce an alternate paradigm that offers practical skills and processes to promote justice and peace within the realities of human behavior. We conclude by highlighting key insights from the study that are critical in addressing the "web of violence" from the interpersonal level to the global level (Turpin and Kurtz, 1997, 2.). Elise Boulding (1990) argues that it is critical to "imagine peace" so that an organic and lasting peace built around social justice and humanity becomes the cornerstone of the survival of our planet and our "species' identity" (158, 64).

Understanding violence is important not only psychologically and sociologically but also economically. Every year violence costs the global economy billions of dollars in damages. Estimates of the cost of violence in the United States, including the prices of prisons, emergency treatment, defense spending, and the police force reach 3.3 percent of the gross domestic product, while in England and Wales the total costs from violence amount to an estimated $40.2 billion annually (World Health Organization 2004). There is also the cost of workers missing work, filing lawsuits due to workplace violence, or simply being less productive at work for fear of danger (Keashly and Harvey 2006). Some large corporations are taking their cue from workplace violence statistics to put in place appropriate policies, task forces, and employee assistance programs to deal with the issue and to improve their bottom line (Braverman 1999). Such alternatives to violence are needed so that people can be trained to deal with this issue proactively and constructively and so that people in pain can be heard before they act out.

## Social Aggression and Violence

Not every person in society behaves aggressively or violently. Aggression is not universal across cultures, although it can be expressed in various forms (Fry 2006). There are such relatively nonviolent and peaceful societies as the Bushmen of the Kalahari, Hopis, Quakers, Mennonites, Hutterites, the Church of the Brethren, and Pueblos. Hunter-gatherer societies generally have lower levels of violence internally as well as among themselves and with other societies (Fry 2006; Ross 1993, 2007).

Since it has been argued that televised sports depict masculine values of using violence to solve problems and since children watch violent cartoons that display aggressive values and behaviors (Wessells 2006), intervention to break the spiral of aggression in society can begin by not rewarding or glorifying that kind of violence in the media or sports (Prothrow-Stith 1991). Since we know that young people can understand and learn from violent stories without becoming violent (Bar-On 2008), the public can put pressure on the corporations that own the television networks not to show gratuitous violence but instead to cover news in ways that show all forms of prosocial and antisocial behavior, indeed Prothrow-Stith and Spivak (2004) argue for showing prosocial messages that young people can mimic.

Teaching violence reduction through prosocial attitudes and actions in the family, in schools, and in places of worship, government, and corporations can also assist parents who themselves are modeling appropriate behavior to help their children. (Vestal 2001). The school culture can work to empower the child's self-esteem and self-efficacy by teaching problem-solving, anger management, and negotiation and mediation skills (Vestal 2001). Over the long term, athletes can work to build a low tolerance among fans and the public for the aggression and violence exhibited by rivals in the stands or on the playing field. Examples of this are the toxic impact of alcohol on violence inhibitions and the correlation between excessive drinking and acting out (Englander 2007). Thus, a key point in peace building has to do with grassroots community and empowerment as part of a holistic process that nurtures relationships and establishes shares goals (Lederach 2005).

It is not necessarily apparent that direct violence is always wholly negative; the right of collective and individual self-defense is recognized in domestic and international affairs. Some insurgent groups also make clear gains and focus attention on unjust conditions through violent resistance (Gallant 2009). Consequently, the study of violence is complex, and there is a good deal of room for hypocrisy as states or actors advocate nonviolence for others but fail to exercise it themselves.

Unfortunately, violence can also be instrumental and rewarding, such as when German, Polish, Lithuanian, and Ukrainian people seized their Jewish neighbors' property during the Holocaust

(Ferguson 2006). Sometimes violence emerges not strictly from the need to dominate but instead from fear, anger (over prior violence received), and insecurity, such as when Chechen separatists held hundreds of hostages in a theater in Moscow on October 26, 2002, and when Chechen fighters held more than a thousand schoolchildren during the Beslan school hostage crisis of September 1–3, 2004. In such instances and others, violence also can result from a seemingly rational cost-benefit calculation, such as in gang-related violence in Bosnia and Thailand over the illicit trafficking of women, weapons, and drugs (Leatherman and Griffin 2009). Some violent groups actually repress certain forms of violence. The Taliban government, despite its perceived subjugation of women, reportedly stopped the rampant rapes of the Afghan Civil War era (Matinuddin 1999). The remedies for violence vary depending on the causes, circumstances, and typologies.

## Organization of the Book

In chapter 2, we discuss the ecologies and root causes of violence and outline a number of the micro (psychological) and macro (structural) theories of violence. We focus attention on the necessity of understanding the linkages between social psychological and social science theories of violence. We are then ready to delve into concrete examples of violence and their prevention in our everyday lives. Chapters 3, 4, 5, and 6 cover case studies of youth violence, violence against women, hate violence, and corporate violence and violence in the workplace, respectively. Contextually, the underlying causes of violence are explored in these four chapters, as is an organic multilevel intervention system to tackle the deep roots of the violence.

The social sciences cover a number of approaches to the study of violence and conflict. One approach has been to present a broad survey of this variety. Three of the best surveys can be found in John Burton, *Violence Explained* (1997); Jennifer Turpin and Lester Kurtz, *The Web of Violence* (1997); and Daniel Christie, Richard

Wagner, and Deborah DuNann Winter, *Peace, Conflict and Violence* (2001). We make no attempt to provide another survey of violence. Rather, we present a number of cases shown to be most useful in the analysis of and prevention of violence. To this end, we include two cases that have recently generated valuable insights about violence. Both examples highlight the deep roots that cause ethnic conflict and war and how to intervene to prevent violence. We take readers through an interesting discussion of both topics in chapters 7 and 8.

In chapter 7 we present the social cubism analytical model—demographics, economics, history, politics, psychoculture, and religion—to understand some of the dynamic and interrelated forces fueling protracted ethnic conflict (Byrne and Carter 1996). In addition, we highlight a multilevel and multimodal intervention system model to build peace in postviolent societies. In chapter 8 we examine the causes of war that highlight the literature, and we provide some new insight within Kenneth Waltz's (1957) three levels of analysis—the individual, the state, and the international system—as well as discuss a multitrack systemic intervention process to end war and create a positive peace.

The connection involving nonviolence, justice, human rights, and social change research and practice is another issue that has aroused our curiosity as scholar-practitioners. The PACS field and most of the social sciences recognize the nexus between theory and practice and also recognize that there cannot be peace without justice. Mohandas K. Gandhi and Cesar Chavez articulated that people must nonviolently cease to cooperate with anything that humiliates them (Hanh and Berrigan 1993). Peace is therefore characterized by shared power, mutual recognition, and awareness of self in context, which sometimes necessitates nonviolent resistance (Senehi 2009b). Injustice involves the violations of the rights of another person or an unjust act that causes abuse, pain, and misery by taking away the dignity of a person (Galtung 1996). Chapter 9 discusses some of the critical moral dilemmas and ethical issues that students, policy makers, and scholar-practitioners must be cognizant of when designing appropriate conflict systems design interventions so that a positive rather than a negative peace (the absence of war) prevails.

Chapter 10 highlights key findings as well as some insights from the PACS field that are critical when addressing the web of violence from the interpersonal level to the global level. We suggest that an interdisciplinary elicitive, creative, and eclectic approach to theory, research, and practice will equip and energize students, policy makers, and scholar-practitioners with new knowledge and skills necessary to deal with the complexity of conflict and violence in our society.

## Conclusion

It is not impossible to create a just and peaceful society where violence is completely eliminated in the long term, yet this remains a challenge to our imagination, behavior, and actions. This chapter has provided an introductory understanding of the complexity of violence in our society. Its conclusion must acknowledge the functional role that violence has played in assisting groups to protect their security. In other words, is it also necessary at times to fight for peace or justice, although the notion is in essence a contradiction, or are there principled and pragmatic nonviolent methods that are more applicable in addressing conflict? Questions related to the causes and remedies of violence are complex and subject to a great deal of debate and testing. Not all answers can be based simply on a peaceful restructuring of society. More practical and immediate concerns of peacekeeping and peacemaking might intrude. We need to engage in considering what sorts of behavior our generation will rethink and what they come to see as violence.

In the next chapter we consider the role of various theories within an ecological framework in order to best understand the complexity and dynamics of violence in our life and our world. Such a typology assists in mapping theory that explains the root causes of violence.

## Websites Related to Violence

The Centre for the Study and Prevention of Violence, University of Colorado at Boulder, http://www.colorado.edu/cspv/

Centre for the Study of Violence, Washington, D.C., http://www.gcsv.org/

Crises States Research Centre, London School of Economics and Political Science, http://www.crisisstates.com/

Institute for the Study and Prevention of Violence, Kent State University, http://dept.kent.edu/ispv/

Peace Research Institute Oslo, Norway, http://www.prio.no/

Prevention Action, United Kingdom, http://www.preventionaction.org

Violence Prevention Alliance, Cape Town, South Africa, http://www.who.int/violenceprevention/en/index.html

## Suggested Questions for Further Discussion

1. What factors tend to activate violent social conflicts?

2. How can storytelling and nonviolence be a potent means of transformation that gets results in society? How can we become aware of implicit cultural assumptions in the analysis and resolution of violent conflicts?

3. In your view, which factors play important roles in the escalation of social conflicts? How does a social conflict become a violent conflict?

4. Why is a multidimensional analytical approach important in understanding and reframing violent conflict?

5. Can the current violent conflicts emanating from capitalist structures be converted to nonviolent conflicts without substantial structural change in capitalism and in the dominance of capitalism on the global market? How can this process be achieved?

6. Are global environmental problems really a shared responsibility of the whole of humanity? What is the responsibility of the global North and the global South and their citizens in providing for

environmental security? Is the nation-state problematic in this re-gard? Would a world government or anarchism be viable alternatives in addressing the tragedy of the global commons?

7. Is it possible to increase the basic standard of living of the world's expanding population without necessarily depleting the world's finite natural resources and, in the process, degrading the environment? Can humanity retreat from the brink of environmental collapse and at the same time lift its poorest members up to the level of basic human health and dignity?

# 2

---

## The Violence Prism

### Framing a Typology of Theories of Violence

Readers are probably familiar with the story of the six blind men who were trying to describe an elephant. Each man came up with an entirely different understanding of the elephant, depending on what part of the elephant they touched. The one who felt the tail said that the elephant was like a rope. The one who felt the leg said that the elephant was like a tree. The one who felt the body said that the elephant was like a wall. The one who felt the ear said that the elephant was like a fan. The one who felt the tusk said that the elephant was like a sword. The one who felt the trunk said that the elephant was like a snake. Rope. Tree. Wall. Fan. Sword. Snake. These are very different interpretations. In disciplinary studies, the same thing can happen. When biologists study violence, they will find biological causes because that is where they are looking. Social scientists find social causes because they are looking at society. Psychologists find answers within individual personality because they are studying the individual personality. This does not mean that their findings should be dismissed but rather that findings from diverse disciplinary approaches need to be integrated so as to gain a wider, more comprehensive perspective on the complexity of violence (Backstein 1992).

Violence is a complex phenomenon rooted in the interaction of many factors, so it is important to use an ecological framework to understand the complex interplay of personal, situational, socioeconomic, political, psychocultural, and historical factors that combine to cause violence. Discussions about violence should include the micro-macro linkage. These are embedded in "entitlement/ownership, the acceptability of hierarchy/superiority/domination, and the legitimacy of violence" (Tifft and Markham 1991, 132).

Conflict and violence exist in society at the interpersonal, group, organizational, and international levels. Conflict can be functional/beneficial or dysfunctional/harmful, so we need to explore the circumstances of each as well as the conditions for replacing conflict with cooperation (Bartos and Wehr 2002). The Carnegie Commission on Preventing Deadly Conflict (1997) found that deadly conflict is not inevitable, yet preventing deadly conflict is increasingly urgent and possible. Humankind needs to understand the processes whereby violence unfolds, escalates, and de-escalates and develop practical approaches to managing or resolving conflict. To begin to offer solutions, it is critical that persons can analyze and map violent situations and understand their background and structure (Sandole 2003). Conflict has important implications for democracy, including questions related to social diversity and violence (Burton 1997).

The struggle against dominant social relations and oppressive cultural norms has existed throughout human history. The large question for Peace and Conflict Studies (PACS) is how we can identify sources of the dominant structure that generate conflict and violence (Jeong 2000b). The deep causes of ethnic violence, violence in the workplace, violence against women, hate violence, youth violence, and violent culture should be understood in terms of the structural conditions of modern society (Sandole, Byrne, Sandole-Staroste, and Senehi 2009).

We need to understand the relationships between types of ecological microsystems and violence and the impact of structural conditions on perceptions and culture (Jeong 2008). The process of creating sociocultural identity is associated with an oppressive structure, and the maintenance of social order is attributed to cultural domination and instrumental rationality (Jeong 2005). Identity construction and politics of discourse are important in understanding transformative possibilities of an unequal power relationship that can escalate into violence (Senehi 2009a, 2009b). Thus, theories of violence and non-violence are central to the PACS field.

Schellenberg (1996, 40) implies that conflict and aggression patterns are very complex and that it is probably dangerous to examine them from only the perspective of individual characteristics and tendencies. Multiple factors correlate with the probability problem to design appropriate preventative interventions and evaluate and replicate them in a holistic multitrack strategy (Reiss and Roth 1993). Using an ecological framework, this chapter draws on the social sciences and the PACS field to explore a plethora of theories about violence.

## The Web of Violence: An Ecological Approach to Theory

People are embedded in several environmental systems ranging from the school, family, and community to the broader culture that includes health and welfare systems, mass media, and cultural customs (Bronfenbrenner 1979). There is a reciprocal interaction and exchange between people and their environment. In the face of "contested ecologies, geographies, and life worlds," particular attention must be paid to "ontological human agency" (Boudreau 2009, 132). We will also consider the genetic and hard-wire questions about violence and humans as well as a comparison of human violence to animal violence.

An ecological approach rests on the idea that human development occurs in a contextual framework of five different levels of environmental influences: (1) microsystem of home, school, and work; (2) mesosystems containing the developing individual; (3) exosystems of two or more interacting systems where one of the systems does not contain the developing person; (4) macrosystem, that is, the overall structural system that develops patterns of education, economy, culture, religion, and government; and (5) chronosystem, that is, the system of change and consistency through the time period of a person's life and in the environment in which he or she lives (Bronfenbrenner 1994; Boulding 2000; Lederach 2005). Understanding is more complete when an ecological framework, entailing most of these various levels, is employed to report the various theories of violence.

This chapter explores a number of different theories that study human conflict and violence. To capture the complexity of violence, we adopt an ecological model that organizes the theories of violence into eight interacting frames: (1) psychology, (2) sociobiology, (3) structural theory, (4) human needs theory, (5) socialization theory, (6) feminist theory, (7) anthropology, and (8) international relations.

## Psychology

Conflict and violence can be examined at different levels of analysis: at the level of the person, the small group, the organization, the cultural group, the social structure, and the international system, etc. Psychological theories usually examine conflict at the level of the person. Psychological theories are used to explain questions such as the following: Why are people violent? What determines the choice people make? How does one's environment shape one's behavior? Why do individuals and groups internalize oppression and accept the mantle of the oppressed?

Social psychologists focus on the processes by which social influences are likely to make individuals behave violently. Behavioral psychologists argue that a system of rewards and punishments as well as social learning determine the behavior of people who are conditioned by their environment and for whom behavior is learned.

Below we provide an overview of some psychological theories in order to serve as a general background on some psychological perspectives on the causes of aggression and violence. Six schools of thought are briefly reviewed: psychoanalytic theory, biopsychology, behavioral psychology, social psychology, humanistic psychology, and political psychology. Clearly, no one viewpoint offers a complete explanation, but each offers insights into different questions and aspects of human personality. Psychological theories often do not provide a consideration of structure, class, gender, or culture, so these factors need to be taken into account in evaluating various theoretical ideas. This review is not intended to be comprehensive but can provide an overview of some of the fundamental ideas that exist concerning psychological explanations of violence.

## PSYCHOANALYTIC THEORY

Psychoanalytic theory derives from the work of Sigmund Freud (1856–1939), who believed that there were important biological bases to the personality. The sciences did not have advanced technologies for studying neuroanatomy, so Freud instead turned to exploring the mind through his clinical practice. He used the term "instincts" to refer to biologically driven personality drives such as hunger, sexual desire, and aggression. Many neo-Freudian psychologists, philosophers, and anthropologists have reinterpreted Freudian theory in a number of important ways. Some feminists have criticized Freud for a masculine bias, while other feminists have engaged psychoanalytic concepts in their critique of patriarchy (Gilligan 1993).

Freud (1949) describes the personality as made up of three components: (1) the id represents biological, instinctual desires that strive to be met; (2) the superego represents parental and societal values as they have been taught to the individual and is usually in direct conflict with the id; and (3) the ego is the conscious sense of self that attempts to balance the id and the superego and deal with the world. The personality is driven by conflict between the id (the drives of the individual) and the superego (the internalized values of the society) as steered and mediated by the ego.

An important Freudian concept is the unconscious. For Freud (1949), the conscious mind represents just the tip of the iceberg, with powerful drives and conflicts submerged below conscious awareness. The idea that human thought and behavior might be driven by impulses, internal conflicts, and past experiences that are out of awareness is the most significant and enduring contribution of Freudian theory and can be used to explain many types of human and social behavior.

For example, anxiety is a state of psychic fear that alerts the ego to danger. Freud (1949) describes different types of anxiety: (1) reality anxiety, when there is a threat from the outside world, and (2) neurotic anxiety, when id impulses threaten to overwhelm the ego.

When anxiety becomes overwhelming, the ego resorts to defense mechanisms including repression, rationalization, denial, regression, projection, displacement, reaction formation, and sublimation.

Freud's theory emphasizes sexuality as a powerful instinctual drive and also emphasizes the importance of early childhood for the adult personality. Freud (1949) describes the life instincts as the libido or eros. These comprise the psychical desire, including sexual desire (in its broadest sense), self-love, love for parents, friendship, and love for humanity in general as well as devotion to concrete objects and abstract ideals. At a later point in his theorizing, Freud (1949) developed the construct of a death instinct. Opposed to eros, thanatos represents another collective of instincts that have as their aim the restoring of living human beings to an inorganic state from which they presumably sprung during centuries past (which Erich Fromm critiqued as rather narrow). Even looking out for oneself or being willing to fight if necessary to retain one's integrity as a person could be seen as a fusion of self-love (eros) and hostility (thanatos). Freud describes the eros and death instincts as rarely appearing in their pure form in human behavior.

Some ideas regarding oral traits, anal traits, early erotic desires, and unconscious factors have held up to empirical tests despite the difficulty of experimental design to test these ideas. The idea that patients talking about their problems could lead to a cure was extremely empowering in Freud's time and place; this is a heritage of contemporary practices that give individuals the power to solve their own problems. The idea that human and group motivations might be influenced by impulses, internal conflicts, and past experiences (i.e., for the person) out of awareness is generally accepted (Volkan 1998). The concept of internalized oppression is based on this assumption. Frantz Fanon (1965), who detailed this phenomenon in *Wretched of the Earth,* was himself a psychoanalyst. Moreover, in any competition between two parties over an object, over time they forget the object, which is replaced by the conflict itself (Girard 1979). Harmony will be restored only if the conflicting parties can vent their anger on a common enemy or scapegoat, as "mimetic violence" divides each against each (Girard 1979, 31). The destruction of the scapegoat produces a unifying experience (Girard 1979). Also, Freud's emphasis on the role of fear and defense mechanisms is of significance to understanding violence and conflict and its resolution at both interpersonal and international levels. This aspect of his theory and its application to PACS could be further explored and developed.

Neo-Freudian scholars build on and critique Freud's psychoanalytic approach. For example, Nancy Chodorow compares the dyadic and triadic experiences of the child's love for her or his mother and father to explain how gender roles are socially constructed, while Vamik Volkan argues that psychoanalysis is of little practical value to diplomats and foreign policy decision makers, as wars are not inevitable because of people's inherent aggressive drives. In addition, Erik Erikson, Jean Piaget, and Lawrence Kohlberg created the stages of cognitive and moral development that correlated to Freud's psychosexual stages.

BIOPSYCHOLOGY

Biopsychology is the study of biological bases for behavior, including chemical and neuroanatomical systems. Modern neuropsychology developed in the nineteenth century from research in France on head injuries that correlated specific types of speech impairment to damage in specific locations in the brain (Chiarello, Senehi, and Nuding 1987). From this beginning, neuroanatomical research has continued to map linguistic and other functions in the brain. These included experiments that attempted to increase knowledge about cognitive functions such as memory and language. Brain research has also led to the development of another branch of research, cognitive science that analyzes cognitive functions such as decision making, problem solving, cognitive maps, and learning. Other biopsychological research has identified chemical and neuroanatomical substrates of many human sensory, emotional, cognitive, and physical processes (Englander 2007). In an attempt to tease apart the influence between nature and nurture, psychologists have studied identical twins separated at birth. Other psychologists have compared children adopted at birth with their adoptive and birth mothers. These studies give evidence of the importance of genetic factors at the individual level but not at the level of the ethnic or regional group (Chiarello, Senehi, and Soulier 1986).

Konrad Lorenz (1937) also studied animals in their natural habitat (etiology) and was able to describe mechanisms of biologically rooted behavior. He demonstrated that baby geese will follow and react to the call of the first moving object they see. The rapid and early establishment of a permanent behavior pattern of this type is termed imprinting. Lorenz (1937) argues that aggression is likewise a biologically rooted behavior, and if the biological drives are repressed rather than released, then conflict will ensue. But humans lack certain innate patterns that inhibit aggression in other animal species. In nonhuman animals, certain stimuli can elicit complex genetically driven, species-specific behavior usually necessary for the survival of individual animals or the species. Mating behaviors offer such an example. In humans, necessary behavior patterns, such as eating and sexuality, are not so specifically determined and encoded and can be expressed in perhaps an infinite number of ways (Reiss and Roth 1993). Frustration aggression theory also ignores the impact of structure and the social milieu on human behavior (Galtung 1996). Biopsychological theories relate to the fields of medicine, biology, chemistry, physics, engineering, computer science, humanities, management, education, and communications.

BEHAVIORAL PSYCHOLOGY

Behavioral psychology focuses on observable behavior rather than on internal, invisible, or unconscious processes. Ivan Pavlov developed classical conditioning theory in 1927 with his famous dog experiment. Certain stimuli elicit automatic responses in the organism; for example, food elicits the salivating response. When this stimulus is repeatedly paired with another stimulus such as a bell, eventually the bell alone will elicit the automatic response (salivating) in the dog (Skinner 1938).

Moreover, B. F. Skinner (1938) developed operant conditioning theory. Using a rigorous scientific method, Skinner focused on the spontaneous behavior of an organism in response to its environment and how the consequences (reinforcement) of that response affected the occurrence of the behavior in the future. Positive reinforcement (reward) encourages more of the behavior in the future. Negative reinforcement discourages the repetition of the behavior. Through increasingly sophisticated experiments, Skinner developed his theory in order to predict behavior based on differing patterns of reinforcement.

In addition, a cluster of experiments by Seligman, Maier, and Solomon (1971) and others drew on conditioning theory to develop the theory of learned helplessness. For instance, if a caged dog was repeatedly given a shock but was not allowed to escape, the dog eventually stopped trying to escape even when the obstruction to escape was removed. Similarly, after repeated failures, a person might develop a sense of hopelessness and give up trying even when solutions are possible. This paradigm has also been used to describe depression.

Behaviorists argue that the environment controls behavior. This line of research and thinking led to increased examination of society and social forces in the field of social psychology.

SOCIAL PSYCHOLOGY

We now focus on some of the classic experiments by a number of social psychologists that seek to explain group behavior. In response to a growing awareness of prejudice in society and in response to the shock of the revelations of the Nazi atrocities in the post–World War II years, a number of experiments in psychology sought to explain how these things could happen (Fisher 1997). For example, the so-called doubling of Nazi doctors in concentration camps allowed the self to split into two parts. One part committed crimes in the camps, while the other part functioned as a normal member of society outside of the camps (Lifton 1997).

In one of the earlier experiments, Solomon Asch (1956) hypothesized that individuals would not shift opinion to keep in line with others when faced with reality. In the experiment, a research subject sat in a room with seven others who were apparently subjects but who were actually Asch's confederates in the experiment. The subject was told that he was participating in an experiment on visual judgment in which he would compare the lengths of lines. After unanimous judgments uttered with great certainly by the confederate subjects, almost one-third of the fifty people tested conformed to the obviously wrong answer. In later studies, if just one confederate gave what would be an obviously correct answer, almost none of the subjects conformed.

Likewise, in Philip Zimbardo's (1974) prison experiment, volunteers were randomly assigned roles as prisoners and guards. Both were placed in the basement of the Stanford University psychology building and given minimal instructions: they were told to assume their assigned roles and were also told that the guards' job was to "maintain law and order." In only a few hours, the behavior of one group had become sharply differentiated from the behavior of the other group, as each conformed to what was considered appropriate for that social role. The guards had adopted behavior patterns and attitudes that are typical of guards in maximum security prisons, with most of them becoming abusive and aggressive. Most of the prisoners had become passive, dependent, and depressed, although some became enraged at the guards. The experiment was intended to run for two weeks, but suffering among the prisoners was so great that one had to be released within 36 hours and others had to be released later, so the experiment lasted for only six days.

That same year Stanley Milgram (1974) investigated obedience, and the results were dramatic. Milgram studied men of all ages and from a wide range of occupations. Each subject was paid to take part in what he was told was a study of the effects of punishment on learning. The experimenter, dressed in a white lab coat, instructed each subject to read a list of word pairs to a learner (really a research confederate) whose task was to memorize the word pairs. The learner was taken into an adjacent room, out of the subject's sight, for the duration of the experiment. Every time the learner made a mistake, the subject was to punish him by administering a shock from an impressive-looking shock generator (which, of course, did not actually administer shocks). The generator had thirty clearly marked voltage levels, with switches ranging from 15 to 450 volts and labels ranging from "Slight Shock" to "Danger: Severe Shock." Whenever the learner made a mistake, the subject was to increase the voltage by one level and administer the shock.

Acting under instructions, the learners made many errors, necessitating increasingly severe shocks. When the shock level reached 300 volts, the learner pounded on the wall in protest and fell silent. At this point, the experimenter instructed the subject to treat the silence as a wrong answer and to raise the voltage. If the subject ever asked to stop the experiment, the researcher sternly told him to go on. Among forty subjects, twenty-six (65 percent) continued to obey the experimenter to the very end. Many subjects showed signs of extreme anxiety and frequently told the experimenter that they wanted to stop. But despite their distress, most of them continued to obey the experimenter's commands.

Another experiment contributing greatly to the understanding of group behavior was that by Jane Elliot. Elliot wanted to give her elementary school pupils direct experience with prejudice (Peters 1971). On the first day of her prejudice experiment, she announced that brown-eyed children were to sit in the back of the room and that they could not use the drinking fountain. Blue-eyed children were given extra recess and got to leave first for lunch. At lunch, brown-eyed children were prevented from taking second helpings because they would "just waste it." Mixing of brown- and blue-eyed children was prevented. The blue-eyed children were told that they were cleaner and smarter.

At first, Elliot had to maintain these imposed conditions of prejudice. She also made an effort to constantly criticize and belittle the brown-eyed children. To her surprise, the blue-eyed children rapidly joined in and soon were outdoing her in the viciousness of their attacks. The brown-eyed children felt very bad. Fights broke out. Test scores of the brown-eyed children fell. Two days later, the roles of the children were reversed. Within a short time, the same destructive effects occurred again but in reverse. In the transference process, the attributes of one group were transformed to another group. The experimenters argue that if these behaviors resulted after a day due to eye color and status inequalities, certainly the effects of a lifetime of real racial or ethnic prejudice are infinitely more powerful and destructive.

Some years prior, Muzafer Sherif and associates (1961) had conducted an experiment with eleven-year-old boys at a summer camp.

When they arrived at the camp, the boys were separated into two groups and housed in cabins that were physically separated. At first the groups were kept apart to build in-group friendships. The boys developed pride and identification with the in-group by participating in cooperative games and activities. Soon each group had a flag and a name and had staked out its own territory. At this point, the two groups were placed in competition with each other. After a number of clashes, the conflict between the two groups was intense. The two groups dehumanized each other so that the conflict escalated without the children having to experience cognitive dissonance over treating each other poorly (e.g., Lord of the Flies). As an experiment in the reduction of intergroup conflict, the social psychologists employed various strategies to reduce tensions. The only strategy that was successful involved the establishment of superordinate goals in the form of staged emergencies, such as damage to the water supply, in a way that required all the boys to work together to repair it for their common interest.

HUMANISTIC PSYCHOLOGY

Humanistic and existential psychologists emphasize the role of meaning in human personality and motivation. Victor Frankl (1984, 26), for example, considered the need to find meaning in life the primary human motive and emphasized the role of humans to give meaning to their lives and thus have the ultimate power to define their identity. Abraham Maslow (1967, 1968) also took an optimistic view of human beings, stressing their capabilities for love, joy, and artistic expression. He believed that there is an active drive toward health in every person, an impulse toward the actualization of one's potential. Still, because human instincts are so weak in comparison with those of animals, a person's impulses toward self-actualization can be distorted by society, habit, or faulty education. Maslow developed a hierarchy of needs divided into two broad categories: basic needs and meta needs. Basic physiological needs include air, food, water, sleep, sex, etc. Meta needs, or higher growth needs, include, in order of more basic to higher needs, safety and security, love and belonging, esteem and self-esteem, and self-actualization. Maslow argued that people would strive to fulfill the more basic needs first before striving to attain the higher needs, although they were still human needs.

Moreover, Carl Rogers (1951) believed that people have an innate impulse toward positive growth. Persons growing up, however, might let people who are important to them guide their behavior rather than trust their own spontaneous perceptions and feelings because they are objects of conditional positive regard. The result of this process is the establishment of conditions of worth, that is, extraneous standards whose attainment ensures positive regard. When an individual is trying to live up to these standards, she or he is likely to misperceive, distort, or deny any experiences that do not meet her or his conditions of worth. The discomfort that an individual might undergo when his or her experiences are denied and distorted can lead the person to become defensive, tense, conflicted, and unable to relate well to others. Such people are often argumentative and hostile, and they may project their feelings onto others. Therapy is client-centered and involves unconditional positive regard.

POLITICAL PSYCHOLOGY

Some political theory draws on the discipline of psychology. For instance, Robert Jervis (1976) argues that it is often impossible to explain crucial decisions and policies without references to the decision makers' beliefs and schemata about the world and their images of others. Cognitive consistency is the norm. Information that conflicts with the decision maker's image tend to be either dismissed, ignored, or reinterpreted in such a way that the information is congruent with existing beliefs.

For example, Irving Janis (1972) examined the tendency for social pressure to enforce conformity and consensus in decision-making groups. He calls this tendency, which people engage when they are part of a cohesive in-group that strives for unanimity over critical reasoning to evaluate alternative courses of action, "group think" (47). Symptoms of group think include illusions of invulnerability, stereotyped views, conformity pressures, self-censorship, illusions of unanimity, and the emergence of so-called mind guards.

Moreover, both individuals and sovereign entities attribute their own behavior to external situational stimuli, while they attribute behavior of others to their internal stable dispositions (Byrne 2003). In other words, people tend to explain their own controversial behavior by saying that they did something because of the circumstances. However, people tend to explain others' controversial behavior by saying they did something because they're bad people.

Margaret Hermann (1986) has also done extensive research on the role of personality in foreign policy. She addresses the question of when decision makers choose international relations as the outlet for their personal emotional needs. She describes six clusters of personality characteristics (nationalism, belief in one's own ability to control events, need for power, need for affiliation, conceptual complexity, and distrust of others) and links them to foreign policy behavior (professed orientation to change, independence/interdependence of action, level of commitment, hostility and friendliness, and type of environmental feedback). She also addresses the question of what kinds of personalities individuals who become political leaders are likely to have. Heads of state, who advocate for nationalism, are in need of power, and distrust of others is more prevalent in nations with lower levels of modernization.

The creation of interactive problem-solving workshop methodologies by John Burton (1997), Ron Fisher (1997), and Herbert Kelman (1991, 1997) improved communication and critical analytical skills as well as provided fresh insight and training to workshop participants to constructively transform international and ethnic conflicts. These unofficial Track II workshops facilitated by knowledgeable third parties, typically conflict resolution academics, brought together middle-tier influential representatives of conflict groups in direct equal-status interaction in a prenegotiation process to build trust, share knowledge creatively, reduce prejudices, and promote recognition to build a framework of joint ideas about their problems to set the stage for a macro-based negotiation process (Kelman 1997).

Violence shapes aggressiveness in children and adults, yet there are many other factors that contribute to violence in general, as the roots of violence lie in society's values about what is important in the life of all its citizens.

## Sociobiology

Sociobiology stresses the role of genes in human conduct so that male and female violence can be explained as a readily available response to genetic programming (Chasin 1998). Neither of these approaches can account for structural violence. Slavery, racism, and sexist domination and control were justified on the basis that they were biological and inevitable (Bjorkqvist 1997). As these claims were found to be untrue, slavery was ended (though it still is seen in various locations where forced labor is practiced), and both individual states and the global community have addressed the problems of ending and preventing racial and sexist domination and control (seen in the past in instances of eugenics research and racism in the U.S. South and in Nazi Germany) (Lifton 1997).

The 1986 Seville Statement on Violence by a variety of scientists challenged a number of biological findings that have been used to justify war and violence (Fry 2006). The Seville Statement claims that war and violent behavior are not genetically programmed into our species' human nature. Genes do not produce people predisposed to violence, nor do homo sapiens (under normal circumstances, as opposed to serial killer psyche) have a violent brain, and humans have not inherited from their animal ancestors a tendency (as opposed to a potential) to make war.

It is important to understand how explanations of the sources of violence and policies for the prevention of violence can be interrelated. Locating violence in biological substrates may lead to suggestions that the cure for violence is in biological prescriptions and policies, some of which may indeed do violence to the individual being treated, as in potential drugs, surgeries, isolation of individuals, and even eugenics (Englander 2007). Biological explanations may suggest that people who commit harmful violent acts are incapable of personal change unless they are changed biologically (Miczek, Mirsky, Carey, DeBold, and Raine 1994).

A thoughtful examination of the biology of violence can lead to other more reasonable conclusions as well. Increasingly, neuroscientists are learning that while the brain may shape thought and behavior, experience actually affects the brain (Miczek et al. 1994). If a young person grows up in a violent household, then the real-life experience of that person will impact the neuronal development of that person's brain so that he or she may develop post-traumatic stress disorder (PTSD).

An example that relates to the effects of violence on the person is what happens to the neurochemistry of people exposed to trauma. What is PTSD?

POST-TRAUMATIC STRESS DISORDER: THE INTERACTION OF CIRCUMSTANCE AND BIOLOGY

PTSD involves the intrusive memory of a traumatic event and a resulting hypervigilance. For example, fifty years after the traumatizing events of World War II, one-third of Holocaust survivors still reported feeling generally fearful (Goleman 1997). Nearly three-fourths said that they became anxious at the sight of a uniform or smoke rising from a chimney or at the sound of a knock on the door or dogs barking. Sixty percent said that they thought about the Holocaust daily. Eight in ten still suffered from repeated nightmares. As one survivor stated, people who survived Auschwitz and claim that they never have nightmares are not normal (Goleman 1995, 202). Traumatic events are also characterized by the traumatized person's sense of helplessness regarding the event. The trauma of these events can carry over even to those who were born afterward in "the transgenerational transmission of trauma" (Volkan 1998, 48).

In fact, the development of PTSD is normal; that is, it is a predictable consequence of trauma. Importantly, PTSD has a neural basis. As Daniel Goleman (1995, 203) proposed, the neural basis for traumatic memories stems from a major change in the chemistry of the brain as a result of a single episode of terror or as a result of repeated sexual, physical, or emotional abuse over many years. The neurotransmitters (chemicals that are part of brain function) that are released during a traumatic event may have a lasting impact on the neurophysiology of the brain (Chiarello, Senehi, and Soulier 1986). Yale psychiatrist Dennis Charney told Goleman

(1995, 204) that survivors of an overwhelming trauma are not the same biologically.

As outlined by Goleman (1995), the reactions involve changes in how brain structures and the brain's neurotransmitters function together. First, there are changes within brain locations, which are associated with nervous system regulation, emotion, memory, and attention (including the amygdala, the locus ceruleus, the hippocampus, and the hypothalamus). These brain centers also communicate with the brain's cortex, which is associated with higher-conscious cognitive functions. These changes are the biological substrates of PTSD symptoms that included anxiety, fear, and hypersensitivity to stimuli; being easily upset and aroused; readiness for fight or flight; and intrusive memories. Catecholamines (adrenaline and noradrenaline) are the neurochemicals involved in the mobilization of the body for an emergency. Vietnam War veterans with PTSD, for example, were found to have 40 percent fewer neural receptors for inhibiting (or stopping) the effect of catecholamines, indicating that their brains had undergone a lasting change (Goleman 1995, 205). In other words, the body's neurochemistry for the emergency response is now on a hair trigger. This hypersensitivity results in the body reacting to what may in reality be trivial events as if they were emergencies.

Another set of changes involves the brain's opioid system, which secretes endorphins to dull feelings of pain. These chemicals are seen as the body's morphine, because in an emergency they dull the pain from any physical or emotional trauma that might result and interfere with the person's survival (Englander 2007). With PTSD, this system is also recalibrated to a hair trigger with the result that there might be an enduring dulling of sensations of pain or even emotional response. Psychological responses associated with PTSD include anhedonia (the inability to feel pleasure) and a general emotional numbness regarding other people's feelings (Reiss and Roth 1993).

This increased sensitivity would furthermore make people sensitive to additional traumatizing, creating a kind of snowball effect. It is also important to note that this biological response can be seen as adaptive (that is, promoting survival). In danger, hypervigilance can be a lifesaver. And a dulling of pain and emotion can help people do what needs to be done during an emergency without falling apart or being overwhelmed by what is happening. However, in the long term the consequences of these biological responses can be damaging but perhaps not life-threatening. The argument can be made that the neurobiology for the fight-or-flight response is much more effective and powerful than the neurobiology for the emotions of security and love, not because people are innately violent or savage (nasty, brutish, or short-tempered) but because in the development of the species (and other organisms), this system is most crucial for survival (Miczek et al. 1994). One needs to be alert to danger, keep one's head, and escape. The research of psychologist Ibrahim Kira et al. (2007) in Dearborn, Michigan, also showed that the violence trauma experiences of Iraqi refugees in Detroit were actually less telling than the humiliation experiences that they suffered.

EMOTIONAL RELEARNING AND RECOVERY

While three-fourths of Holocaust survivors were found to have PSTD symptoms fifty years after the event, one-fourth were found to have largely overcome the effects of trauma. Daniel Goleman (1995) argues that this suggests that emotional relearning is possible. He reviews several strategies for recovery. Thousands of former child-soldiers are also suffering from physical as well as emotional and physical traumas (Beah 2007). Traditional healing is used to restore their spiritual harmony and emotional relearning so that they can integrate back into their communities (Wessells 2006).

*Games and expressive forms.* Especially for children, playacting fantasies that allow the children to relive and examine a traumatic event in a safe place helps them analyze and gain mastery over the traumatic event. Art or other expressive forms can also function in this way. Goleman (1995, 209) writes that the emotional brain (i.e., the systems that are involved in emotional processing, including the hippocampus) is highly attuned to symbolic meanings in the messages of metaphor, story, myth, and the arts. For example, storytelling is used in some forms of therapy for survivors of political violence and for children who were seriously neglected or traumatized by ethnic violence or civil wars (Senehi and Byrne 2006).

Goleman (1995) outlines five critical steps in emotional relearning and recovery:

Step 1: *Regaining a sense of safety.* Strategies need to be found to calm and sooth in the event of easily triggered emotional reactions.

Step 2: *Unlearning the lesson of helplessness.* Taking effective action removes a sense of helplessness. A woman dealing with a stalker might have the support of the police. If the police ignore her, she might enlist the help of family and friends to serve as protection in the face of this fearful event. Perhaps any form of empowerment involving increased skills, community ties, and political access might be helpful. In the face of a terrible tragedy, political action—such as lobbying for laws to prevent similar tragedies—might serve to remove one's sense of helplessness. In several cases the police denied women who were harassed by stalkers protection because the stalkers hadn't broken any law. When their stalkers killed some of these women, their loved ones successfully lobbied for laws to make stalking itself illegal (Tifft and Markham 1991).

Step 3: *Medication and relaxation techniques.* Drugs may serve to rebalance the neurochemistry of the brain. Relaxation techniques may help to counter anxiety and stress reactions.

Step 4: *Retelling and reconstructing the story of the trauma.* Talking about trauma seems to be an essential part of dealing with it, although the pace of this telling may be slow and may need to involve the alternation of telling and resting from telling (Senehi 2009a, 2009b). Helen Bamber, for example, worked with victims of torture worldwide for more than fifty years. She describes their need to repeat their complete stories in complete detail again and again, to "vomit" out the stories of their appalling experiences (Belton 1999). Moreover, in a Tanzanian camp where Rwandan refugees were told not to discuss their experiences, women cured their insomnia by telling the stories of the atrocities they had experienced to a so-called story tree (Anderson and Foley 1998).

Goleman (1995) thus argues that by discussing the event, individuals gain mastery over it. By putting the event into words and dealing with it cognitively, the event is more likely to come under the control of the cortex (the part of the brain associated with higher-conscious functioning). In this way, while the brain's emotional response system may remain somewhat on a hair trigger, the person is more able to respond to this internal response in a way that involves self-soothing or brings this response under control (Miczek et al. 1994). We find it interesting that the need to tell about trauma (even though this process is sometimes very difficult) seems universal, because this can also be seen as an adaptive response. By telling a story about a particular hazard, others are warned and thus protected to avoid that hazard.

Step 5: *Mourning*. It is necessary to mourn the losses that resulted from the traumatic event so that the person can heal. Healing encourages the person to reclaim her or his life.

### Structural Theories

Structural theorists suggest that individuals are constrained by the set of options and outcomes they perceive as available to them (Turpin and Kurtz 1997). Conflict sociologists such as Louis Kriesberg (1998) argue that violence is organized around social cleavages such as race, class, ethnicity, and gender in which elite groups use power or the threat of power to maintain their privileged positions. Johan Galtung (1996) argues that direct violence is horrific and brutal. Structural violence, however, "is almost always invisible, embedded in social structures and normalized by institutions and cultural norms, and kill people slowly" (DuNann Winter and Leighton 2001, 100). "Direct and structural violence operate together, forming an interlocking system of violence" (Christie, Wagner, and DuNann Winter 2001, 10).

Direct forms of violence are the most recognized and abhorred by the global community. A useful definition of violence needs to focus our attention on the interpersonal, cultural, and structural forces that make people's lives more dangerous and less healthy. Consequently, Johan Galtung (1996, 197) argues that direct violence (e.g., genocide, domestic violence, hate crimes, and ethnic violence) is intentional, immoral, and kills people quickly. Structural violence targets women, children, and the elderly in particular as people die through poverty or hunger, and cultural violence blinds us to other cultures (Jeong

2000a). Societal structures and institutions produce oppression, exploitation, and dominance that "curtail life spans by depriving people of material and nonmaterial resources" (Christie, Wagner, and Du-Nann Winter 2001, 9). This has "the effect of denying people important rights such as economic opportunity, social and political equality, and a sense of fulfillment and self-worth" (Barash 1991, 8). Moreover, structural violence is almost always invisible and frequently leads to direct violence (DuNann Winter and Leighton 2001). The underlying violence that contributes to indirect or structural violence is less overt and more controlled (Galtung 1996).

Direct, structural, and cultural violence is built into the rules of our institutions that deny people economic opportunity, fulfillment, social equality, human rights, and dignity (Galtung 1996). "Society brings violence upon human rights and dignity when it forcibly stunts the optimum development of each human being, whether because of race, religion, gender, sexual preference, or age" (Barash 1991, 8). Examples of this are global economic oppression of citizens in the global South, violations of indigenous people's rights, apartheid, militarization, poor health care, globalization, and poor nutrition (Barash and Webel 2002). Thus, structural and cultural violence stemming from the economic system and government is built into all of the social, political, and cultural institutions in society that deny socioeconomic and political equality (Barash 1991, 8); promote repression and alienation of elders, women, children, same-sex couples, and people of color; and deny education and housing to the poor (Galtung 1996). Consequently, people who "share subjectivities that justify and legitimize inequitable power relations in political and economic structures" such as "just-world thinking" also "rationalize disparities in power" (Christie 2001, 277), limiting the scope of justice to include only certain people such as with ethnic and religious ethnocentrism, cultural intolerance, and symbols such as flags, colors, and national anthems (Jeong 2008).

Galtung (1996) also distinguishes between negative peace, or the absence of direct violence such as war, and positive peace, or building equal relationships in a democracy. Just peace can only be accomplished by ending direct structural and cultural violence expressed through hunger, poverty, ethnocentrism, sectarianism, militarism, patriarchy, misogyny, heterosexism, and unequal access to education, health care, and resources (Webel and Galtung 2007). Positive peace overlaps or is identical with justice (Miall, Woodhouse, and Ramsbotham 1999, 18). Positive peace is related to overcoming oppression and is based on democracy, justice, freedom, dignity, human rights, and equality (Galtung 1996, 1).

Furthermore, research and theory indicate that the roots of war or the sources of conflict that lead to war are often to be found in structural violence, that is, in economic and social injustice (Jeong 2000a). Wars are frequently traceable to elites trying to retain and enhance illegitimate power and to oppressed groups rebelling against those elites. Structural violence actually does more harm than war (Barash and Webel 2002). Territoriality and security also play a key role (Senese and Vasquez 2008). More people die due to preventable hunger, disease, and other unjust conditions than die in wars (Barash 1991, 11). Feminist scholars are particularly sensitive to this issue, since women and children suffer disproportionately from structural violence (Boulding 2000; de Lauretis 1987; Enloe 2000) and since civilians have become the greatest victims of civil wars.

Structural violence primarily affects the poor, the working class, and minority groups and is a direct result of decisions made by society's economic and political elites and often ignored by the media (Chasin 1998). We need to search for new possibilities not based on hegemonic power that promote gender and economic justice (Tickner 1992). In our turbulent world there is a need to build cooperative understandings and transform values and behavior and the interlinking oppressions within patriarchy (race, class, and gender) (hooks 1990; Stephens 1994). However, competition arises regardless of gender; women are fully capable of victimizing other women in the workplace and in politics.

Moreover, Marxists who advocate for a classless noncapitalist society argue that the economic structure leads to certain types of behavior, including the objectification of the working class whose continual poverty, alienation, and degrading lifestyle are the result of an economic system riddled with clashing contradictions and internal tensions (Agnew and Corbridge 1994). Karl Marx suggested that the workers were alienated from each other and that overproduction and underconsumption would eventually result in class confrontation and revolution by the proletariat.

Is it possible to create a paradigm shift in how we think about power and violence as ways to solve conflict? Can we protect human rights and promote prosperity without a complete paradigm shift (for example, jurisprudence and the building of law). The PACS field provides a philosophy of hope as well as pragmatic conflict intervention tools, skills, and processes for personal and community empowerment. PACS also gives the tools for social transformation to actively promote sustainable participatory democracy (Lederach 1997, 2005).

### Human Needs

Echoing Galtung's concept of structural violence and human needs (survival, well-being, identity, and freedom), Burton (1997) argues that political and socioeconomic structures frustrate people's basic human needs, such as the needs for recognition and identity, leading to frustration, conflict, and violent responses. This is in contrast to Ted Gurr (1970), who argues that when frustration is prolonged, it often results in anger and eventually flames into violence. Burton distinguished among three types of human motivation: needs, values, and interests, as opposed to the traditional idea that conflicts are about interests only. He contends that one of the primary causes of protracted or intractable conflict is people's drive to meet their needs on the individual, group, and societal levels. Needs, unlike interests, cannot be negotiated; they must be satisfied (Burton 1990a). Burton (1990a) identifies eight human needs: safety and security, belongingness/love, self-esteem/recognition, personal fulfillment, identity, participation, freedom, and fair allocation of resources.

Basic needs are common and universal across cultures and need to be satisfied for individual development and socialization to occur (Burton 1990a). If these needs are not satisfied, deviant behavior and political and social conflict may result. The violation of human needs leads to conflict and violence, and the satisfaction of needs through problem-solving processes prevents violence (Burton 1997; Dunn

2004). Problem-solving approaches analyze the deep roots of conflict and take into account its complexity of, including interests and human needs. The analytical problem-solving process allows the parties to see the sources of problems in relationships and to find and develop appropriate mechanisms to meet the needs of all the parties (Burton 1990a; Dunn 2004).

The focus on individual agency must encompass a multidisciplinary approach to the study of identity, nationalism, poverty, and violence among others (Burton 1990b). Policy makers need to use problem-solving processes rather than an adversarial approach in domestic, national, and international relationships. Burton (1997) argues that diverse problems such as family conflict, workplace conflict, and ethnic conflict have the same source—human needs—and may be amenable to resolution through a problem solving interactive process.

### Socialization Theory

Socialization is learned behavior, norms, and values obtained through agents such as peers, the media, parents, schools, and churches (Englander 2007). Wittingly or not, various socialization agents teach aggression, which creates a culture of violence that impacts children and adults growing up in society (Kriesberg 1998). This approach contends that only the personality and genetic factors that lead to violent behavior need to be understood because genetic and psychological differences cause the person to behave in different, even antisocial, ways (Englander 2007).

Others argue persuasively that aggression and violence are not universal across cultures because they can be expressed differently (Fry 2006; Ross 2007). For example, the Kwakiutl Indians of the Pacific Northwest give away their property to express their resolution of conflict, while the Punans of Borneo represent a nonaggressive culture in which there is no intragroup conflict (Ross 1993). Cultural agents, such as elders, undoubtedly have perpetuated these conflict styles by passing them down through family lineages and in group dynamics (Rice 2011; Tuso 2011). The way that individuals deal with conflict may be affected by their cultural norms about social conflicts and how to deal with them (Avruch 1998; Lederach 1995). This argument is counter to the idea that conflict processes—such as aggression—are rooted in nature or even in genetics. (The prevailing view is that genes allow for violence but that social triggers determine the outbreak.) Rather, how we deal with conflict can be learned and can be affected by our training within society as a member of a particular cultural or gender group and by our personal experiences growing up within a family and our more immediate social circle (Fry 2006).

Elders play a key conflict resolution role in indigenous communities (Tuso 1999). For example, Marian Wright Edelman (1992), president of the Children's Defense Fund and considered to be the most influential children's advocate in the United States, writes about how her work for positive social change is grounded in the teaching of her parents and the elders in her community. These elders can be seen as community builders and peace builders because their everyday actions, choices, examples, and lessons created a community based on the everyday nurturing of relationships and conscious meaning-making that involved positive and powerful values and ideas (e.g., Chief Oren Lyons of the Onondagan nation of the Iroquois Confederacy).

### Feminist Theory

Feminists make the point that the dominant male patriarchal paradigm includes those who have forged the world, constructing sexism and its justification and inventing the categories to promote their interests (Spender 1990, 107). The patriarchal paradigm labels the difference between the genders, with female subordinate to male in a dominant-subordinate power imbalance. Male privilege is perpetuated by a patriarchal structure that is woven into the fabric of society, resulting in a power imbalance (Enloe 2000). Male elites create institutions in the structure of society that reinforce their superiority and other groups' inferiority (hooks 1990; Sylvester 2002).

Thus, the phenomenon of violence is mostly, though not exclusively, practiced by men, and the patriarchal culture, in which masculine dominates feminine, creates both microlevel violence against women and children and macrolevel violence such as war (Turpin and Kurtz 1997). Turpin and Kurtz (1997) argue, for example, that sexist ideology perpetuates systemic violence from the household to the global political order. Other feminists such as Anna Snyder (2003) examine the important role of women in peacemaking. Hence, there is a need for intercultural respect to promote peace on the one hand (United States and Iran, for example) and tolerance for cultures such as Islam, orthodox Judaism, and Hinduism in which women appear to be consigned to lesser positions (although again many Islamic, Jewish, and Hindu women defend the system, and some rise to positions of power).

### Anthropology

Anthropologists explore the relationship between culture and social structures (institutions) and people's lives. Douglas Fry (2006) argues, for example, that while human beings have a capacity for aggression, they also possess an ability to prevent and resolve conflict without resorting to violence. Consequently, Kevin Avruch (1998) highlights the centrality of culture in conflict resolution, while John Paul Lederach (1995) and Raymond Cohen (1997) distinguish between elicitive (what is present in a cultural setting) and prescriptive (explicit model of conflict resolution with implicit cultural assumptions) models and between low-context (a predominantly verbal and explicit style typical of individualistic societies) and high-context (a style associated with nonverbal and implicit communication more typical of traditionally interdependent societies) cultures.

Language, tools, technology, and culture have made war possible (Fry 2006). As Marc Howard Ross (1993) points out, warfare is not inevitable, since as we have seen there are cultures that have not engaged in warmaking, such as the Hopi and Navajo Native Americans, the aboriginals of Australia, and the aboriginals of Canada. Other cultures that engaged in war at certain times have conflicts but now generally live in peace with each other. One example of this is Germany and France, which traditionally were enemies but now are allies within the European Union.

Rapoport (1992, 7) makes the point that "it has been said that war begins in the minds of men. If so, then, perhaps so does peace." States are formed by people to provide for their security, particularly against violence, and for their collective welfare. In a semianarchical international milieu, as states compete with each other, violence is often used to further state interests, and a balance of power by rival alliances is sought or created to preserve order (Kegley and Wittkopf 2006). Traditional, as opposed to structural, realists further argue that human beings have an inherent urge for power as an end in itself in a world absent of a central authority, resulting in conflict and ultimately in war and violence (Goldstein 2003). Order rather than necessarily human rights and justice is pursued at the international level, while the criminal justice system curbs criminal violence at the domestic level (Turpin and Kurtz 1997). Realists also tend to eschew moralistic arguments or debates about ethical issues of justice, concentrating instead on the realities of power competition seen so often in political contexts (Kegley and Wittkopf 2006). Balances of power, deterrence, and inducements versus costs are thought to be the language that leaders understand and to hold in the hopes of preventing or ameliorating violence (K. Boulding 1990).

Critics of realism argue that the war system will end only when it runs out of adaptations, when the global community becomes more integrated and interdependent, and when calculations also include factors such as effects of policy on human lives (Rapoport 1997). The protection of the life-sustaining planet through principles of social justice are necessary to end all organized violence and radically transform the global society and the ideological framework of humanity (Boulding 2000; Rapoport 1997). Thus, Rapoport (1997) calls for a science of peace that embodies both theories of conflict and conflict resolution that recognize the key role of language in shaping a social reality dominated by an addiction to power that operates in socioeconomic and political systems that can be transformed by tolerance, cooperation, nonviolence, and peace education. Furthermore, Bondurant (1988, 5) points out that Gandhi's "experiments in truth" to effect powerful sociopolitical change remain far from complete, as both the philosophy of action and the technique of nonviolence have an important role to play in the creation of ideal society.

## Conclusion

Lewis Coser (1965) argued that conflict is functional and is the by-product of human interaction in which the parties have a divergence of interests. This chapter has explored a typology of violence theories to understand some of the underlying causes of violence in society. The typology is not an exhaustive one; however, the range of theories covered in this chapter provide an understanding of the interrelated environmental systems and key micro and macro theories of individual behavior, group behavior, and structural behavior leading to violence. These approaches assist in our understanding of how the individual is impacted by psychological, group, and structural dimensions of conflict that may influence that person to be violent; how and in what circumstances specific forms of violence arise; and how physical and structural violence interact. Acknowledging how micro and macro factors shape and mold the individual's behavior in society ensures that we can more effectively work to create constructive change in society. Violence is caused not simply by individual psychological factors, biological impulses, or social-structural factors alone but rather by a web of causal connections between personal-level and global-level structures, processes, and behaviors (Turpin and Kurtz 1997). Solutions to the problem of violence must address all levels as well as the interactions between them.

We must focus on the means of changing institutions, substantive issues, structures, and relationships to build trust and a just and sustainable culture of peace. This process entails an inclusive, participatory, nonviolent, and evolutionary process that acknowledges and respects differences and agency, encouraging cooperation among groups engaged in protracted conflict (Bjorkqvist 1997).

Subsequent chapters discuss violence in different settings to explore the interrelated causal linkages and circumstantial triggers as well as the multitrack intervention processes needed to prevent violence.

## Websites Related to Theories of Violence

Centre for the Study of Violence, Washington, D.C., http://www.gcsv .org/

Centres for Disease Control and Prevention, http://www.cdc.gov /ncipc/dvp/dvp.htm

Institute for the Study and Prevention of Violence, Kent State University, http://dept.kent.edu/ispv/

LaMarsh Centre for Child and Youth Research, York University, http://www.arts.yorku.ca/lamarsh/

National Centre for PTSD, United States Department of Veterans Affairs, http://www.ncptsd.va.gov

National Consortium on Violence Research, http://www.ncovr.heinz .cmu.edu/

Te Awatea Violence Research Centre, University of Canterbury, http: //www.vrc.canterbury.ac.nz/

## Suggested Questions for Further Discussion

1. According to basic needs theory, what fundamental needs are necessary for individual or communal survival? How are basic needs that are not met likely to be expressed in violence?

2. Why is an ecological approach that rests on the idea that human development occurs in a contextual framework of different levels of environmental influences critical to our understanding of violence?

3. If a system's approach is a constructive approach to frame and analyze violent conflicts, then why are so many violent conflicts perceived as social relations problems?

4. How are direct, cultural, and structural violence related to positive and negative peace?

5. Why is it important to have a multidimensional analysis of violence? Do you think that any conflict is ever intractable?

6. How does the intersection of gender, race, class, and culture explain microlevel dominant-subordinate power relations that often result in violence? Is it possible to realize the feminist notion of security in today's global context?

7. How can ethnography and narrative methods improve the analysis of violent conflicts? What are some potential limitations?

# 3

## Violence Unveiled

### Causes and Varieties of Youth Violence and Strategies for Intervention

In 1991 Sybil, a fifteen-year-old Protestant teenage woman who was living on the Shankill Road, attended an integrated school in Belfast, Northern Ireland. One day while she was hanging out with her friends they came upon a group of emotional young men who lived in their neighborhood. These young men were active in the Loyalist Ulster Volunteer Force and were planning to go across to the Falls Road and abduct and shoot a young Catholic man, a known Republican who was part of a gang who hurt a friend of theirs. A neighborhood friend had been badly beaten by young Republican men active in the Provisional Irish Republican Army. Both of his legs were broken with iron bars. Sybil went up to the group and said that she knew a lot of Catholic people who attended her integrated school and who were all right. She said that they shouldn't go across to the Falls Road to hurt any young Catholic people. The young Protestant men listened to what Sybil had to say and decided that they weren't going to use violence against the young Catholic man (Byrne 1997a, 1997b).

Biological, physical, and hormonal changes impact young people in various ways that ultimately also relate to violence potential. These changes affect sexual motivation, which in turn relates to capacities for either physical or structural violence in the form of male or female competition. Moreover, their cognitive and social development ensures that they learn to think more rationally and perhaps less emotionally so that they can consider multiple perspectives (Garbarino 2003). Adolescents experience major changes relating to their identity and self-esteem and especially around age thirteen have a strong tendency to be swayed by and conform to peers. By midadolescence there is a greater possibility of independent decision making (Coles 1986).

All of these factors can affect conflict and violence as well as conflict resolution propensity. Girls spend more time in intimate relationships and interdependent activities and communication. Boys prefer to spend time in larger group activities (using linear legalistic language) that are physically arousing and more likely to involve physical aggression (Garbarino 1999). Patterns of conflict resolution begin to emerge, with girls more likely to demonstrate increasing emphasis on interdependence and relationship (Wessells 2006).

A study by Howard and Wang (2003, 525) identified several risk factors associated with physical dating violence. Teens who had reported sad or hopeless feelings, attempted suicide, physical fighting, multiple sex partners, and not using condoms were more likely to report dating violence and were more at risk. Carrying guns, fighting, drinking alcohol, smoking cigarettes, using cocaine or inhalants, or engaging in risky sexual behavior were all associated with teen dating violence (527). These findings support the notion of an at-risk profile of problem behavior.

Though not necessarily severe, conflicts are normal among all young people as well as among adults (McEvoy-Levy 2006). Most conflict does not escalate to violence. In conflicts involving parents, adolescents are more likely to demonstrate low compromise and high submission or disengagement (Bemak and Keys 2000). Children in families in which there is domestic violence are at greater risk of violent abuse (Gelles and Strauss 1989; Mitchell and Finkelhor 2001).

This is a very important aspect of learning violence as well, perhaps more than movies and TV.

Children are affected by abuse (Benda and Corwyn 2002; Mitchell and Finkelhor 2001). A National Crime Victimization Survey of fifty thousand homes found that for all youths, living in a home in which there was domestic violence increased the risk of being victims by 158 percent, whereas living in a non–domestic violence home meant an increase of 107 percent (Mitchell and Finkelhor 2001). Notably, girls in a domestic violence home had an increase of 229 percent of being at risk (Mitchell and Finkelhor 2001). Girls in particular identify with the primary female adult victim and learn to accept the inevitability of victimization, or they acquire other attitudes that ensure that self-protection becomes more difficult (Mitchell and Finkelhor 2001, 960). In conflicts with their close friends and nonsibling peers, adolescents are more likely to demonstrate a higher rate of conflict resolution, perhaps reflecting that young people are very aware that disputes may rupture their affiliations (Vestal 2001). Given these facts, why are young people getting into so much trouble over violence?

This chapter explores some causes of youth violence including youth political violence, war, gangs, and violence as it relates to minority males and examines a multitrack intervention system that explores the range of actors and interventions to transform youth violence of all types.

## Some Causes of Youth Violence

Young people's socialization and emotional development is critical to the formation of identity and a moral sense of self (Coles 1986). This is especially critical for young people growing up in the global North as well as in the global South where direct, cultural, and structural violence trickles down into the very fabric of society. According to the Global Burden of Disease data issued by the World Health Organization (WHO), around 875,000 children and adolescents aged eighteen years died as a result of an injury or violence in 2002 (Mathers 2005). WHO estimates cited in the United Nations (UN) Secretary-

General's Study on Violence against Children indicate that nearly fifty-three thousand children are murdered each year, and sexual violence against boys and girls under age eighteen is 73 million and 150 million, respectively (Pinheiro 2007). On November 27, 2007, the Third Committee of the UN General Assembly approved the resolution on the Rights of the Child, which includes a focus on the elimination of violence against children.

Adolescence is a time of change during which one or more parents are overprotective and teens are confused about their sexuality, independence, and future. Teens are beginning to mature and become less dependent on their parents but are also at risk. A study by Paige Hall Smith (2003) found that women from fourteen years of age to college age in the United States who were physically assaulted in adolescence were more likely to be revictimized in their first year of college as well as in subsequent years, and adolescent victimization was a better predictor of future victimization than was childhood victimization. However, adolescents who have been victimized can also become victimizers (Garbarino 1999). Being victimized in both childhood and adolescence was the strongest predictor of future victimization in college, and those who had been victimized in the year prior to attending college were at a growing risk of being revictimized in their four years at college (Smith 2003). Physical and sexual dating violence is common, with results showing that 88 percent of women experience one incident of violence between adolescence and college (1107).

These findings indicate a need for programs to teach prevention of and intervention in dating relationship violence situations in high school and college. Teens also join gangs because gangs give them an identity, take care of their needs, and provide a chance for economic mobility benefits that families would normally be expected to provide (Prothrow-Stith and Spivak 2004). Gang members may also rebel against conformity by wearing different clothes and by trying drugs, sex, and alcohol; indeed, a degree of rebellion may be a normal stage of adolescent development. Teenagers may reject mainstream culture and create a counterculture, as in the punk rock movement of the mid to late 1970s.

# Figure 3.1. Systems view of violence, aggression, and youth
## Heather Tanksley, April 2003

### Types of Violence

- Weapon possession/use (guns, knives, razors, clubs)
- Burglary, theft, larceny
- Vandalism to property, lockers, vehicles, facilities, grounds, classrooms
- Drug and alcohol possession/use/distribution
- Assault and battery, pushing, shoving, kicking, biting, hitting, bullying
- Threatening, verbal abuse, intimidations, stare downs, disruption of classes, uproars
- Sexual assault
- Post-traumatic stress disorder, guilt, anxiety, fear

### Violent/Aggressive Youths

- Individual personality factors
- Peer group factors, identity, status, power, cultural differences/beliefs/values, acceptance of violence as a "good thing," gang influences
- Community and neighborhood norms, history, climate, resources, access to "bad" things
- Influence of family and parents, modeling behaviors, rituals, and passage
- Influence of teachers, counselors, community leaders, clergy
- Influence of media, sports, games, toys, music
- Influence of police and legal institutions
- Poverty/socioeconomic factors, cost of violence
- Educational and learning factors
- Deficient problem solving and interpersonal communication skills (vital skills for living)
- Deficient intervention programs, short-term vs. long-term effectiveness, scope of programs, funding and strategic implementation issues

### Interveners and Strategies

- Involve parents, communities, health organizations, businesses, schools, counselors, clergy, peers, teachers, youths in examining the current situation
- Assess a variety of contexts and situations; behaviors and needs may differ in each
- Examine other systemic components for efficacy, such as procedures, rules, resources, facilities, funding, individual student situations/needs
- Identify ways to build trust and alliances, break through windows of emotional chaos, dialogue
- Put safety of others, self, and property at the forefront
- Know thyself and own cognitive biases/fears
- Stay calm; model effective problem-solving behaviors
- Take small steps, set realistic goals, celebrate successes, work as a team
- Demonstrate and encourage human/systemic interdependence vs. independence

In previous eras, children also saw and experienced cruelty. Today's youths are bombarded with negativity and both direct and indirect societal cruelty and systems that seem to lead to a place of no return (Prothrow-Stith 1991). Some youths in North America are "shell-shocked soldiers" who have grown up in a violent society filled with violent images, toys, and leaders; they see violence as the most viable mechanism for dealing with conflict (Prothrow-Stith 1991, 68). The roots of such emotions grow very deeply, and violence becomes an acceptable norm if not checked. Research shows that child and adolescent rates of post-traumatic stress disorder (PTSD) are linked to higher levels of exposure to traumatic events (Stewart 2004, 325). Children separated from their parents are at a greater risk for PTSD, and it follows that homeless youths are particularly vulnerable, especially when they are intentionally removed from their family (325–26). Homeless adolescent youths are more prone to becoming victims of physical assault and sexual exploitation (326). Bemak and Keys (2000) suggest that the solution requires a full community of teachers, students, parents, business leaders, community leaders, healthcare practitioners and others working together to resolve this very critical problem. Nonetheless, it is likely that schools will remain danger zones if some of the aforementioned systemic aspects of the problem go unresolved (Prothrow-Stith and Spivak 2004) (figure 3.1).

Schools in North America and Europe today have become potential danger zones for students, teachers, and the community at large (e.g., the Colombine school shootings in the United States and the recent mass murder of youths in Norway by a right-wing sociopath). Some of the most frequently encountered incidents or acts of violence and aggression that contribute to schools being viewed as danger zones include possession or use of weapons; assault and battery; vandalism of property; theft; intimidation and verbal threats; possession, sale, and/or use of drugs, guns, and alcohol; gang formation and expansion; sexual assault; hate crimes; and incidences leading to anxiety and PTSD (Byrne 1997b; Prothrow-Stith and Spivak 2004). The victims of these types of aggression include fellow students, teachers, parents, law enforcement officers, community members, and perhaps even the perpetrators. While the problem proliferates within schools, it may both originate and end not only with the individual but also with society as a whole (Prothrow-Stith and Spivak 2004). The Canadian Centre for Justice Statistics and the 2004 General Social Survey found that 653,000 Canadian women aged fifteen and older experienced and reported spousal violence by a current or previous partner in the previous five years (Brzozowski and Brazeau 2008). Young people globally are exposed to violence and are living in a violent society because to a large extent neither students, teachers, counselors, parents, police, nor the community can single-handedly solve all of the systemic problems and factors that may contribute to student aggression and violence (Wessells 2006). Violence relates to a complex mix of factors, including individual factors (biological and/or social), peer group factors (identity group, status, power, group norms, economics), family factors (parents, models, leaders, cultural norms, acceptable behaviors, religion), community factors (history, group norms, family norms, economics, resource availability, education, jobs, social programs), and larger societal factors (media, political institutions, legal institutions, history) (Grossman and DeGaetano 1999).

With respect to individual factors, a number of scholars question the degree to which violence and aggression may be attributed to either biological factors or social factors (Garbarino 1999; Burton 1997; Cairns 1996; Fry 2006). Although there is some argument that aggressive behavior is possibly linked to hormone levels, enzyme levels, psychological or neurological genetic disorders, or even exposure in utero to androgens (especially in males), the degree to which aggression and violence are genetically or physically rooted is highly debated (Miczek, Mirsky, Carey, DeBold, and Raine 1994; Englander 2007). The research also demonstrates that related behaviors are socially conditioned or learned, based on each individual's experiences within and perceptions of her or his milieu (Fry 2006; Jenson and Howard 1999). Children and youths living with both parents in tight-knit communities are also resilient in the face of ongoing violence (Cairns 1996).

Questions are frequently posed regarding social conditioning and factors such as poverty and lower socioeconomic advantage that may induce greater disposition for aggression and violent behavior (Levitt and Dubner 2009; Raine 2002). Does poverty create violence, or is it a risk factor that may lead to violence? If a child grows up in a poor neighborhood, is she or he automatically destined to be aggressive (Levitt and Dubner 2009)? Poverty is perhaps only a part of a larger systemic problem. What if the person grows up in a poor but intact household in which the parents learned to deal with anger effectively, model appropriate behaviors for dealing with anger and aggression, and promote the values of education (Cairns 1996)? Will the child then automatically also be able to deal with such anger and despair effectively? Do some children remain resilient in the face of these challenges? These questions lead to additional questions about the child's ecological environment (Bronfenbrenner 1979).

Poverty alone is not always a root of the problem, as youth violence has often been perpetrated by middle-class youths (e.g., Jason Derek Brown). However, the general effects of poverty cannot be denied. Poverty may induce feelings of desperation and hopelessness, which in some individuals may lead to aggressive or insensitive violent behavior (Prothrow-Stith 1991). Poverty may exclude an individual from particular opportunities, such as good education and mentoring, community activities and involvement and community-based resources, and getting out of a generally destructive and dangerous milieu that is rampant with crime and violence (Levitt and Dubner 2009; Prothrow-Stith 1991). Violence might result from relative rather than absolute deprivation (Horowitz 2000) in which individuals envy or resent the success or opportunities of others. Thus, while the cyclical effects of poverty and its contribution to aggressive and violent behavior in youths cannot be underestimated, poverty does not appear to be the only cause, because not all poor people are necessarily violent (Garbarino 2003; Levitt and Dubner 2009; Prothrow-Stith 1991).

Some of the key elements pointed out by Bemak and Keys (2000) regarding the roots of violence involve the degree to which parents and others with whom the youths interact are role models in teaching young people effective coping strategies for dealing with anger and aggression. The concern is that if youths do not have positive role models or if they have the wrong role models (such as gang leaders and hate mongers) or unskilled role models (such as inept parents), then they may be unable to learn nonaggressive behaviors or may learn that violence is an acceptable option to problem solving (Howell 2003; Prothrow-Stith and Spivak 2004).

The media promotes the violent conditioning of youths through generally violent television shows, movies, and some music types, which often demean women, ethnic groups, and authority or otherwise serve to marginalize certain members of society (Prothrow-Stith 1991; Ury 2002). Yet delinquency and the desire to hear rap or punk music may not always correlate and could both stem from other ecological causes. Children who play with war toys and watch violent cartoons may be predisposed to long-range negative consequences (Garbarino 1999), though certainly those who witness actual violence in their homes and lives may be even more prone to negative consequences (Prothrow-Stith 1991). The media often tends to glamorize violence by showing it, making light of it, making violent perpetrators seem cool, perpetuating negative stereotypes, and using narratives that appeal to violence such as profane language and sexist comments (Prothrow-Stith and Spivak 2004; Prothrow-Stith 1991).

Homicide rates in the United States are six times higher than in Canada (Hagan and Foster 2001). Female victims of homicide are about ten times more likely to have been killed by an intimate partner than are male victims (Hagan and Foster 2001). American public policy punishes young offenders through waivers and transfers from juvenile to adult courts. Some argue that this reduces street violence; others argue that more prevalent birth control did so as well (Levitt and Dubner 2009). In some large American cities, adolescents may observe someone being shot (Prothrow-Stith and Spivak 2004). Young people have easier access to handguns than in countries such as Canada, England, and Ireland that have restrictive gun laws (Harper 2004).

Violence is learned at home, where teenagers and children are repeatedly exposed to it and have the opportunity to model it (Englander 2007). Antisocial behaviors (e.g., violence) are widespread in the general population. Adolescent males may be more likely to engage in violent behavior than adolescent females, while youths living in low-income housing are more at risk of later violence than youths from middle-class backgrounds (Mason 2004; Prothrow-Stith 1991). Younger adolescents with a father who is better educated, especially those who have stronger attachments to their mothers and better self-esteem, are less at risk of later violence (Benda and Corwyn 2002). The anger of young people is also expressed in their music (Prothrow-Stith 1991). Heavy metal and punk music reflect working-class anger, while hip-hop and rap music reflect what is happening in the poor inner-city communities (Prothrow-Stith 1991). Adolescents who listen to heavy metal and gangster rap music may be more prone to "delinquency, antisocial behaviors, poor academic achievement, and substance abuse" compared to other adolescents (Miranda and Claes 2004, 113). Youth music often seems to condone violence and also shows the alienation of young people.

Violence against youths also includes violence that is structural and hidden, expressed as poverty, hunger, racism, sexism, heterosexism, oppression, and victimization (Galtung 2006). Violence easily becomes a way of life for children living in the inner cities in Western countries, including concentrations of ghettoized and alienated immigrant youths in Western Europe and North America. Adolescents are afraid to function as violence becomes normal for those living in a war zone; there is no escape from the violent neighborhoods as young people feel abandoned and oppressed (Wessells and Jonah 2006). Peer pressure to commit violence pushes young people over the edge as their environment reproduces the cycle of victim and offender (McEvoy-Levy 2006). Young males from minority groups have no strong economic support base and may feel that they have no meaningful role in society (e.g., recent riots in Birmingham, London, and Manchester in England) (Garbarino 1999). Television and movies promote a culture of dominance that socializes young people who spend too much time watching TV and may lash out as a result of the power of suggestion of violence (Englander 2007; Prothrow-Stith 1991). Antiviolence efforts also need to extend to sports-related models that often prove to be an out for young inner-city children (Foer 2004). These include officials taking more action more quickly, making education about sports violence mandatory, providing training for coaches, banning parents for unsportsmanlike behavior, and prosecuting professionals for violent behavior (Schoenfelder 2001, 156).

## Youths, Political Violence, and War

Youths who are exposed to political violence in civil wars and ethnic conflicts become both victims and perpetrators of the violence (Wessells 2006). Repeated exposure to political violence increases the risk that young adults will engage in future violent and antisocial behavior (McEvoy-Levy 2006; Raviv, Oppenheimer, and Bar-Tal 1999). Young people are socialized into a sociocultural environment that shapes their individual experiences and melds and infuses their ideas about violence and peace (Byrne 1997a, 1997b). Young people can also learn to develop coping and resiliency skills through the mentoring of family, friends, and community (Bicksler 2002; Cairns 1996). Insights into the worldviews of youths exposed to violence have implications for policy that is intended to end direct and structural violence so that our children can live in a new peaceful world (Polkinghorn and Byrne 2001).

The proliferation of civil wars and ethnic conflicts has resulted in the use of children as soldiers. Violence is common against women and children in these wars. Hundreds of thousands of children were co-opted to fight in civil wars in countries such as Sierra Leone, Sri Lanka, Liberia, and East Timor (Beah 2007; Dodge and Raundalen 1987; Keethaponcalon 2001). Underage soldiers hail from economically disadvantaged families, are uneducated or have had their education forcibly interrupted, and are forcibly recruited into armed militias where they are indoctrinated with the group's violent ideology and sometimes into a drugged condition of obedience and frenzy (Wessells 2006). Child-soldiers are easy to control in the execution of horrific atrocities and ultimately are expendable. Many child-soldiers returning from wars suffer from symptoms of PTSD (Cohn and Goodwin-Gill 1994). The younger the child-soldier, the deeper the psychological damage. Children's stress reaction, however, varies according to their emotional and cognitive maturity (Garbarino and Kostelny 1997). Children who have tight family and social networks tend to be more resilient and better able to cope with the stress and anxiety than children who do not have such networks (Cairns 1996). In a study of youths in South Africa's townships, Straker (1992) noted that black children were caught in a dual world that consisted of both narcissistic fantasies and traumatic deflation. These highly traumatized children operated within a war mentality that related to violence as a form of self-defense and as a channel for revenge. Garbarino and Kostelny's (1997) study of children living in Chicago found that inner-city children were impacted by gang members who plague those communities with drugs, guns, and power.

Children express anxiety and fear when confronted by stressors of direct and structural violence in urban areas (Prothrow-Stith 1991). Children and adolescents in the United States have become more aggressive, impulsive, disobedient, lonely, and sad (Vestal 2001). Young people begin to accept and expect violence as normal and are continually exposed to it on television and in the neighborhood (Prothrow-Stith 1991). Youths are modeling their behavior on aggressive role models and are acting out aggression in antisocial ways (Prothrow-Stith 1991). Youths believe that violence is an integral part of society, which impacts the moral development of very young children (Coles 1986). Repeated exposure to violence in all its forms can lead to a child's feelings of withdrawal, helplessness, and hostility (Garbarino and Kostelny 1997). Parenting practices that include corporal punishment, spanking, or other punitive styles of discipline model for children that violence is an acceptable means of social control (Ellison and Bartwoski 1997). Homicide is also the leading cause of death for young men of color in the urban inner cities of the United States (Hacker 1995; Prothrow-Stith and Spivak 2004). New skills of conflict resolution and peace education can be taught to children in the schools to build emotional competence to handle anger and resolve conflict (Brown 2000; Macbeth and Fine 1995; Vestal 2001).

## Gangs

Gangs use cultural symbols and colors to denote their geographic territory and to demonstrate their values and beliefs (Nordstrom 2006). In Northern Ireland and Sri Lanka, gangs scribble graffiti on the walls of buildings to mark their territory and to warn other gangs not to trespass (Wessells 2006). Gang member profiles suggest that typical gang members are working-class youths who join to achieve status and develop opportunities (Prothrow-Stith 1991). They are socially isolated, deviant, and mistrustful (Byrne, McCleod, and Polkinghorn 2004). More female gang members join in urban areas. Those in their early teens and adult members are the core leaders of the gangs, and gang members are usually ethnically segregated, reflecting working-class origins (Jenson and Howard 1999). In the United States they provide protection for their "local neighborhood" and for local businesses (Prothrow-Stith 1991, 99).

Deborah Prothrow-Stith and Howard Spivak (2004) note that the social characteristics of gangs are reflected in the fact that gangs are isolated from the conventional adult world. They perceive adults as unwilling to help them. In Canada, gang recruits are school dropouts, aboriginal youths, and new immigrants (Stein et al. 2007). Some gang members may have experienced physical or psychological abuse in their families and lack the encouraging support of a mentor (Prothrow-Stith 1991). Moreover, the gang member's family may be under economic stress and without parental supervision (Prothrow-Stith 1991). Relatives may also be gang members so that there is a tradition to be followed with a gang culture (Prothrow-Stith 1991). Gangs predominate because of the social isolation of the urban underclass who reside in deteriorating neighborhoods (Prothrow-Stith 1991). The failure of schools and the family to provide an adequate mechanism of opportunity and positive mentoring is also a systemic part of the problem (Prothrow-Stith and Spivak 2004).

Recruitment into the gang is informal via family members or peers, and the inductee must have courage and be able to physically fight (Prothrow-Stith 1991). Gangs recruit actively in schools and in the neighborhood. Prothrow-Stith (1991) identified three types of gangs in the United States: the scavenger gang, which is loosely organized; the territorial gang, in which the members identify with territory; and the corporate gang, in which crews sell drugs to make money. Some adolescents join gangs for support, entertainment, or economic organization. Kevin Yoder (2003) also outlines three models of gang membership: selection, facilitation, and enhancement. In the selection model, gangs "attract and recruit youth who are already delinquent"; in the social facilitation model, gangs "train youth to be delinquent"; and in the enhancement model, both elements of the previous models are evident. It is when gangs "provide further training that . . . delinquency and drug use" are exacerbated (443). Other members join gangs to achieve personal goals such as to traffic drugs, to survive, or just to hang out (Prothrow-Stith 1991). Typically members come from communities struggling with the same problems of poverty, racism, and demographic changes (Beah 2007). Youths, including the homeless or runaways, also join gangs because membership provides them with a sense of community, as these young people are isolated from schools and law enforcement (Yoder 2003). The movement of businesses from the community, in part due to the shift of the job market from industrial to service-type jobs, impacts young people's employment opportunities (Prothrow-Stith 1991; Sachs 2006). Population change has also witnessed rapid ethnic changes in American neighborhoods, as the flight of middle-class residents to the suburbs has also ensured that there are few leaders left to mentor these young people (Prothrow-Stith 1991). Residents tolerate the gang in their neighborhood because it protects businesses from rival gangs and because they also identify with the economic challenges faced by gang youths (Prothrow-Stith and Spivak 2004; Prothrow-Stith 1991).

The needs and desires of gang members are many: identity, recognition, protection, love, hope, and understanding (Prothrow-Stith 1991). Gang members also seek status, money, opportunity, acceptance, and belonging (Prothrow-Stith 1991). Members who come from dysfunctional families and who are fed up with the hopelessness of urban life or who are school dropouts also search for power, discipline, shelter, food, and self-esteem within the gang structure (Prothrow-Stith 1991). Gangs may become an "ethnocultural enterprise with a strong ethnic identity," customs, practices, and network of friends as they set up an underground economy as the chief means of survival for scores of poor teenagers in the United States (Prothrow-Stith 1991, 99). Prothrow-Stith (1991) found that the gang has regulations that prevent male members from having girlfriends or other distractions so that the male members can go out on the streets to make money for the gang. The schools may also not be providing these young people with the cultural capital of a sound education to prepare them for future employment (MacLeod 1995). Yet lack of job opportunities to generate a living and the resulting hopelessness relate to Belfast, Gaza city, and American inner cities perhaps in contradiction from assumptions about poor school experiences (Monti 1994). Thus, the structural constraints of the education and economic systems ensure that these adolescents are frustrated over their lack of prospects in the job market (MacLeod 1995).

During apartheid in South Africa and out of a sense of hopelessness, young people joined ethnic gangs and did not perceive their behavior as an act of delinquency, deviance, or failure; rather, membership in the ethnic gang represented the only course of action available because it assisted young people in challenging existing constraints and domination by mainstream society (Straker 1992). Poor experiences in school and with adults also encourage young people to rebel against and resist the system (Hacker 1995; MacLeod 1995).

The socialization process and experience is critical in shaping the perceptions and behavior of young people. The school experience may involve labeling young people as deviant as they receive poor treatment from their teachers (Hacker 1995; MacLeod 1995). Youths may act out the deviant label assigned to them in the classroom and seek refuge with others also so labeled (Prothrow-Stith 1991). If the police harass young people in the neighborhood, they may turn to the gang for protection and solace, becoming entrapped in gang life (McEvoy-Levy 2006; Prothrow-Stith 1991). Later it is difficult for members to pull out of the gang because older gang leaders need the younger members' labor (Prothrow-Stith 1991). In reality, gangs are franchised businesses rather than stemming from culture (Levitt and Dubner 2009). Younger members eventually realize that they are taken advantage of and may return to the mainstream world that they earlier opposed because they realize that the gang has not been a liberating mechanism (Conly et al. 1993; Prothrow-Stith 1991). It is hard for them to cut their ties with the gang (Welch 2003), as they have a gang identity and a reputation that is not respected by mainstream society, and their lack of education and work skills keeps them in a working-class context (Prothrow-Stith 1991).

The gang provides a mechanism for survival for young people who face very difficult circumstances in their everyday lives (Prothrow-Stith and Spivak 2004). Gang members form friendships and assist one another. It is demoralizing for young people to be deprived of economic and other resources (Polkinghorn and Byrne 2001). When youths respond to these conditions by organizing themselves into a cohesive communal type of organization because they feel that society has abandoned them, they may be stigmatized as criminals (Prothrow-Stith 1991). They may need to insulate themselves from the negative judgments that people have made about them (Prothrow-Stith 1991). They are not psychopaths because they are striving to care for themselves and others (Garbarino 2003; Prothrow-Stith 1991).

Gang members have a history of negative experiences with adults, especially regarding the need for job skills (Prothrow-Stith 1991). Former members of gangs are afraid that employers will not be understanding about their past experiences; they have a need for positive role models to guide them and help them to restore their confidence (Prothrow-Stith and Spivak 2004). Globally gangs are more violent than in the 1950s because some gangs traffic drugs for survival and have more access to lethal weapons such as machine guns (Prothrow-Stith 1991). Consequently, there is an increased possibility for violence as rival gangs compete for resources and territory (Prothrow-Stith 1991). Being in a culture of violence lends street youths to be especially sensitive and responsive to attacks (Baron 2001).

### Violence and Minority Males

In the United States, African American males in inner cities are "shell-shocked soldiers" who are desensitized to violence because they live in war zones where violence is normal (Prothrow-Stith 1991, 68). This is also true for minority urban youths living in Belfast, Jerusalem, and Johannesburg who suffer from PTSD (Jenson and Howard 1999). They are enraged because they feel helpless, and as a result they lash out at others. They typically live in the inner city, usually in poor households headed by a single parent or by grandparents (Prothrow-Stith 1991). Prothrow-Stith (1991) makes the critical point that in the 1970s the international economy began to stagnate as a result of the Organization of Petroleum Exporting Countries (OPEC) oil crisis and as multinational corporations moved overseas. As a result, people in the manufacturing industry lost their jobs, which destroyed inner-city economies (Prothrow-Stith 1991). In the United States, African American families began to collapse as men became unemployed and lost their self-respect and dignity and left their families (Prothrow-Stith 1991). Thus, the single working-class American mother ended up living in poverty and had to find employment to care for her family. The community also fragmented as middle-class African Americans and churches moved out to the suburbs, leaving behind impoverished schools (Prothrow-Stith 1991). Young black males joined gangs out of despair because they felt that they had no future, and the rituals, se-crecy, and colors of these gangs gave them a sense of identity as well as strong leaders who gave them a sense of leadership (Anderson 1999; Prothrow-Stith 1991).

In Northern Ireland the search-on-sight policy ensured that the Royal Ulster Constabulary (RUC) perceived all Catholic inner-city kids as violent members of the Provisional Irish Republican Army (Byrne 1997a, 1997b). When the RUC and the British Army searched Catholic males, hostile relations were created because the searches were perceived as harassment. In the United States, young black men are described as an "endangered species" because of the life-and-death challenges faced by them in the inner city (Prothrow-Stith 1991). Black males are unemployed and may feel helpless as violence shapes their lives and they see no hope of a bright future (Liebow 1967; Prothrow-Stith 1991). Consequently, they abuse alcohol and drugs.

Gang violence is prevalent in inner-city neighborhoods, and there is peer pressure to commit violence and crime (Wessells and Jonah 2006). Adolescents lash out at others because they feel anger and rage. Gangs compete for the control of territory to sell drugs in neighbor-hoods (Prothrow-Stith and Spivak 2004). New members behave in a macho way so as not to appear weak to other members while they gain material rewards from the gang to satisfy their basic human needs (Prothrow-Stith 1991). As a result, there is a high rate of lateral violence as crime increases because of economic deprivation and the absence of authority figures (Prothrow-Stith 1991). In the United States the police use excessive force on young African American males in the inner city; the police treat African American males in a humiliating way (Anderson 1999; Prothrow-Stith 1991; Zimring 1998). Similarly, the neighborhood military incursions into black townships in apartheid South Africa created hostile relations between the police and young black males as rage became a catalyst for youth violence against the South African Defense Force (Straker 1992).

## Youth Violence Intervention and Prevention

A number of social forces that cause youth conflict and violence and that interact together can be analyzed through the lens of social cubism (Byrne and Carter 1996) if we are to increase the range of interventions in local community disputes. The complexity of youth violence necessitates a multifaceted grassroots and elite social movement approach that works cooperatively with young people to devise an appropriate intervention and prevention strategy (Prothrow-Stith and Spivak 2004; Senehi and Byrne 2006). A multiplicity of intervention efforts must engage at all levels to transform the underlying nature of youth conflict over time. Such a multimodal and multilevel coordinated approach to youth conflicts includes many actors and approaches (Byrne and Keashly 2000). For example, Deborah Prothrow-Stith (1991) proposes a multidisciplinary intervention model by health departments at the primary level to educate the general public, the secondary level aimed at young people at risk, and the tertiary level that combines strategies to prevent those who are at risk of dying on the streets.

Conly et al. (1993) also outline a multitrack prevention and intervention systems approach to target street gangs, in contrast to the law enforcement suppression model, that involves high-risk youth programs, organizing a community response, school-based strategies, family interventions, and employment and training strategies.

We have added a peace education and conflict resolution component to the Conly et al. (1993) process discussed below. This combined intervention approach can be expanded to address situations in which children are drawn into paramilitary organizations as combatants. We now outline in more detail and discuss the (Conly et al. 1993) model.

## High-Risk Youth Program

Peripheral gang members have to be reached to reduce the appeal of gangs for potential new recruits (Conly et al. 1993). The goals of the intervention program are to give all young people positive experiences and skills to avoid commitment to negative behavior (Macbeth and Fine 1995). Conly et al. (1993) suggest that an inclusive intervention process that targets all children in the local neighborhood may prevent labeling one group of young people as deviant. It is important to involve all members of the community, such as the police, trade unions, and private industry in a multimodal intervention process (Conly et al. 1993).

According to Conly et al. (1993), the goals of a high-risk youth program would be to: (1) establish a community center to bring the local community together; (2) provide job-training skills and placement; (3) set up mentoring and tutorial programs with the local schools and youth centers; (4) set up clubs and after-school programs in sports, reading, music, etc.; (5) establish conflict resolution and Big Brother/Big Sister mentoring programs in the schools to teach young people about anger management, problem-solving, listening skills, etc.; (6) formulate a substance abuse counseling program in local health centers; (7) establish a program in which the police can visit families to discuss how guns kill young people; (8) create vibrant and community-led sports programs; and (9) set up new norms to change the cultural environment so that young people can turn to people in the neighborhood for support and for role models.

## Community-based Programs

It is important for a community as a third-party intervener to organize itself because it is the entire community's responsibility to prevent the spread of youth violence in their neighborhood, raise community awareness about gangs in the area, and organize community leaders in schools, businesses, churches, local politics, education, and the police to take action (Conly et al. 1993; Saunders 2001). The goals of the intervention program are to institutionalize the program in communities in which youth violence problems have not become entrenched, because it is easier to organize the whole community as an inclusive strategy for community-based empowerment (Conly et al. 1993).

According to Conly et al. (1993), the community-based program components might include the following interventions: (1) a referral service to a neighborhood mediation center to assist residents by having community training sessions to address youth violence in the neighborhood; (2) a twenty-four-hour hotline that residents can use if they anticipate a youth violence problem (e.g., the police could arrive before gang violence erupts); and (3) the development of new norms in key institutions such as the family, schools, and places of worship to provide new opportunities for young people to bond with positive role models and to give them new skills to uphold the new norms of behavior; (4) the development of superordinate goals to create shared tasks leading to shared goals and meaningful contact; (5) healing groups for victims to allow the community to acknowledge suffering and to grieve a loss by participating in rituals such as candlelight vigils so that they can heal from the trauma (Carter, Irani, and Volkan 2009); and (6) police officers on the beat trained in conflict resolution and community policing in order to help build community and prevent crime and improve contact with the young people to build rapport.

Reverend Bill Chapman goes into the prisons in St. Louis to teach young men new skills of problem solving and communication through the elicitive storytelling conflict intervention process. Moreover, taxi drivers in Belfast take young children from both sides of the intercommunal divide out of the city into the countryside, teaching them new norms of cooperation.

Participation in youth sports is generally viewed as a positive experience. Sports can have both positive and negative effects in conditioning about violence or offering productive time. In urban inner-city areas, sports play an even larger role, keeping young people away from drugs, gangs, and violence and thereby building their confidence and self-esteem.

Local community leaders could get the community involved in environmental action to gather up trash and use music, quilt making, posters, and T-shirts to get the community together to address environmental issues that impact everyone. Police officers in Syracuse, New York, for example, take inner-city children to Adirondack Park every summer to play sports and to learn problem-solving skills.

Establishing a Victim Offender Restorative Program (VORP) brings survivors and perpetrators together in a restorative healing process.

### School-based Programs

A third-party intervener must also organize the schools to improve the educational services in communities in which there is youth violence so that the quality of life can be improved for all children in the neighborhood (Conly et al. 1993; Ury 2002). The school needs to keep minority children committed to education (MacLeod 1995). This is difficult in schools in which there is youth violence activity. Schools need to focus on dropout prevention and on improving academic standing. Eliminating the portion of local (city and county) property taxes that goes to supporting schools and instead using a federal-level tax to support schools would enhance all schools' resources in the United States by creating an equal playing field and providing a fair opportunity for all children to succeed so that no child is left behind (Kozol 1991).

The goals of a school-based intervention program might include a conflict systems design of the needs assessment focusing on the local community (Ury, Brett, and Goldberg 1993). It is critical to examine the structural and cultural roots of conflict and realize that many youths live in poor areas of the city and are open to individual "spirit murder" as a result (Prothrow-Stith 1991). The program could also encourage youngsters to see that the school is not an alien place. Educators need the youths' attachment to the school to improve the relationship between the schools and the community (Prothrow-Stith

1991). The school could provide reading classes and sports and drama opportunities for the parents and the children, and parents could sit together in night class to study for extracurricular education or to complete a high school diploma (Conly et al. 1993). Lagan College, the integrated ethnoreligious school in Belfast, provides these types of events for its students and their parents (Byrne 1997a, 1997b).

According to Conly et al. (1993), the program components of a school-based intervention could include the following: (1) a drug abuse program that would involve parents and teachers with the young people in the community; (2) a conflict resolution training program to provide new values and ethics for children to resolve conflict nonviolently; (3) a multicultural training program for teachers so that they are sensitive to minority children and to eliminate cultural biases (Prothrow-Stith and Spivak 2004); (4) a nonviolence program for young people in the community; (5) a demarginalization of potential youth recruits by providing family counseling, tutoring, sports, and music; (6) the establishment of youth clubs to meet twice a week to build young people's self-esteem and leadership skills; (7) a planning and management team to review the goals of the school in meeting community needs and to prevent the streaming of children into "smart" and "not smart" classes (e.g., Prothrow-Stith 1991); (8) the development of parent outreach to involve parents in their children's education; and (9) police programs on violence whereby police can go into the schools to talk to young people and provide a violence prevention curriculum to train children in violence prevention skills.

Professor Neil Katz from the Program on the Analysis and Resolution of Conflicts (PARC) at Syracuse University set up a teaching nonviolence through sports program for young inner-city children in Syracuse. Play therapy through sports and music opens up the creative possibilities of deprogramming former child-soldiers so that they can see outside of their milieus (Wessells 2006). Youth workers are positive role models for young people and can build up their skills. PTA workshops could be provided for the parents to develop their math and reading skills so that they can mentor their children.

*Family Intervention Programs*

Family life is difficult once the youths becomes involved with violence, as the parents may have lost control of the situation (Conly et al. 1993). The father needed to socialize male youths to manage aggression oftentimes is not available (Prothrow-Stith 1991). The goals of a family intervention program would concentrate attention on families with young children because parental influence is at its peak when children are young and would also provide parents with better parenting skills so that they can teach their children expectations for behavior and provide positive reinforcement for desired behavior (Conly et al. 1993; Prothrow-Stith 1991; Prothrow-Stith and Spivak 2004). Important questions to consider in designing such a program include the following: Is the best location to conduct parent training a church, synagogue, mosque, clinic, or community center? How can parent networks increase parent participation (Conly et al. 1993)?

The family intervention program components might include providing incentives such as free childcare, transportation, and financial aid to get parents to participate in the program; connecting families with their communities by integrating families into social services; and providing workshops on how to control funding resources (Conly et al. 1993). This is especially significant for working mothers, as it demonstrates that the community wants them to participate in the program (Conly et al. 1993).

*Employment and Training Intervention Programs*

There is a need to build sustainable employment opportunities for young people in their local communities (Byrne, Thiessen, and Fissuh 2007). Research on ethnic violence demonstrates that external economic aid assists in building the peace dividend and in providing employment for young people typically drawn to paramilitary organizations (Byrne and Irvin 2001, 2002; Matic, Byrne, and Ghebretsadik 2007). However, it is important to point out that creating employment opportunities is not itself a panacea to ending youth violence in the community. Youths who are employed may continue to commit crimes, such as the outbreaks of riots in London, Manchester, and

Birmingham in England and two years ago in Lyons, France. Some young people may benefit more than others from on-the-job training or classroom training. The goals of an employment and training intervention program (Conly et al. 1993) should include: (1) creating employment maintenance and development in communities with high levels of unemployment to turn young people away from illegal economic activities toward embracing employment opportunities that are accessible to all youths in the neighborhood, (2) promoting indigenous businesses to change the social structure of communities to employ their own people, and (3) creating apprenticeship scholarships to forge partnerships between private industry and trade unions to find employment for young people after they graduate from high school.

The employment and training intervention program components might include a work program for gang affiliates and potential gang recruits in the local community center so that they get social skills training, participate in recreational activities, and receive counseling and vocational training instruction (Conly et al. 1993). It is most important to saturate a neighborhood with positive educational and economic opportunity programs to address poverty and with programs to address drug and alcohol addictions as well as to establish support groups in health care, housing, and family services (Conly et al. 1993; Byrne, McLeod, and Polkinghorn 2004). The idea is to create choices for young people who begin to perceive that joining gangs or militias and becoming embroiled in violence is not inevitable.

### Peace Education, Restorative Justice, Conflict Resolution, and Violence Prevention

Increasingly, students seek to make sense of complicated and perilous events in their society. Meanwhile, they may feel helpless in the face of these powerful social and political forces and the conflicts they experience in their own homes, schools, and communities (Wallach 2000). Peace education addresses these student needs, and peer mediation has been used with great success in schools. Students and teachers are provided with a nonviolent alternative to the traditional system of discipline to resolve conflict in the schools (Brown 2000). Students develop skills and enhance self-esteem and self-efficacy through using the problem-solving process to resolve conflict creatively (Vestal 2001). The current research shows that schools that are conducted democratically result in greater success in peacemaking, teaching tolerance, and violence reduction (Johnson and Johnson 1996). Peer mediation programs assist in creating a more positive school context, teaching students creative skills to manage conflicts constructively, and providing them with a process to address violence in their own lives (Bowling and Hoffman 2003). Schools also report a decrease in violence and an overall improvement in the general school climate (Bekerman 2009). Young children learn conflict resolution skills that can impact the images that they have of violence as the only technique to solve conflict (Polkinghorn and Byrne 2001; Vestal 2001).

Peace schools' policies and practices are inherent in the operation of the school. Peace education assists in building a nonviolent classroom and community through a peace curriculum that introduces students to standards of social justice, human rights, and nonviolent ethical principles (Bekerman 2009; Vestal 2001). Dr. Jessica Senehi's Storytelling for Peace and Renewing Community (SPARC) Institute, housed in the Arthur V. Mauro Centre for Peace and Justice at St. Paul's College, University of Manitoba, combines the storytelling process with peace education tools to provide the teachers who take the SPARC Institute courses with innovative and creative ideas and practices to engage their students in an authentic way to cocreate new spaces (Senehi 2009b). SPARC also includes an annual Winnipeg International Storytelling Festival (WISF) involving thousands of schoolchildren and their teachers and parents based on the idea that providing spaces for children and citizens to define their experiences, identities, and vision for the future in a public context is an essential part of global citizenship, democracy, and establishing and maintaining human rights, peace, and social justice (Senehi 2009a). Peace educators also use cooperative learning methodologies to empower their students to resolve conflict nonviolently and to construct a better world based on the promotion of human rights and ecological sustainability (Harris and Morrison 2003). More research is needed to reconsider whether cooperative learning research truly substantiates the outcomes (Brown 2000). Does the creation of a democratic milieu foster the development of social and civic responsibility within the school as a holistic system? The federal Head Start program in the United States is a unique effort to provide low-income children with a comprehensive intervention program involving their parents and the community in order to promote social competence and nonviolence and to prepare at-risk youngsters for school (Vestal 2001).

Violence intervention and prevention programs can also be tied into the education system. Colette Daiute (2003) created a yearlong literacy-based violence prevention curriculum focusing on discrimination in third and fifth grades in an urban setting in America. On the basis of the findings, Daiute argues that a major goal of programs should be to assist teachers and students to examine values rather than merely conforming to a set of them (99). Hence, a values negotiation sociocultural model including students and their families must be part of the curriculum and interrelationships within the school (100). Butts and Mears (2001) suggest that there are four main important elements to successful juvenile justice. First, accurate assessment is necessary to screen for co-occurring disorders such as mental health and substance abuse (188). Second, it is crucial that criminogenic needs, or factors that predict recidivism and are amenable to change, are targeted. Factors that may discourage criminal behavior should be investigated (183). Third, "general responsivity" programming that is grounded in cognitive-behavioral treatment modalities addressing the needs of youths should be in place (184). Fourth, intervention programs should be located in the same communities in which the offenders reside.

In contrast, Karp and Breslin's (2001) study of American restorative justice programs in the statewide school system in Minnesota, fifteen schools in the metropolitan Denver area, and a small cluster of six alternative facilities in southeastern Pennsylvania suggests that restorative justice reduces delinquency, finds just solutions, empowers the community to respond to problems without always resorting to the criminal justice system, and creates a safe and supportive learning environment to promote positive cultural values. The comprehensive and prominently instituted family model of restorative justice is brought into the school environment.

Restorative justice differs from traditional systems in three ways. First, attention is focused on all stakeholders in a conflict. Second, the basis for working through the conflict is in already-established natural or community relationships; these relationships are morally interdependent (Karp and Breslin 2001, 252). Third, the focus of the process extends beyond the offender's needs to the larger social context of a community (Karp and Breslin 2001). When a criminal law is infringed upon, harm is defined in terms of its effects on other members of the community and not as a technical infraction alone. Strategies based on authoritative control, with liaisons between schools and private security agencies, are more common, as these systems are based on fear rather than care. This tension is an enduring issue between traditional and restorative justice systems and leads to more marginalization and even greater social-psychological deficits (254). Restorative techniques covered included healing circles that bring together victims, offenders, their supporters, and others from the community to discuss the effect of the incidents; they also find strategies for making repair and reintegrating the offender and in building community (256).

The drawbacks of certain techniques (conferencing, circle sentencing, etc.) used in this system are that they preclude any immediate solution to problems, and the majority of school personnel are unfamiliar with their philosophy (Karp and Breslin 2001, 267). Some teachers in the schools in the study have attempted to offset any potential problems by having group conferencing and discussions with their classes at the opening of every school day. The process also takes time (typically one to three years) to see a meaningful change, time to train facilitators and peace builders and time to "repair specific harms" (269). Moreover, the program has an awkward relationship with other institutional policies grounded in retributive justice, so the need to produce clear standards is pressing (269). In any case, the whole process enjoins the student to consider the consequences of bad behavior and to reevaluate and rebuild social ties in the context of student life. According to the authors, this system encourages students to identify compelling alternatives (270).

# Conclusion

This chapter calls for a paradigm shift that transcends the current state of reality from a culture of violence to a culture of peace (Harris and Morrison 2003). Young people must be energized to be the vanguard of such a paradigm shift in order to be included in a process that transcends ethnicity, race, gender, culture, sexual identity, and class in the process of building a new society. Such a paradigm shift would first and foremost require the training and development of adolescents and children in a less violent and more nonviolent philosophy so that they can be directed into channels for peacemaking and become instrumental in introducing the changes in their communities (Senehi and Byrne 2006). However, such a paradigm shift also necessitates adults ending direct, cultural and structural violence, and adults must also confront the genuine insecurities and transitional disruptions that teenagers face. Constructive inclusive mechanisms have to be found to allow young people to participate in the political and economic process, to develop themselves through education, and to have access to viable career opportunities. The myriad of socioeconomic and personal issues identified as important to these young people must be considered and further developed.

The next chapter explores some of the causes of violence against women and also outlines a multitrack intervention and prevention process.

## Websites Related to Youth Violence

Centre for Effective Collaboration and Practice, American Institutes for Research, http://cecp.air.org/

Centre for the Prevention of Youth Violence, John Hopkins Bloomberg School of Public Health, http://www.jhsph.edu/Prevent-YouthViolence/

National Centre for Mental Health Promotion and Youth Violence Prevention, http://www.promoteprevent.org

Ontario Ministry of Children and Youth Services, http://www.rootso-fyouthviolence.on.ca/

Peel Youth Violence Prevention Network, http://www.endyouthvio-lence.ca/

Southern Poverty Law Center, Teaching Tolerance, http://www.teach-ingtolerance.org

Striving to Reduce Youth Violence Everywhere, Centers for Disease Control and Prevention, http://www.safeyouth.org/

UN Department of Economic and Social Affairs, Economic and Social Council, Youth Social Policy and Development Division, http://www.un.org/youth

Violence Intervention Project, Scarborough, Ontario, http://www .violenceinterventionproject.com

## Suggested Questions for Further Discussion

1. Why is there an epidemic of violence that is decimating a gen-eration of minority young men and women in North America? How do distorted images of violence, the lack of nonviolent role models, and the brutal tactics of gangs and drug dealers impact these young people who are filled with aggression and anger?

2. Why is youth violence a more complex and multifaceted prob-lem, with many interrelated factors contributing to its causes? Are boys who are abused in the home more at risk of delinquency and in joining gangs than girls? What are some of the common misconcep-tions of the relationship between gangs and violence in society? What purpose do you see gangs serving for young people?

3. Do you think that spanking, violent television programs, mov-ies, and video games socialize young people to behave violently? Why do schools continue to be danger zones for young people? How can youths be expected to focus on learning if they live in constant fear of bullying, bodily injury, or even death on school grounds?

4. Is the availability of guns really the issue when it comes to ado-lescent violence, or are guns merely the most accessible tool for vio-lence? Even if all the guns were taken off the streets, would this be

enough to prevent youth violence? How do unmet needs and relative deprivation lead to the violent expressions of frustration and hopelessness among youths?

5. Are young people caught up in ethnic conflicts and civil wars resilient in the face of grave violence? How should child-soldiers be reintegrated back into their own communities after the violence has ceased?

6. Why is it important for the medical, business, police, school, and trade union communities to be part of the movement to end youth violence? What skills can we develop within ourselves to better equip us for working with youths who are at risk and have been abused and neglected?

7. If you could design an innovative and multidimensional grassroots intervention program that dealt with violence and youths, who would be your target audience? What would your benchmarks for such an intervention program be?

# 4

---

# Understanding and Preventing Violence against Women and Interpersonal Violence in the Home

During the genocide, Berthe Kayitesi was a young student in Rwanda who decided to visit her grandparents in the countryside. Berthe, a Tutsi, hid in the local convent while the Impuzamugambi and Interahamwe militias put all of the women, children, and nuns on a bus and took them to a killing field, where the militia members raped and killed the women. The abbess, a Hutu, implored the militia to stop, and she was in turn murdered. Berthe held on tight to the hand of one of the genocidaires, who put her on the bus. The other militia members goaded him to rape and kill the "cockroach." Instead, he drove Berthe back to the convent. She survived the genocide and was able to get out of Rwanda, but her family perished there. Today Berthe is working to provide access to education for young people in Tubeho whose parents were killed during the genocide. Her Tubeho, a nongovernmental organization (NGO), means "let's live" and is a community of child-headed households. Today Berthe works to encourage the resilience and empowerment of these young children through education and community renewal (Berthe Kayitesi, personal communication, May 9, 2008).

Violence too often is viewed as a legitimate way of solving problems. The media creates public narratives that frame problems and solutions so that some violence is legitimized if it is placed in an acceptable narrative form that is good or evil or bad and good (Elias 1997). Violence is used to keep power, not to solve problems, and permeates society through sports, media, film, cartoons, and corporations. War is declared on poverty, drugs, terrorism, and crime as a patriarchal war model socializes us to behave violently. Violence is used to preserve the control of males who batter so that women are physically, psychologically, and sexually abused (Tifft and Markham 1991). As Kay Harris (1991, 85) argues, "the personal is political." A husband beating his wife is a clear case of male privilege and interpersonal violence, and when "one million husbands keep one million wives in ignorance, this is structural violence" (Brock-Utne 1997, 153). Violence against women is rooted in socioeconomic and sexual inequality (Caringella-MacDonald and Humphries 1991, 112). According to the United Nations Development Fund for Women (2007, 1), violence against girls and women is a problem of pandemic proportions. Women are beaten, sexually abused, burned, harassed, and impoverished by males and the oppressive institutions of patriarchy (Honey-Knopp 1991). A study conducted in Tanzania in 2001 found that HIV-positive women were 2.5 times more likely to have experienced violence from their current partner than other women experienced (UNIFEM 2007). Bulubulu is a Fijian indigenous peace-building intervention process to resolve local minor disputes whereby the perpetrator apologizes and reconciles with the father of the victim (Merry 2006). This practice is now used by the government to resolve rape cases (Merry 2006). Rape is connected to social, cultural, and structural problems related to misogyny and the devaluation of women, children, and men (Allen 1996). This is why an epidemiological and multidimensional approach is needed to identify the risk factors associated with the causes of violence in rape-prone societies (Englander 2007).

Sexual assault prevention is still the responsibility of the woman at risk, and this reality continues to take shape as repressive restrictions on personal conduct (Caringella-MacDonald and Humphries 1991). Myths about women's complicity in sexual assault and about false accusations are deterrents to reporting on the microlevel (Brock-Utne 1997). On the macrolevel, rape accompanied by murder as an instrument of war in Bosnia and Rwanda has ensured that there are few survivors to tell their stories of mass rape (Allen 1996). Violence against women during or after ethnic violence has been reported in a number of war zones, including Afghanistan, Burundi, Chad, Colombia, Côte d'Ivoire, the Democratic Republic of the Congo, Liberia, Peru, Rwanda, Sierra Leone, Chechnya, Darfur, Sudan, northern Uganda, and the former Yugoslavia (UNIFEM 2007, 8). The international community is intolerant of sexual violence and war crimes yet turns a blind eye to the trafficking of young women to work in the sex industry in the developed world; trafficking is often connected to organized crime and is a very profitable business that generates an estimated $7 billion to $12 billion per year (UNIFEM 2007, 5).

The term "wife battering" can no longer be used to define the problems of domestic violence, as abuse crosses all lines of economic and educational status, age, race, religion, geography, and sexual orientation (Lundy 1993, 276). However, Gelles (1997), Gelles and Strauss (1989), and Englander (2007, 88) suggests that most perpetrators of homicides, assaults, and rapes are primarily males, since women's aggression is less severe and less fatal and results more from self-defense. Heterosexual and same-sex domestic violence is caused by coercion and illegitimate power by one partner over another (Lundy 1993, 275). Power in violent same-sex relationships may also be rooted in the ideas of hierarchy, ownership, entitlement, and control (Herek and Berrill 1992; Lundy 1993). The underlying beliefs that support a heterosexist and misogynist patriarchal culture are developed through the socialization process (Enloe 2000). Thus, some same-sex partners who are raised in a patriarchal society and have not had the opportunity of being exposed to positive role models may internalize the power-over model (Silver 1997). Heterosexual and lesbian battering differ in that same-sex batterers oftentimes may use homophobia to maintain a power imbalance in relationships (Lundy 1993, 282). Lesbian battering, like all domestic violence, affects all segments of the community and demands a holistic approach that involves multimodal interventions (V. Coleman 1994; Lundy 1993; Renzetti 1992).

Steinmetz and Straus (1973) have called the family a "cradle of violence" because the problem of violence and aggression in children originates in the home when parents and other family members use corporal punishment or verbal and/or physical violence against each other. The creation of a space that is home shelters the man (Price 2002, 45). Domestic violence today affects a large percentage of American households (Englander 2007). Globally, violence is apparently so common that domestic violence can be classified as lower-level direct violence or extreme deadly violence (Vallee 2007).

Substance abuse (drugs/alcohol), economic or social deprivation, and immature parents increase the risk of violence at home (Dutton 2007). Domestic abuse is prevalent because it often takes place behind closed doors, and women often keep it to themselves (Gelles 1997). Corporal punishment against children often produces future abusers of children and/or violent tendencies in future generations (Ellison and Bartowski 1997). It is also one element of a much greater system of influences that create angry and violent children. Corporal punishment may produce the transgenerational transmission of violent attitudes and behaviors among children as well as their long-term insensitivity to various types of violence (Ellison and Bartowski 1997).

Domestic violence cuts across all socioeconomic, cultural, and ethnic dimensions, such that even though the aforementioned are noted as risk factors, they are not the only factors (Merry 2006). Other factors include individual and familial belief systems, such as beliefs that the husband is the authority to be obeyed (Enloe 2000). Another reason why domestic violence proliferates is sheer fear of abandonment, poverty, and homelessness (Gelles and Strauss 1989). Some women also believe that placation of the perpetrator is in the best interests of the household, that taking the beating is better than solving the problem (Vallee 2007).

In terms of reducing the risk of violence to family members, the first key step is to highlight the problem of domestic violence in society. Domestic violence came to be made visible as a form of violence due to the first explicit anti–wife battering campaign organized by a small group of women in Britain in the 1970s (DeKeseredy and Schwartz 1991). Stalking, sexual harassment, and gay bashing, each of which was only made to be seen as specific forms of violence in the 1970s and 1990s in certain regions and countries, is still not so perceived in others (DeKeserdy and Schwartz 1991; Jenness 2007; Wall 2000).

This chapter provides a short overview of sexual violence against women (global violence against women, rape as violence, domestic family violence, violence in the home) and outlines some of the specific intervention strategies for preventing violence against women.

## Sexual Violence against Women

This section discusses a few of the many issues in this very broad and complex subject area that is worthy of a book in itself. Sexual violence against women and children reinforces destructive stories of male power and female and children's inferiority (Caprioli and Boyer 2001). The media sexualizes women and children; this is reflected in the trafficking of women as well as in child prostitution, white slavery, sexual offenders, child-soldiers, and child molesters (Snyder 2003). Currently the literature on war does not cover the fact that women's bodies are the site for interstate and intrastate wars constructed by a masculinized, racist, misogynist, and violent patriarchy (Koo 2002, 527).

In developing countries, a better standard of living may favor some men, as females are often perceived as being burdens on their family's scarce resources; better health care is provided for male infants, which results in a higher infant mortality rate for females (Abernethy 1993; Richey 2008). In Afghanistan during the Taliban's regime, only boys had the opportunity to go to school. Female children toil long hours in sweatshops in Africa, Asia, and Latin America (Williams 1999). Young at-risk homeless girls are murdered on the streets of Brazil (Huggins and Mesquita 2000, 258). Parents in some developed and developing countries also perceive that it is more expensive to marry a daughter off with a dowry (Escobar 1995). Female infanticide is reflected in the reaction to the Chinese government's policy that prevents couples from having more than one child. In rural China, a household without a son is considered dishonorable; pressure is on the wife to have a baby boy (Junhong 2001, 275).

Similarly, in India the desire to have sons has forced some expecting mothers to abort female babies after amniocentesis testing shows that the developing baby is female (Bandyopadhyay 2003). In fact, sex-selective abortion, or female feticide, is increasingly occurring because of rapid economic development, progress in technology, and the decline in fertility (912). Indian women will continue bearing children until they have sons because of the prestige that comes with having male children, including socioeconomic, cultural, and political power (923). The continuity of the lineage depends on sons, as daughters are transitory members of a household (923). In Calcutta, Mother Theresa often took baby girls out of trash heaps. In traditional villages in India, the practice of suttee—whereby women have to throw themselves on their husband's funeral pyres and be burned to death because their spouse's family will not take care of them—still exists (Wadley 1994). As a result of these and similar practices, it is estimated that globally many millions of females are missing from the human population (Bales 1999).

Sexual slavery impacts women in both economically developing and developed areas of the world. Only recently has the Japanese nation come to terms with the history of comfort women from Korea, China, Holland, and England who were forced into prostitution for Japanese troops during World War II (Snyder 2003). Currently in countries such as Moldova, Nepal, and Ukraine, young women are trafficked by sexual enslavers. In Thailand and South Africa, a large population of female child prostitutes are prisoners of the sex industry (Bales 1999). Sex tourism represents a leading global industry that exploits these young women (Bales 1999). A significant majority of these prostitutes are HIV-positive (Ford 1990).

Complications in pregnancy lead to more deaths of women in the global South compared to women in the global North (Snyder 2003). For example, the latest estimate is that 536,000 women died in 2005 from complications of pregnancy and childbirth and that 400 mothers died for every 100,000 live births; 99 percent of the women who died were from developing countries (United Nations Children's Fund

2008, 8). Especially in situations of poverty, if the mother dies, then the children may suffer from abuse, neglect, malnutrition, and even death (Snyder 2003). The WHO calculated that by 2000 more than three million women in Africa would die of AIDS, leaving many millions of orphans behind (Williams 1999). A 2005 WHO multicountry study on women's health and domestic violence against women reported that nearly one-third of Ethiopian women had been physically forced by a partner to have sex against their will within the twelve months prior to the study.

It is estimated that worldwide, one in five women will become a victim of rape or attempted rape in her lifetime (UNIFEM 2007, 2). Rape in the context of war has been used as a political act of violence and torture against women and men in Bosnia, Kosovo, and Rwanda (Conroy 2001). In Bosnia, rape was used as a deliberate policy by the Serbian government to promote genocide (Power 2007). Women were raped systematically by groups of men whose agenda was to impregnate them and prevent them from aborting the children (Allen 1996). The logic of the Serbian rape war strategy was that the children of non-Serbian women who were impregnated by Serbian men would have a Serbian identity (Volkan 1998). In Bosnia, Kosovo, Rwanda, and Sudan, women were raped repeatedly, tortured, and killed. Meanwhile, women survivors of the rape camps were perceived as defiled by their society, and often they and the children of the rapes were not accepted into the society after the war (Sylvester 2002). This behavior also constitutes a deliberate strategy of ethnic cleansing (driving particular ethnic groups from a particular region), since women and some men were raped in public view and then the terrified women and other residents were offered safe passage out of their homes and territory (Allen 1996). More than twenty thousand Bosnian, Serbian, and Croat women were raped during the war in the former Yugoslavia (Allen 1996). According to Boose (2002, 93), in ethnic wars the vengeance of male-male rape on the replacement targeted victim is legitimated by the patriarchal culture as the construction of women's bodies as property signify male honor so that women become the targets of enemy rape (93).

In the United States, a National Victim Center (1992) survey of 4,008 participants representing a cross-section of the society found that a woman is beaten every fifteen seconds, 1.3 adult women are raped every minute, 74 percent of all murders of women due to domestic violence occurred when the women left the relationship, 30 percent of all murdered women are killed by their boyfriends or husbands, five million women are beaten by their partners each year. Thirteen percent of the sample was made up of survivors of forcible rape, and 25 percent of those women had been raped more than once.

Consequently, it is necessary to examine the larger sociocultural contexts of political, historical, religious, and economic factors affecting attitudes on violence against women (Nayak, Byrne, Martin, and Abraham 2003, 333). Violence against women has tended to fall into the private sphere of intimate relations, where sociospatial characteristics, such as the "private patriarchal boundary," may keep others from interfering if they perceive the perpetrator to be victimizing his or her intimate partner (Youngs 2003, 1212). It is important to challenge the distinctions made between these public and private framings and instead focus on the continuity of violence against women, children, and men that transcend public/private boundaries (1216). There is an existing continuum between state-perpetrated violence and violence in the personal sphere (Youngs 2003). The state has two roles. One role is as the perpetuating patriarchal figure that sees that male violence is part of the state and is authorized by the state, as patriarchy is linked to violence that is linked to the state (Youngs 2003). Thus, the state is part of the problem and prevents change. The other role is as representing the "key site, in institutional and legal terms, for exposing and attacking it" (1223).

## Rape as Violence

Male and female batterers use violence to maintain control and use the ideology of obligation to coerce their partners into sex (Gelles and Strauss 1989; Strauss and Donnelly 2000). The marital rape exemption in many states in the United States encourages rape, as male perpetrators feel that using force is a normal behavior (Gelles and Strauss 1989; Strauss and Donnelly 2000) (figure 4.1).

Outside of marriage, the interpersonal context of rape varies depending on whether or not or how well the perpetrator and the survivor know each other (Suresh and Seksari 1993). Rape may involve spontaneity or not; an individual male or multiple males plan some rapes, while other rapes are unplanned (Gelles 1997). Rapists will also transform the perpetrator-survivor relationship by framing rape as a date (Buchwald, Fletcher, and Roth 1995).

In a study by Bradley and Davino (2002) of sixty-five women incarcerated in a medium-security prison for women with mental and physical health problems in the United States, 55 percent of the respondents reported childhood sexual and physical abuse, just over 60 percent reported childhood and adult sexual assault, and 43 percent reported all four types of abuse. The women all had a common perception that prison was a safer milieu than was childhood or adulthood (Bradley and Davino 2002, 354). Furthermore, Bradley and Davino (2002, 357) recommend that programs concentrate on increasing the safety and support of incarcerated women's future environments, addressing violence and poverty, providing alternatives to incarceration, and encouraging substance abuse treatment.

### Domestic Family Violence

Law does not punish the so-called little rapes in which women experience fear and harassment every day (DeKeseredy and Schwartz 1991). Violence is interwoven into the fabric of our intimate relationships in the private institution of the family (figure 4.2). Yet the nature of battering women and the battering of developing nations is essentially the same (Tifft and Markham 1991). Historically, violence and domination represent the foundation of man's power against women, children, the environment, indigenous peoples, and weaker nations. Both spheres of battering have common structural sources, and within each sphere similar processes are involved in establishing and maintaining arrangements that foster battering (Tifft and Markham 1991). Private/domestic violence is a private matter that allows male batterers to batter and subordinate women, while public/military violence is a legitimate and acceptable mechanism to exploit and dominate developing nations (Enloe 2000; Tifft and Markham 1991).

*Figure 4.1. Systems view of sexual assault and rape*
**Source: *Compiled by Heather Tanksley, April 2003.***

---

### Types of Sexual Assault Violence and Key Subjects

- Sexual assault/rape of dates, nonspouses, unknowns
- Sexual assault/rape of women in war (sex slavery in war)
- Sexual assault of children
- Infanticide (female)
- Sexual assault across cultures/ethnicities
- Sexual assault of spouse (so-called intimate rape)

---

### Some Statistics/Issues:
### Sexual Assault

- According to biosocial model, men are more at risk of being predisposed to violent/aggressive tendencies; chromosomal differences, testosterone, exposure to in-utero androgens; highly disputed area
- Men are traditionally more socially conditioned to be violent (upbringing, toys, dress, roles, dominance/authority, patriarchy).
- Thailand, U.S., and Bosnian sex slave trade and HIV (critical economic and health issues prevail),
- Infanticide in India and China; son is better; may lead to conflict over time due to population imbalance

---

### Offender Patterns/Beliefs

- Men assault primarily out of domination and power; not an act of love, but act of hatred and marginalization of women, gays, children; violent rapist = battery and rape, power rapist = rape without battery
- Rapists lack ability to empathize with other/victim and often believe in rape myths:
- Sexual violence is justifiable (she asked for it; it was the alcohol)
- No such thing as sexual violence (women want it, not in marriage, only between strangers)
- Sexual assault isn't hurtful (making a fuss about nothing)
- Available services

## Intervenors and Strategies

- Involve communities, health organizations, businesses, counselors, victim/offenders in examining the current situation and taping/creating resources for change
- Assess a variety of contexts and situations; behaviors and needs may differ in each
- Examine other systemic components for efficacy, such as institutional procedures, rules, resources, facilities, funding, reporting and data accuracy (i.e., examine macro/micro)
- Work to diminish patriarchal institutions that devalue women
- Work to empower women's voices, elderly voices, victims' voices
- Shift men's paradigm about power and violence
- Promote positive peace
- Stop hiding/isolating the problem

## Statistics/Issues:
## Sexual Assault

- Women most at risk may be those with developmental disabilities, prior victimization history, tourists, homeless
- Alcohol is often a contributing factor
- Other factors include sexism, racism, poverty, exposure to pornography, drugs
- Violence against women may be rooted in economic, social, and sexual inequality (paradigm)

## Victim Patterns/Beliefs

- Currently, it seems that the victims are "responsible" for all prevention, often via personal conduct and expression.
- It seems that the degree to which a woman resists is her largest safety net in exercising one's legal rights.
- Many women won't press charges to prevent being re-victimized (double victimization); they fear for their continued safety and doubt the system will work for them, system will make it look like its her fault.
- Would-be rapist are not deterred by laws.
- Statutory reform has NOT altered the range of coping options open to women, nor has it improved community options to confront rape problems.

## Resources to address problem

- Rape crisis centers
- Take Back the Night marches
- Counseling, psychological
- Counseling, legal
- Community education from sexual assault centers
- Dispel myths about rape
- Disseminate reliable information about rape
- Citizen watchdog programs
- Form task forces such as Kalamazoo Task Force 1988
- Start small, use subcommittees
- Reexamine laws regarding the punishments for rape; examine enforcement and ethics of advocacy

## Figure 4.2. Systems view of spouse abuse
### Source: *Compiled by Heather Tanksley, April 2003.*

### Types of Domestic and Family Violence and Key Subjects:

- Sexual assault of spouse (so-called intimate rape)
- Spousal Battery, "normal = minor= pushing, slapping, shoving, throwing things" or "deviant = major = kicking, punching, stabbing, choking, burning, etc."
- Spousal Homicide, Spousal Suicide, Teen Suicide, Elder Abuse and Neglect
- Child Discipline and Punishment (hitting, slapping, spanking) versus Child Abuse (beating, burning, torturing, depriving, etc.)
- Religious and cultural beliefs/norms and predominant views of power and authority vs. love

### Statistics/Issues: Child Abuse and Punishment

- Most American parents believe that spanking a child is acceptable punishment
- Some children are more susceptible to abuse: ill, behaviorally challenged, handicapped, boys vs. girls.
- Abusers include: substance abusers, adolescent or unskilled parents, immature parents, parents with rigid belief systems (such as religious) about authority, parents distressed by financial, social, or emotional woes
- Conclusions about the linkages between physical punishment and later aggression and transgenerational trauma and behaviors are mixed; may lead to adult depression

### Key Arguments & Issues

- 3 Key Theories include:
1) spanking increases aggressive or violent tendencies, 2) nonspanking results in "unchecked behavior" leading to aggression or violence, 3) either excess or insufficient spanking results in aggression/violence (balance is key)
- **What distinguishes punishment from abuse:** 1) degree of aggression, 2) potential for harm, 3) degree of atypical, generally unacceptable behavior, 4) intention of the parent
- **Family factors are relevant:** socioeconomic status, cultural norms, family size/norms, marital satisfaction, parenting skills, conflict management skills, parental warmth and affection, willingness to discuss issues with kids, consistency, safety, religious beliefs may play role.

### Interveners and Strategies

- Involve communities, health organizations, businesses, churches, counselors, victim/offenders in examining the current situation and taping/creating resources for change
- Assess a variety of contexts and situations; behaviors and needs may differ in each
- Examine other systemic components for **efficacy**, such as institutional procedures, rules, resources, facilities, funding, reporting and data accuracy (i.e. examine macro/micro)
- Work to diminish patriarchal institutions that devalue women
- Work to empower women's and children's voices; expose the problem
- Shift men's paradigm about power and violence

A World Health Organization (2005) study found that more than 50 percent of women in Bangladesh, Ethiopia, Peru, and Tanzania reported having been subjected to physical or sexual violence by intimate partners, with figures reaching 71 percent in rural Ethiopia, 20 percent in Japan, 30 percent in the United Kingdom, and 22 percent in the United States (UNIFEM 2007, 1). Domestic violence or intimate femicide includes partners who live together in a common-law relationship and ex-couples either separated or divorced (Gelles and Loeske 1993). Domestic violence includes physical abuse (assault, abandonment, and restraint), emotional and psychological abuse (intimidation, humiliation, silencing, and isolation), and sexual abuse (nonconsensual sex) (Bregman 1991; Gelles 1997).

Militarism is perpetuated by a sex-based patriarchy embodying violence and aggression that subjugates women in the developed world as well as exploits the cheap labor of women in developing countries (Tifft and Markham 1991). Drawn into the wage market, women have challenged patriarchal dominance and enhanced their legal and economic independence, which has led to conflict with traditional demands on women's time, attention, and work in the home (Tifft and Markham 1991). Tifft and Markham point out that the parallels between militaristic and domestic violence are uncanny.

Feminist scholars argue that there is a systematic unequal power distribution between males and females (that is, patriarchy), as a patriarchal society emphasizes male dominance and aggression as well as female victimization (Tickner 1992). The war culture ensures that women and minorities are pushed to the margins of society (hooks 1990). Moreover, there is an unequal distribution of power between parents and children. Children are socialized into sex roles so that boys get toy guns and girls get toy dolls as gifts (Nighswander and Proulx 2007).

The batterer who isolates his spouse from her family and friends is a key ingredient in domestic violence (Gelles 1997). The male batterer uses physical violence to gain control of his wife or girlfriend, and threats and psychological abuse are intricate parts of the batterer's repertoire (Gelles 1997). A batterer acting like the master of the castle implies that the spouse or partner is the servant (O'Donnell, Smith, and Madison 2002). Immigrant women are also more at risk from battering than a spouse or partner from the culture of the batterer (Ramdial 2002). The survivor who is isolated by ethnicity and language will fear the police and courts because of a fear of deportation (Cameron 1995).

The batterer's violence has serious ramifications for the survivor and her family, who are most affected in terms of their physical and emotional well-being (Riger 2002, 198). Many women are unable to complete their education or hold a job due to battering (194).

Lenore Walker (2000) outlines three phases in the cycle of battering described in her classic study, *The Battered Woman Syndrome*:

1. Tension building: There is stress within the family or work milieu for the male who becomes irritable. The female partner provokes an attack by her angry partner.
2. Explosion: The batterer detonates because there are no releases for his frustration and rage. His partner defends herself.
3. Honeymoon: The male abuser feels ashamed and fears that his wife will leave him. He tries to make up by showering her with gifts.

Furthermore, socialization within the family provides norms and values that legitimate the violence (Gelles and Strauss 1989). A person learns violence through mimicking role models in the family (Gelles 1997). A pattern of repeat family violence ensures a continuing relationship between batterers and vulnerable survivors (Nayak, Byrne, Martin, and Abraham 2003). Women seek medical attention for assault injuries (Gelles and Strauss 1989).

Globally, it is difficult to obtain accurate and reliable information about family violence (Garbarino 1999). There is underreporting of battering as the victim conceals the facts (Elsaas 1997; Gelles and Strauss 1989). "Victims of domestic violence must wrestle with feelings of fear, loyalty, love, self-blame, guilt, and shame all at the same time" (Burgess and Roberts 2002, 5). Home is a dangerous place for domestic violence victims (6). "Staying means abuse and violence, but leaving may mean death" (Englander 2007, 175). Women who are extremely battered, tortured, and assaulted often use lethal force in self-defense (Gelles and Strauss 1989).

Who are the survivors of domestic violence? Children are also victims of intrafamily violence. Parents and step-parents use lethal force against children. For example, in 2009 each state's Child Protective Services (CPS) agency reported to the U.S. Department of Health and Human Services' National Child Abuse and Neglect Data System that six million children in the United States were allegedly maltreated by parents (81 percent), with women representing 54 percent and men representing 44 percent of perpetrators and with 83 percent of the perpetrators being between twenty and forty-nine years of age. The most common forms of maltreatment included neglect (75 percent), physical abuse (18 percent), sexual abuse (10 percent), and psychological abuse (8 percent). Boys accounted for 48 percent of survivors and girls 51 percent, while the highest rate of victims were white (44 percent) compared to African American (22 percent) and Hispanic (21 percent) (Gaudiosi 2009).

Similarly, the Fourth National Incidence Study of Child Abuse and Neglect, or NIS-4, collected data between 2005 and 2006 from 126 CPS agencies (Sedlak et al. 2010). NIS-4 used the Harm Standard and the Endangerment Standard to analyze the 6,208 completed data forms of CPS agency professionals. During 2005–2006, using the Harm Standard, 1,256,660 children were found to be maltreated in the United States. Of the 44 percent of abused children, 58 percent were physically abused, 24 percent were sexually abused, and 27 percent were emotionally abused (5). Of the 61 percent of neglected children, 47 percent survived educational neglect, 38 percent survived physical neglect, and 25 percent survived emotional neglect (5).

In addition, the Incidence of Endangerment Standard during the same period found that three million children experienced Endangerment Standard maltreatment. Of the 29 percent of abused children, 57 percent were physically abused, 36 percent were emotionally abused, and 22 percent were sexually abused (Sedlak et al. 2010, 6–7). Of the 77 percent of neglected children, 53 percent were physically neglected, 52 percent were emotionally neglected, and 16 percent were educationally neglected (6–7). Children from lower socioeconomic households who were living with a single parent and cohabiting partner or living in a large family in a rural area and were not attending school were more at risk of abuse and neglect across both definitional standards (8–13). The study's findings have implications for trying to understand the complexity of child abuse and neglect, highlighting the interdependent relationships of several variables to incidences of the maltreatment of children (19–21).

In addition, corporal punishment trains youngsters in violence by establishing a connection between love and violence and by encouraging the view that might is right (Ellison and Bartowski 1997). Children who are exposed to harsh or abusive parenting are at risk for a number of negative developmental outcomes. Responsible child rearing is reflected in a child's warm, loving, and close relationship with her or his parents (Reiss and Roth 1993).

Even though some children are resilient, young people are impacted by violence in the home (Englander 2007). Studies have found that boys show more aggression, while girls show more distress (Garbarino 1999). The violent home milieu may become even more toxic if the stressed-out mother abuses her already traumatized children (Burgess and Roberts 2002). Children who live in violent homes have a higher likelihood for later delinquent and violent behavior (Reiss and Roth 1993).

Intersibling violence is another form of intrafamily violence, as teenagers have physical strength differentials and considerable time together and have the opportunity to abuse each other (Hoffman and Edwards 2004, 185–86). Sibling violence is related to violence in adulthood, and the practice of violent behavior toward a sibling may lead to future aggression against family or others (187). These violent experiences may justify future aggressive and abusive behavior and may also increase the tolerance and use of violence to solve conflict (Hoffman and Edwards 2004).

Sibling violence clearly represents the victimization of female and male children (Gelles and Loeske 1993). This is a pandemic situation, because most often the victim cannot leave the abusive situation. Langhinrichsen-Rohling, Hankla, and Stormberg (2004) asked 110 students from a first-year psychology class in a large Midwestern

American university to complete a sorting task that measured certain given actions at certain points on a spectrum of intensity of violence. Sixty-five percent of the sample was female. The study sought to determine how negative relationship behaviors are structured in the semantic networks of young adults from violent versus nonviolent homes. "Seventy words or short phrases describing different relationship behaviors were put on cards, and each respondent had to categorize them" (Langhinrichsen-Rohling, Hankla, and Stormberg 2004, 144). The results of the study indicated that only individuals from nonviolent households differentiated clearly between violent and nonviolent behaviors and that violent behaviors were more likely to be blurred with other nonviolent behaviors by those from violent backgrounds.

Violence against the elderly is another form of intrafamily violence in the home. Either a younger member of the extended family or the spouse expresses intrafamily violence and neglect against her or his elders (Bergeron 2002). Typically the abused elder lives with the perpetrator, who is abusive as a result of stress or changing family relationships, and elder abuse is also manifested as a result of a pattern of marital violence extending over years (Bergeron 2002). Elder abuse is subcategorized into five basic categories: neglect, physical abuse, financial exploitation, emotional abuse, and sexual abuse (548). The risks are greater for women because of their greater life expectancy. Elders may also not wish to leave their abusers because they may be dependent on them for their basic human needs or also feel responsible for providing for their abuser's daily needs (547). Elders are often abused by other family members so that necessary intervention must be based on a family system's approach.

## Intervention to Prevent Violence Against Women and Domestic and Family Violence

In terms of short-term intervention policy, governments must make efforts to provide safety for battered women in shelters as well as to educate police, lawyers, judges, and women advocates about domestic violence (Honey-Knopp 1991, 187). Prisons could be reformed to rehabilitate the offender, and restorative justice programs must be introduced into male batterer programs and women's prisons to change the thinking about using personal violence to solve problems (Honey-Knopp 1991; Strahl 2004). Moreover, the media should protect the right of free expression and provide programming that does not use sex and violence that normalize violence against women (Turpin and Kurtz 1997).

Having a comprehensive intervention strategy ensures that more comprehensive data is collected on domestic violence and that survivors have safe places to come to, that crisis centers are used more effectively, that men are better educated about how they perceive women and behave toward them, that destructive stereotypes against women are reduced and eliminated, and that the voices of women and those abused domestically are empowered (Kuypers 1992).

Joseph Kuypers (1992, 111–20) argues that we must place men's will to hurt at center stage if society is to change how men think and act about violence and presents four key intervention strategies. First, it is important not to glorify violence or justify the use of force to solve international conflicts (Kuypers 1992). Men must challenge men and question the use of violence to resolve conflict. Consequently, he argues that society needs to monitor male language that reinforces the belief that male violence is both necessary and inevitable, which is illustrated by some of the following everyday expressions: "only mad men do it" and "violence keeps the peace and is necessary" (Kuypers 1992). In the process, fathers must mentor their boys and talk to them about using violence to hurt other human beings (Garbarino 1999).

Second, it is important to redefine international law away from the idea that "might is right" so that violence is not used to solve international conflicts (Kuypers 1992). An example is recognition by the United Nations that genocidal rape must be considered a gross violation of human rights because it is part of a systematic policy to annihilate a whole population, so all rapes carried out in war must be considered a violation of human rights (Mertus 2008). As Campbell (2003, 509) has noted, sexual violence constitutes a crime against humanity, and rape used against a civilian population in armed conflict is a serious violation of international humanitarian law, that is, trauma to a social body is denial of the humanity of others.

Third, it is critical to destroy conventional as well as nuclear weapons and in the process eliminate "the profit that comes from pain" when weapons are sold by the developed world to developing countries (Kuypers 1992, 116). Politicians need to challenge the myth of vulnerability put forth by the realist pundits that states need to be prepared for war (Kuypers 1992). Costa Rica does not have a standing army because it does not need one. State legislatures could forge policies banning guns in every country. Finally, Kuypers (1992, 119) asks that we "think partnership" by creating a shift in our worldview from aggression and force to interdependence by preventing the creation and demonization of the Other. Practically, this means supporting women's claims for equality and safety as well as recognizing that we are all interdependent parts of a larger system (Kuypers 1992).

It is also critical to recognize the symptoms of trauma and violence and assess the types of interventions that may be needed in the short and long term (Elsaas 1997). Ledray (1994) makes the point that survivors of sexual violence need to tell their stories to close friends and/or family members so that they can heal from the trauma. Telling the story to a trusted individual is therapeutic and critical to the survivor's recovery from the traumatic experience (Senehi 2009a, 2009b). This constructive process is also important to the survivor's self-esteem and self-worth, for the trusted individual assists the survivor by reflectively listening to her story (Laurer 2002; Ledray 1994).

In terms of education to empower, the Domestic Abuse Intervention Project in Duluth, Minnesota, uses the Duluth Model of intervention to educate abused women about the power and control of males who batter using threats, coercion, intimidation, emotional abuse, isolation, the children, male privilege, economic abuse, denying, and blaming to wield his power and control (Pence and Paymar 1993). The Duluth Model promotes a nonviolent alternative whereby the male partner uses negotiation and fairness, nonthreatening behavior, honesty and accountability, responsible parenting, shared responsibility, economic partnership, and respect, trust, and support to create an organic and equal partnership (Pence and Paymar 1993).

In addition, male batterer programs seek to reform batterers and end men's violence through counseling, self-help groups, reality therapy, and relaxation training (Warters 1986). The "insight-oriented small group format" resocializes men to think about their childhood experiences and attitudes toward women through interpersonal skills training, anger management, "self observation of behavior chains that precede, occur with, and follow violent events, training in relaxation, and a cognitive restructuring of irrational belief systems and family thinking styles" through a process of social unlearning (Warters 1986, 20). The batterer is forced to take responsibility for his behavior through confrontation by the group and through the role modeling of the counselor (Warters 1986). The structured treatment format also uses antisexist education to challenge the batterer's belief that violent and abusive behavior is legitimate (Warters 1986). Men who engage in more external change processes, including being socially supported by the community, may in fact hold themselves more accountable for their own abusive behavior and seek validation for their decision to change (Eckhardt, Babcock, and Homack 2004, 91). The use of external change processes may be contingent upon their first using internal processes, which may emphasize more empathy with the victim (91). Moreover, 60 percent of battered American women in a study by Burgess and Roberts (2002, 20–21) believed that their batterers had made improvements upon taking part in education and group counseling, and 80 percent found that improvement resulted from the combined involvement of the police, the courts, group counseling, and shelters.

Culture also shapes how women and men understand domestic violence. Shame and self-blame may be buttressed by cultural vales that ensure that a woman survivor cannot or will not seek help (Cameron 1995). In some cultures, the local community imposes sanctions on a batterer (Merry 2006). In rural communities in Togo, for example, where women weave the roofs of homes, if a man beats his wife, the women in the village come and remove the woman from the home and tear down the roof. Alternatively, religious leaders may call out the name of the batterer in church, thus placing the perpetrator in a moral Coventry. According to the Johns Hopkins University School of Public Health's Population Information Report (1999), gender-based violence is a human rights violation and a public health issue. The report concludes that ending violence against women necessitates changing the community's cultural norms that give rise to the perception that women are of less value than men, which permits men's violence against women to persist. In this way women can be empowered to gain control over their own socioeconomic and family resources and their own bodies (38).

Some states that are making little headway in the protection of women tend to blame a culture that is considered patriarchal and unchanging (Merry 2006). Yet universal gender equality and standards of human rights focus on changing laws and cultural and institutional practices that facilitate violence against women (Merry 2006). Human rights law as part of international law applies universal principles to all contexts. The Convention on the Elimination of All Forms of Discrimination Against Women (CEDAW) is an international bill of rights for women whose aim is to eradicate discrimination against women and protect the principle of equality of rights and respect of human dignity for all (Merry 2006). CEDAW and its articles on violence stress individual autonomy and physical safety over the unity of the family. As Merry (2006) astutely observes, translating transnational universal initiatives into local cultural practices creates many problems. Some states articulate a position to not employ CEDAW articles because customary patriarchal traditions are deeply entrenched in the culture even though they permit violence against women (Merry 2006). The challenge is to change governments' perceptions of these so-called traditional indigenous cultural practices that conflict with CEDAW articles. Thus, human rights and peace-building NGOs generate public support.

Merry (2006, 220) articulates that rather than replacing political and legal processes, the human rights framework adds a new critical dimension to the way individuals perceive local problems. According to Merry (2006), the adaption from the universal to both national and local communities necessitates three important changes in the form and presentation of human rights and peace-building ideas. First, changes must be framed in terms of image, religious, and secular stories, and symbols must resonate with the local community. Second, changes must be tailored to local structural conditions that embrace economic and political systems. And third, the target population must be carefully defined. Consequently, human rights and peace-building ideas are then repackaged in culturally appropriate and specific stories challenging patriarchy, which is embedded in local cultural customs and traditions of the grand narrative.

With regard to elder abuse protection, governments generally see their function as threefold: (1) receive and investigate reports, (2) provide intervention and referrals to community services, and (3) interface with the justice system and law enforcement bodies where the victim is in need of a guardian (Bergeron 2002, 548). The perpetrators are required to be involved in the process and are notified of allegations, interviewed, and assessed to see how their situation affects the abuse (Bergeron 2002). Perpetrators are engaged in the process of finding a solution. Elder protection agency workers worked from a strengths perspective to engage the whole family in problem solving (Bergeron 2002). As Bergeron (2002) has noted, such agencies work from the perspective that clients can change and become partners in formulating solutions to problems and in developing mutual respect.

Developing a universal practice model means necessarily building on strengths within a family. In one instance, Dr. Cathie Witty brought together faculty and students from the Department of Marriage and Family Therapy and the Department of Conflict Analysis and Resolution at Nova Southeastern University's Graduate School of Humanities and Social Sciences to develop the Violence Outreach in Communities through Education and Services (VOICES) program. The VOICES program was funded by a $250,000 grant from the U.S. Department of Justice to address family violence in southern Florida. VOICES combined the interdisciplinary problem-solving approach of conflict resolution with the clinical practice of family therapy to the family system in order to resolve the deep roots of family conflict and to provide violence prevention and problem-solving training.

In addition, women survivors need to be empowered and provided with financially accessible and safe alternatives for providing care for their children (Riger 2002, 200). Extended families need to be protected from batterers because they often provide support for a woman and her children postshelter (200). In addition, probation officers need to be assigned to domestic violence cases to increase victim safety and to be trained to realize that the abuser's threats, intimidation, or even neutral contact with the woman's family can jeopardize both victim and family safety (201).

## Conclusion

The core values of our society are the birthplace from which family violence stems (Burton 1997). This reflects the realities of structural suffering and the necessity for both personal and social structural change. Tracing violence, the acceptance of violence, and battering of women, children, and men to a male character trait has limited validity (Gelles 1997). It implies that there are traits, aside from physiological and procreative differences, that differentiate male and female (Gelles 1997). It also implies that gender structures are natural or essential and that some males create gender realities, identities, and inequalities (Brock-Utne 1997). It leaves unexplored the diverse cultural, historical, economic, political, and social processes through which sex-based structures are created and reproduced (Merry 2006; Sylvester 2002). To stop violence against women, we need to explore more fully micro-macro interdependent linkages and similarities that promote violent behavior (Turpin and Kurtz 1997). In the words of Tifft and Markham (1991, 139), "both private policy—individual battering—and public policy—collective battering—have similar structural sources."

Some violence intervention and prevention policies and practices are chosen, and others are not. The process depicts battery as a choice-behavior that reflects and is created and enforced through specific values and social processes (Tifft and Markham 1991). Violence on a larger, more global scale should be seen in the same power frame of dehumanization as is the domestic batterer on the microlevel of society (Burton 1997; Turpin and Kurtz 1997). There is a need to establish the link between violence at all levels of society and address issues of aggressive and violent compliance strategies that lead to alienation, revenge, and learned power orientations that affect behavior later in life (Burton 1997; Tifft and Markham 1991).

The next chapter outlines some approaches to the analysis of hate crime and xenophobic violence and some of the preventive measures and intervention that can be used to address hate crime.

## Websites Related to Violence Against Women

Amnesty International Stop Violence Against Women Campaign, http://www.amnesty.ca/campaigns/svaw_overview.php

Canadian Research Institute for the Advancement of Women, http://www.criaw-icref.ca/

Canadian Women's Foundation, Violence Prevention Fund, http://www.cdnwomen.org/EN/section05/3_5_1_1_violence_facts.html

Centre for Research and Education on Violence Against Women and Children, http://www.crvawc.ca/

Intimate Partner Violence Prevention, http://www.cdc.gov/ncipc/dvp/vawguide.htm

Pacific Institute for Research and Evaluation, http://www.pire.org/

Stop Violence Against Women. A Project of the Advocates for Human Rights, http://www.stopvaw.org

United Nations Entity for Gender Equality and the Empowerment of Women, http://www.unifem.org/

United Nations Secretary General's Campaign to End Violence Against Women, http://endviolence.un.org/

## Suggested Questions for Further Discussion

1. Given the urgency and gravity of violence against women, what are some of the subtle and overt ways that culture condones and perpetuates violence against women? Why is the home the cradle of violence? What are some of the characteristics of men and women who

abuse? Is intrafamily violence linked with other forms of violence outside of the home?

2. How can individuals, groups, and societies accept greater responsibility for preventing and reducing those conditions, values, and structures that produce and support violence against women? Do you think that spousal abuse is a power issue, a social issue, an economic issue, a cultural issue, a political issue, an anger issue, or a combination? What are some of the triggers of domestic family violence?

3. Is there room for interventions and practices that respect the uniqueness of cultures but simultaneously protect women from violence? Can you provide some examples?

4. Is there a relationship between militarism, patriarchy, and violence against women? Do private policy individual battering and public policy collective battering have similar structures? Do social, cultural, legal, economic, and political structures in society maintain and encourage violence against women?

5. How can communities organize to break the cycle of battering women, or is it too woven into the very fabric of society? How can society prevent the negative portrayal of women by the media and the negative socialization of young boys and girls in society? Why do women remain in abusive relationships?

6. Should batterers and rapists be restrained and confined or restored back into the community? What are some important intervention strategies and treatment techniques for men and women who batter?

7. Why is there a need to make a broader connection between micro and macro intervention strategies in addressing violence against women? Are structural changes needed in society if we are to comprehensively address the abuse of women?

# 5

## Understanding and Preventing Hate Crimes in Communities

### Xenophobia, Homelessness, Racism, Soccer Hooliganism, Anti-GLBT, and Neo-Fascist Violence

Matthew Shepard was a twenty-two-year-old undergraduate student studying international politics and languages at the University of Wyoming in Laramie. On a cold October night in 1998, Aaron McKinney and Russell Henderson brought Matthew from a local bar to eastern Laramie. They tied him to a split-rail fence, beat him, called him homophobic names, and left him to die. Eighteen hours later, a passing cyclist found Matthew's body tied to the fence. Matthew's funeral was attended by friends and family and received international media attention that brought his story to light in the struggle to end intolerance and hate. The tragic death of Matthew Shepard clearly illustrates that hate and discrimination need to be addressed in families, schools, and communities. The Matthew Shepard Foundation, founded by Matthew's mother, Judy, seeks to create a movement of people to work together to end hatred in society. The Matthew Shepard Foundation equips people with the necessary antihate and pro–human rights tools to deal with hateful speech and actions and promotes discussion and dialogue that address hate violence in society (Loffreda 2001).

Hate crimes can be characterized as violence against a person who is seen as a member of an out-group toward which there is some measure of socially approved hostility (Gerstenfeld and Grant 2003). Hate crimes might also be referred to as ethnoviolence. The attacker perceives the targeted out-group as a threat to the attacker's identity and values (Staub 1992). The ideas that justify violent crimes are promoted by prominent persons in society (e.g., political leaders) and/or popular culture (e.g., folklore, films, TV, and advertising) that portray stereotypes (Gerstenfeld 2003). Even the homeless are subjected to hate crimes and are often held "liable for societal ills such as sin, urban disorder, crime, disease, and poverty" (Barak 1991, 8). Oftentimes, for ordinary people such as the Nazi doctors in the concentration camps to commit horrendous acts of violence, a duality of identity must take place (Lifton 1997).

Two features distinguish hate crimes (Southern Poverty Law Center 1999). First, the attacks are vicious, especially considering that the survivors did nothing to the attackers. Second, hate crimes are often committed by large groups of assailants, which ensures lack of personal responsibility felt by any individual for his or her role in the attack. Hate crimes are committed against individuals on the basis of their sexual orientation, gender, ethnic and/or religious group affiliation, or disability (Perry 2001) (table 5.1).

Hate crimes are committed against the dignity and human rights of an individual person (Barash 1991; Galtung 1996). Human rights are essential to our understanding of the dignity of human persons, which is essential to intervening in ethnic, gender, racial, and religious conflict (Gerstenfeld and Grant 2003). These rights are essential to the roots of conflict, because conflict may escalate into violence if human rights are trampled on (Merry 2006). Resolutions reached on nonlevel playing fields usually suffer fundamental flaws and do not promote sustainable peace between disputants (Lederach 2005). The denial of human rights therefore works against the goals of peace (Barash 1991). In contrast, globally nonviolent direct action and related social movements for socioeconomic and political change have forged people power in support of civil and women's rights, disability rights, the environment, and human rights (Sharp 2005). Human rights are critical in the development of economic and social justice that fulfills human needs and expands people's critical and creative consciousness to end hate crimes and violence (Merry 2006).

This chapter addresses some of the multiple causes of hate crime by exploring the media as well as racial, ethnic, and political violence and violence against gay, lesbian, bisexual, and transgender (GLBT) people and also discusses the impact of violence in society by soccer hooligans, skinheads, and neo-Fascists. In addition, this chapter outlines some interventions to prevent hate crimes.

## Causes of Hate Crimes

Hate violence is the systematic abuse of a targeted group that generates inaccurate information about these people (Perry 2001). Hate crimes and hate violence hurt all members of the community (Kivel 1997) (figure 5.1).

### Racial and Ethnic Hate Crimes

The extent and nature of hate crime against racially diverse groups is on the increase globally (Barkun 1996, 2003; Klein and Bromberg 2003). In the United States, Native Americans, Latinos, and African Americans perceive that racial prejudice and discrimination are both significant problems and are more likely to be psychologically damaging than non–hate crimes for the survivor (Rayburn, Mendoza, and Davison 2003, 1058). The persistent problem of racism is directed specifically toward black, Hispanic, and native peoples on the North and South American continents (Boudreau 2003). Race as a biological concept or reality has no meaning (Davis 1991). The social construction of race has magnified intergroup conflict especially when the economic interests of the powerful are threatened (Boudreau 2009), with racism as a direct consequence of this power asymmetry. The most intractable causes of human rights violations are those of racial violence in North America and against four hundred million indigenous people globally (Boudreau 2003). Thus, racism can best be understood within the complexity of socioeconomic, historical, religious, cultural, and political intergroup

## Figure 5.1. Systems view of hate crimes and socialization
### Heather Tanksley, April 2003

### Types of Hate Crimes and Abuse

- Verbal abuse
- Threats of physical violence
- Vandalism of property
- Followed, chased
- Intimidated, harassment
- Stoned or hit with objects
- Spat upon
- Punched, kicked, beaten

- Assaulted with weapon
- Familial verbal abuse
- Familial physical abuse
- Murder
- Rape (as in prisons)
- Symbol taunting (swastika)
- Cross burnings
- Bombings

- Genocide
- Xenophobia
- Police beatings
- Against GLBT
- Against Jews, Asians, other ethnic minorities
- Against people of color
- Against women

### Statistics/Issues: Antigay Violence

- 1984: 19% punched, hit, beaten, kicked; 44% threatened with violence; 94% victimized
- Verbal abuse is highest
- Most GLBT are still afraid and modify behavior to hide
- Gay men of color at highest risk, then gay men (public), then gay women (home) (why: gender stereotypes, social role stereotypes, religion, patriarchy, androcentrism)
- Violence in many contexts: school, home, prison and jails, public
- Is AIDS epidemic a new focus of long-standing hatred?

### Perpetrators/Causes

- Perpetrators are largely young white male strangers
- Neo-Nazis (Aryan Nation, White Patriot Party, Identity Followers, KKK)
- Skinheads (most brutal)
- Police and prison guards; often look the other way, encourage, perpetrate
- Prisoners, white heterosexual males; power over, identity, control and dominance
- Doubling; maintenance of cognitive consistency
- Specialists; encourage and proliferate hate
- Specialists; organize global hate activities
- Media, news, Internet are key transport mechanisms of hate messages

### Intervenors and Strategies

- Involve communities, health organizations, businesses, counselors, victim/offenders in examining the current situation and taping/creating resources for change
- Examine other systemic components for efficacy, such as institutional procedures, rules, resources, facilities, funding, reporting and data accuracy (i.e., examine macro/micro)
- Work to diminish patriarchal institutions
- Work to empower victims' voices
- Shift men's paradigm about power and violence
- Stop hiding/isolating the problem
- Teach tolerance, create positive websites
- Speak up, lobby leaders, unite against hate, get involved

# Table 5.1. Ten-year comparison of FBI hate crime statistics in the United States (2006–1997)

## ADL Ten-Year Comparison of FBI Hate Crime Statistics in the U.S. (2006–1997)

| | 2006 | 2005 | 2004 | 2003 | 2002 | 2001 | 2000 | 1999 | 1998 | 1997 |
|---|---|---|---|---|---|---|---|---|---|---|
| Participating Agencies | 12,620 | 12,417 | 12,711 | 11,909 | 12,073 | 11,987 | 11,690 | 12,122 | 10,730 | 11,211 |
| Total Hate Crime Incidents Reported | 7,722 | 7,163 | 7,649 | 7,489 | 7,462 | 9,730 | 8,063 | 7,876 | 7,755 | 8,049 |
| Number of States, including D.C. | 50 | 50 | 50 | 50 | 50 | 50 | 49 | 49 | 47 | 49 |
| Percentage of U.S. Population Agencies Represented | 85.2 | 82.7% | 86.6% | 82.8% | 85.7% | 85.0% | 84.2% | 85.0% | 80.0% | 83.0% |

## Offenders' Reported Motivations in Percentages of Incidents (2006–1997)

| | 2006 | 2005 | 2004 | 2003 | 2002 | 2001 | 2000 | 1999 | 1998 | 1997 |
|---|---|---|---|---|---|---|---|---|---|---|
| Racial Bias | 4,000/51.8 | 3,919/54.7 | 4,402/57.5 | 3,844/51.3 | 3,642/48.8 | 4,367/44.9 | 4,337/53.8 | 4,295/54.5 | 4,321/55.7 | 4,710/58.5 |
| Antiblack | 2,640/34.2 | 2,630/36.7 | 2,731/35.7 | 2,548/34.0 | 2,486/33.3 | 2,899/30 | 3,884/35.8 | 2,486/33.3 | 2,901/37.4 | 3,120/38.8 |
| Antiwhite | 890/11.5 | 828/11.6 | 829/10.8 | 830/1.1 | 719/9.6 | 891/9.1 | 875/10.9 | 781/9.9 | 792/10.2 | 993/12.3 |
| Anti-Asian/Pacific Islander | 181/2.3 | 199/2.8 | 217/2.8 | 231/3.1 | 217/2.9 | 280/2.9 | 281/3.5 | 298/3.8 | 293/3.8 | 347/4.3 |
| Religious Bias | 1,462/18.9 | 1,227/17.1 | 1,374/18.0 | 1,343/17.9 | 1,426/19.1 | 1,828/18.8 | 1,472/18.3 | 1,411/17.9 | 1,390/17.9 | 1,385/17.2 |
| Anti-Semitic | 967/12.5 | 848/1.8 | 954/12.5 | 927/2.4 | 931/12.5 | 1,043/10.7 | 1,109/13.8 | 1,109/14.1 | 1,081/13.9 | 1,087/13.5 |
| Anti-Semitic as Percentage of Religious Bias | 66 | 69 | 69 | 69 | 65 | 57 | 75 | 79 | 78 | 79 |
| Anti-Islamic | 156/2.0 | 128/.8 | 156/2.0 | 149/2.0 | 155/2.1 | 481/4.9 | 28/0.35 | 32/0.40 | 21/0.27 | 28/0.35 |
| Ethnicity/National Origin | 984/12.7 | 944/13.2 | 972/12.7 | 1026/13.7 | 1,102/14.8 | 2,098/21.6 | 911/11.3 | 829/10.5 | 754/9.7 | 836/10.4 |
| Anti-Hispanic | 576/7.5 | 522/7.3 | 475/6.2 | 426/5.7 | 480/6.4 | 597/6.1 | 557/6.9 | 466/5.9 | 754/9.7 | 491/6.1 |
| Sexual Orientation | 1,195/15.5 | 1,017/14.2 | 1,197/15.6 | 1,239/16.5 | 1,244/16.7 | 1,393/14.3 | 1,299/16.1 | 1,317/16.7 | 1,206/16.2 | 1,102/13.7 |
| Disability | 79/1.0 | 53/0.74 | 57/0.74 | 33/0.44 | 45/0.59 | 35/0.36 | 36/0.45 | 19/0.24 | 25/0.32 | 12/0.15 |

dynamics (Boudreau 2009). Specific policy issues are characterized by deep discrimination (Boudreau 2003) that disproportionately impact white people, people of color, and indigenous people who reside on the margins of society (Kivel 1997; West 1994, 2001).

These uneven policy issues include (1) police enforcement against minority communities; (2) the impact on minority communities of building major roads, incinerators, and toxic dumps in their neighborhoods; and (3) employment opportunities for minority peoples compared to the white dominant group (see also Beckwith and Jones 1997; Frederickson 1995; Gates 1986; Jones 1997; Marable 1997; Mills 1997). However, as a result of the 1964 Civil Rights Act and other federal legislation local, state, and federal governments do not tolerate racial discrimination when those laws are violated (Boudreau 2009; Rutstein 1997). Of all crimes, hate crimes are the most likely to "create and exacerbate conflicts that could undermine the socioeconomic foundation of a state" (Espiritu 2004, 198).

New computer-mediated forms of communication help build a "spirit of community and civility," providing an outlet to express "anger, outrage, and frustration over hate crime attacks," but the remoteness and anonymity of the Internet leads to the expression of more extreme views and behavior (Coffey and Woolworth 2004, 2). The U.S. protection of the First Amendment is making it difficult for other nations "to pursue alternative measures of dealing with hate crime" (Bailey 2003, 63). Technology appears to have overpowered public regulation, and the "inadequate substitute" of private regulators appears to be useful in limiting the spread of hateful material on the Internet (Bailey 2003, 63).

Global white supremacist websites grew to four thousand in 2001, twenty-five hundred of which were based in the United States (Bailey 2003, 64). Globally, thus far the focus of law enforcement and justice agencies has been on racist propaganda. In 2001 the Council of Europe met in an international forum in which racist propaganda was the main policy-making issue (65). A number of international states signed the Additional Protocol to limit racist and xenophobic acts, a document that Canada has yet to sign (Bailey 2003; Perry 2008).

Canada initially dealt with Internet hate propaganda via the formulation of the Anti-Terrorism Act. Two amendments are being taken into consideration: changing the Criminal Code to "eliminate online hate propaganda" and instituting the Canadian Human Rights Act to prohibit the spreading of repeated hate messages by telephonic communications, which includes all telecommunications technologies (Bailey 2003, 67).

In regard to concrete steps to be taken to address Internet hate propaganda, Canada's suggestion to the World Conference Against Racism Advisory Committee was that the United Nations (UN) could create "an independent coordinating agency" to create a "code of conduct," monitor and report on propaganda, and develop educational programs to illustrate to government officials the impact of these sites on their citizens (Bailey 2003, 101). A certain degree of monitoring and consideration of which topics are appropriate for online discussion must be done to encourage positive dialogue between people (Coffey and Woolworth 2004, 12).

Ethnic segregation can lead to an escalation of hate crime in deeply divided societies. Since the peace process began in Northern Ireland, arson and vandalism have been occurring more on Catholic and Protestant properties because individuals fear losing particular privileges or are reacting to acts by other spoiler groups (MacGinty 2001). Compared to racial hate crime in the United States, hate crime in deeply divided societies is politically motivated.

All hate crime is political insofar as it carries a statement that gives more weight to a crime than just its actual perpetration on a survivor. As MacGinty (2001) has noted, hate crime involves the identification, objectification, and depersonalization of the targeted survivor. Oftentimes, hate crimes have a public aspect that conveys a warning to the wider community and also sends a message of dominance and control (MacGinty 2001, 650). In the United States, hate violence is interpreted in emotional and personal terms (650).

In Europe, an annual report by the Office of Democratic Institutions and Human Rights (2006) of the Organization for Security and Cooperation in Europe (OSCE) found that racist and xenophobic attacks against Africans, Jews, Muslims, Romas, and Sintis was on the rise in Europe. Hate-motivated attacks targeted individuals, sites, symbols, and property. The media, especially the Internet, was used to transmit hate discourse and propaganda as well as incitement to commit violent acts against minority groups. The report found that some European governments did not always respond adequately, transparently, or effectively; instead, they presented the hate crimes as isolated cases carried out by hooligans or so-called yobbos. The report also found that law enforcement agencies and the courts demonstrated inadequate first responses and issued lenient sentences for violent hate crimes.

### Political Violence and Hate Crimes

A whole generation of children can be socialized to hate other ethnic groups. German children were traumatized by the events of World War I. In postwar Germany after the 1929 stock market crash, the German Weimar government could no longer repay its debt to the Allies, and many German people went hungry. In addition, the war-guilt clause in the 1919 Treaty of Versailles that ended World War I directed hatred toward the United States and the Entente Cordiale (Britain, France, and Russia), who explicitly blamed Germany for causing the war (Ferguson 2006). As a result, Germany's alienated youths joined the Nazi Party (Loewenberg 1971). Political socialization begins in early childhood, and the historical context is also very important in shaping a child's worldview (Byrne 1997a). For example, the Great Depression in the United States impacted the age cohort that grew up in that particular historical period (Elders 1974).

Socialization may involve internalizing group trauma (Volkan 1998). The famine-causing droughts in Ethiopia and Somalia during the mid-1980s impacted an entire generation of young people. A national catastrophe can also impact the life cycle of a group of young people. In China, the 1934–35 Long March affected those who were to become part of the Cultural Revolution. During the late 1960s, Gerry Adams and Bobby Sands were children living in Belfast when the British Army broke into their homes and took away their fathers and brothers (Adams 2003; O'Malley 1992). During the apartheid era in South Africa, Bantu children in Soweto were traumatized by the violence of apartheid (Coles 1986; Straker 1992).

### Leaders Foment Hate Violence for Particular Outcomes

Political leaders seeking to maintain or create political and economic power foment hate violence. Paul Brass (1997) and Ervin Staub (1992) discusses the specialist type of leader who uses hate violence as a political tool to strengthen her or his political position. Specialists organize and instigate riots and engage in specific activities such as providing rumors and shouting slogans. Specialists keep tensions at a certain level by transforming trivial incidents to spark a riot. First, specialists in towns and villages construct differences and prejudices to accomplish the following objectives: structure intergroup relations and distribute rewards and punishments, politicize prejudice by forming political organizations and by creating slogans such as "the foreigners are taking our jobs," and transform the environment into a sociopolitical problem. The media may be directed by specialists to magnify these problems. The media may also generate narratives and destructive stories (or discourses) that perpetuate and instigate violence by its focus on events (Senehi 2009a, 2009b). In India, television had a role in precipitating riots during 1981–85. During the Bombay riots of 1984, the Muslim community was infuriated because Muslims kept seeing their mosques destroyed on television (Brass 1997). Nationalism may also be an instrumental force in the processes of division and exclusion. Specialists foment certain kinds of emotions and fears to solidify the in-group by projecting its anger against an out-group.

Ervin Staub (1992) and Paul Brass (1997) argue that there are three outcomes of hate violence. First, specialists label the victims, organize and motivate the crowd, and attack the targets to create the riot. The crowd is rational, not irrational (Rude 1959). The riots in South Africa that pitted the African National Congress (ANC) against the Inkatha Freedom Party are a good example of this point. In London, the Brixton Riots of 1981 were part of continuing violence between the police and blacks in Britain, while in Belfast during the 1970s the specialists organized gangs to burn neighbors out of mixed religious neighborhoods. In the Middle East, the 1988 Intifada was a riot organized against the Israeli police and army to draw world attention to the conflict between the Israelis and Palestinians.

Second, in a pogrom victims are targeted by the state, which ignores the activities of its soldiers and police force (Brass 1997; Staub 1992). Local authorities manipulate the situation for political gain as minority groups become the state's scapegoats. During the nineteenth century, Russian anti-Semitism exploded in the form of Cossack violence against the local Jewish population (Ferguson 2006). Leaders use the prejudices that were taught during childhood to attack an out-group. These prejudices may be molded by elites and the state and turned against the out-group, while a divide-and-rule discourse ensures that the state cures its ills by targeting the out-group (Staub 1992). Thus, throughout the world in former colonies, intergroup conflicts are often seen as the legacy of colonialism (Tuso 1997, 2000). During the colonial period in India, the British influenced intergroup prejudices between the Hindus and Muslims and fomented pogroms in order to control the region. In Cyprus, the British manipulated the relationship between Turkish and Greek Cypriots during the 1960s, which led to a civil war in 1974 (Byrne 2007). People assume that the violence is pathological and normal, while the passivity of internal bystanders is seen by the perpetrators as tacit approval of their actions (Staub 1992). In reality, the state has a monopoly over the meaning of violence as it uses its power to protect its authority (Brass 1997). Violence-legitimating narratives in civil society have helped to limit the power of the state so that violence must be a last resort taken by a quasi-heroic figure against an evil figure (Smith 1997). There is a constant struggle between different actors in civil discourse over the narration of the events and legitimacy (Senehi 2002).

Third, the following elements lead to genocide (Brass 1997; Staub 1992). Difficult life conditions, such as severe economic problems, affect basic human needs and impact whole generations. The 1929 Wall Street stock market crash impacted the ability of Germany's Weimar government to make its reparations payments to the Allies, which resulted in political instability and conflict in which minorities were excluded from politics, economics, and culture (Ferguson 2006). The Weimar Republic was unstable, comprising a weak political party system that resulted in the Communists and the Nazis competing with each other for power. Alienation affected the German people's connections to other people, leading to a breakdown of community. Rapid social change in Germany affected individuals and groups, who used an us-versus-them mentality to deal with all of the confusion and chaos (Staub 1992). When the Nazi Party came to power in 1933, economic reform and the creation of the autobahns were accomplished by creating a war economy that resulted in Nazi Germany having to eventually go to war (Ferguson 2006).

Fourth, psychological processes such as social identities play a role as people turn to their own groups for identity needs and the creation of shared meaning (Brass 1997; Staub 1992). The state engages in scapegoating by identifying some group to blame and target and also deals with difficult situations by fostering an ideology such as Nazism to create a positive social identity for the group or nation (Brass 1997; Staub 1992). The state sees the out-group as unable to fulfill the ideology, so the out-group has to be eliminated (Staub 1992). Hence, the state mobilizes the in-group by fomenting hatred of the out-group while devaluing or demonizing the out-group through the use of stereotypes and mimetic violence (Girard 1979). The state may also decide to expand the victim group. The Nazis added Romas, intellectuals, liberals, Slavs, Communists, and GLBT people to the list that also branded the Jewish community as out-group (Staub 1992). It becomes difficult to critique or to devalue your own group in its devaluation of the out-group (Staub 1992). Anyone doing so is called a traitor; such traitors are tarred and feathered, imprisoned, fined, or shot.

### Anti-GLBT Violence, Soccer Hooligans, Skinheads, and Neo-Fascists Hate Crimes

Anti-GLBT violence is more harmful because these crimes may be linked to the survivor's "core identity" and a "heightened sense of vulnerability" that typically follows victimization and can exacerbate the survivor's own tendency to self-blame (Rayburn, Mendoza, and Davison 2003, 1056). Anti-GLBT violence is widespread globally. Males tend to experience greater levels of anti-GLBT harassment, threats, and victimization in school and by the police (Herek and Berrill 1992). Lesbians generally experience higher rates of verbal harassment by family members. Lesbians and gay men of color are at increased risk of violent attack because of their sexual orientation (Herek and Berrill 1992). The general profile of perpetrators of anti-GLBT violence is young white males often acting in concert with other young males, all of whom are strangers to the victim (Silver 1997). Of all hate crimes reported to law enforcement in the United States between 1991 and 1998, 16.2 percent were hate crimes based on sexual orientation (Federal Bureau of Investigation 1997). However, the data is incomplete since many GLBT people grow up in and are exposed to a hostile environment, so they may chose to remain in fear their entire lives.

## Soccer Hooligans

In Britain during the 1970s, armed gangs used knives, bottles, bicycle chains, and steel pipes to fight each other at soccer games in the guise of rival groups supporting different soccer teams (Giulianotti, Bonney, and Hepworth 1994). The members of these loosely organized groups were working-class youths looking for thrills in the face of poverty and alienation. In the 1980s, soccer violence spread to continental Europe and Latin America as rival groups of supporters traveled looking to instigate trouble with supporters of rival teams. In 1985 at the Hysel Stadium in Belgium, fifty Inter-Milan fans were killed by Liverpool fan members of the National Front neo-Fascist movement in Britain (Kerr 1994).

## Skinheads

The skinheads are hostile to authority. More than seventy thousand skins worldwide in thirty-three different countries are linked together (Suall 1995). Most skinheads live in Germany, Britain, Brazil, Sweden, Hungary, and the United States (Suall 1995). White power Oi or Ska music connects the skinhead movement internationally, and the music supports the violence and gives the skinheads a collective identity (Suall 1995). Skinheads wear Bovver boots (Doctor Marten boots), have shaved heads, and wear braced shin-length jeans. Violence blends with xenophobia, and in Britain skinheads go bashing, targeting ethnic minorities and GLBT citizens, while in Germany the skins are anti-Semitic and attack foreign workers (Knight 1983).

The skinheads originated as working-class British youths of the 1970s reacting against the hippie drug culture movement (Suall 1995). The skinheads are typically youths from broken homes and families who are rebelling against authority (Knight 1983). Membership in the skinhead movement helps the members to combat low self-esteem because they feel they are part of a worldwide social movement (Watson 2001). Class is not the identity factor, but race and nation are factors (Suall 1995). Skinheads attack people of different races, religions, and sexual orientation and are strongly anti-Left; skinheads are "the shock troops for xenophobia" (Suall 1995, 11).

Ideologically the skinheads identify and have links with right-wing groups and political parties (Watson 2001). In Britain, the National Front is connected to the Ulster Volunteer Force (UVF), a Protestant paramilitary group in Northern Ireland (Guelke 1988). The skinheads worship young German Nazis (Watts 2001). The slow response of the German government during the 1990s encouraged the skinheads to align with the neo-Nazi movement (Ridgeway 1995). This small international group of seventy thousand will not overthrow the state; the aim of the skinheads is to create fear in the local population and tear at the fabric of civil society (Suall 1995). Skinheads wish to punish and hurt the out-group, whom they hate, so the violence is very personal (Cooper 1998; Suall 1995).

In the early 1990s, 38 percent of those arrested in Germany for anti-immigrant violence were skinheads (Watts 2001, 605). Prior to this, the term "skinhead" was not very connected to anti-Semitic or anti-immigrant violence; 90 percent of the perpetrators were identified with neo-Nazi or other right-wing extremist groups (605). German data gives the reason for committing violent acts as "thrill-seeking" or attacking as part of an ideological "mission" (605). Watts (2001) argues that some skinheads are racists, but most racists are not skinheads. However, the skinheads have played a growing role in xenophobic violence (606). According to the German Federal Office for the Protection of the Constitution, "right-wing extremist potential" increased consistently in the later half of the nineties (606).

The three-part poison of aggression, xenophobia, and ideology will continue to produce subcultures in which contempt is held for cultural scapegoat outsiders (Watts 2001). As Watts (2001, 600) has noted, xenophobia is connected to local and international ideological networks, as the Internet gives political and commercial elements of skinhead and right-wing cultures a means of growth and support.

## NEO-FASCISTS

Immigration has become a political issue in Austria, Britain, France, Germany, Holland, Ireland, Italy, Sweden, and Switzerland, where the neo-Fascist parties argue that foreigners have contaminated the national culture (Fanning 2002). Neo-Fascists have desecrated Jewish cemeteries; attacked Romas, North Africans, Eastern Europeans, Arabs, Turks, and refugee shelters with petrol bombs; and covered the walls of immigrants' homes with hate slogans (Merkl and Weinberg 1997). On April 21, 2002, Jean Marie Le Pen of La Front National contested the French presidential election with Jacques Chirac. Le Pen was noted for his most infamous and evil remark that the Nazi concentration camps were merely a "detail of history" (Masson 2002, 384). He later apologized for this remark and condemned revisionist historians (Masson 2002, 386). Le Pen maintained that "only illegal immigrants have no place in France" and that immigrant communities want to live in peace and are the "totem" for his party; he maintained conservative same-sex adoption rights, which was not a progressive stance (386). In 1994 the Italian prime minister Silvio Berlusconi formed a coalition government with the right-wing National Alliance and Northern League. From 2000 to 2002 the extreme right-wing Austrian Freedom Party of Jörg Haider formed a coalition government with Wolfgang Schussel's People's Party on a political platform that was anti-immigrant and anti–European Union.

The neo-Fascist movement has a hatred of government and multicultural society and is anti-Semitic. The recruits for the neo-Nazi movement in Germany are disaffected youths looking for an identity who are indoctrinated by old Nazis who deny that the Holocaust ever happened (Merkl and Weinberg 1997). These young people have training sessions in Nazi ideology, read *Mien Kampf,* and watch

Joseph Goebbels's Nazi propaganda films from the 1930s (Merkl and Weinberg 1997). The neo-Nazi movement is an international organization that provides hate materials in a variety of languages for neo-Nazis worldwide (Barkun 1996).

## How Can We Intervene to Prevent Hate Crime?

In *Roots of Evil*, Ervin Staub (1992) speaks about a "critical loyalty" to humankind (280), that is, "creating positive connections between groups by expanding contact, positive reciprocity, cross-cutting relations, and superordinate goals" to challenge intergroup stereotypes (278). Just speaking out may be enough to prevent violence from escalating. Ingo Hasselbach was a leader of the neo-Nazi movement in Germany who now speaks out against the organization. During the 1970s, the ban on South Africa's athletes and musicians showed the South African government that the world community did not support apartheid.

Nations need a way to respond to the violence. The global community should develop an early warning mechanism to detect the escalation of conflict and use a UN Rapid Deployment Force to intervene to prevent conflict (Byrne, Fergusson, Ben-Ari, and Michael 2006). Early intervention may prevent the escalation of violence. In 1992 the UN deployed troops in Macedonia to prevent the conflict in Bosnia from spilling over into both Macedonia and Greece (Pearson and Rochester 1992).

Healing-survivor groups are also an important intervention, as people need to participate in public, collective, private, and personal rituals for healing (Staub 1992). Survivor groups could become future aggressors if their suffering is not acknowledged. "To reduce the probability of genocide and war, helping must be inclusive, across group lines, so that the evolving values of caring and connection ultimately include all human beings" (Staub 1992, 276). In Argentina, the Mothers of Plazo del Mayo created rituals to remember the disappeared and to grieve over the loss of loved ones. Perpetrators must also be held accountable for their actions and punished (Staub 1992). It is necessary to expose the perpetrators of violence by asking what is gained and by whom (Staub 1992). Perpetrators must be made to explain why they committed violence (Staub 1992). It is dangerous not to hold perpetrators accountable for their actions because this promotes the so-called Eichmann defense: "We were just doing what everyone else was doing" or "I was following orders" (Arendt 1994).

It is important to create dialogue groups to bring people in the middle ground together. For instance, Israelis and Palestinians, involved in the 1993 Oslo Peace Accords, were impacted by Herbert Kelman's (1991, 1997) dialogue groups that created intergroup understanding and identified common ground between the workshop participants. Creating meaningful contact between groups using superordinate goals or shared tasks that lead to shared goals can be very powerful (Rothman 1997). In communities plagued with violence, this is urgent. The leadership has to create a powerful vision that is inclusive.

What should be done to prevent anti-GLBT violence in society? It is important to make people aware of the problem by creating networks within the community to create relationships and by lobbying leaders to speak out against hate (Kivel 1997). Communities need to build programs to establish policies in schools that prohibit discrimination against same-sex couples and programs that enable students, both straight and GLBT, to interact and learn about each other and break down and challenge stereotypes (Rayburn, Mendoza, and Davison 2003). Politicians need to examine states' laws and policies and other institutions to see where they may be systemically fueling hate-crime and anti-GLBT violence (Green, Strolovitch, Wong, and Bailey 2001). The local community can also form and participate in peace rallies and marches that support and promote both individual choice and interdependence and speak out against the violence. An organized local community can also lobby against a medium that promotes stereotypes and glamorizes hate crimes against same-sex couples. It is every individual's responsibility and civic duty to take action. The statistics used to measure this type of violence are incomplete because victims may be unwilling to report assaults due to fears of publicizing their cases, because of distrust of the reporting agency, or out of the understanding that little would be achieved in doing so (Green, Strolovitch, Wong, and Bailey 2001, 282; Herek and Berrill 1992).

The following short-term interventions were made to decrease soccer violence (Perryman 2002). Soccer clubs have changed the rules and have strictly enforced them. Soccer players are now banned and fined for displaying violence on the field. Aggressive behavior is not rewarded because the players are role models for children. Fans have to produce their photo IDs to get into soccer grounds in Britain and Europe. Alcohol is not sold at the soccer grounds. In the stadium, fans are segregated to minimize riots. Police use metal detectors to search fans going into games and video surveillance of fans inside the stadium, while special antiriot police patrol the grounds during games. A team with a history of soccer violence may have its ticket sales limited so that only a certain amount of tickets are available for an away game. Soccer clubs with a history of fan violence may be banned from international competition for a number of years. For example, because of the Hysel Stadium tragedy, Liverpool could not play in European competitions for several years, which impacted its revenue flow. Perryman (2002) argues that long-term interventions necessitate that sports journalists should not focus their reports on yobbo violence so as to prevent publicity for soccer hooligans. Moreover, it is important to change the perceptions of fans, athletes, management, corporations, and media to have a no-tolerance policy for sports violence or hate violence of players (eg kick racism out of football and the recent Luis Suarez and John Terry incidents in England).

Worldwide law enforcement agencies know that the skinheads are an ideological group that must be monitored very carefully (Suall 1995). There are interventions that can be used to prevent skinhead hate crimes and violence. The community can intervene to mobilize tolerance and to support survivors of skinhead violence in the community to illustrate solidarity. When a Jewish youngster was attacked in Idaho in 1994, every member of the community put a menorah in their windows to show solidarity with the local Jewish community (Suall 1995). In addition, African and Turkish guest workers in Germany have founded self-defense groups (Watson 2001).

Governments and the wider community can intervene to prevent neo-Nazi and neo-Fascist violence. The German Constitution limits free speech when it threatens democracy by banning the dissemination of Nazi symbols and propaganda (Barkun 2003). A political party in Germany has to win 5 percent of the votes to elect politicians to the Bundestag and the Bundesrat. The so-called 5 Percent Rule election threshold restricts the National Socialist German Workers Party and the Communist Party from electing members to office. Community support for victims of neo-Fascist violence is illustrated by the hundreds of thousands of Europeans who take to the streets in candlelight marches to protest violence against communities in the wake of attacks and pogroms against East European, Roma, Jewish, Arab, Turkish, and African immigrants (Barkun 1996).

Instead of asking what causes hate violence, Brass (1997) argues that we should ask "What is violence?" This task can be accomplished by examining the discourse of various parties locally. It is critical to get a local interpretation of events to get a clear picture of what is going on (Brass 1997). It is arguable that the level of violence in society remains constant. What changes is the name put on it. In Britain, the warfare against blacks in urban areas is continuous (Vogler 1991). Labeling violence may lead to ignoring other types of violence (Staub 1992). By focusing on a particular situation or event and giving violence a particular label, we may in fact be allowing violence to continue in our societies (Staub 1992). The state holds a monopoly over the meaning and use of violence (Brass 1997; Smith 1997).

## Conclusion

Hate violence is one consequence of a self-perpetuating imbalance in socioeconomic and political power (Perry 2001). According to the Montgomery County Government (1995), hate violence progresses from acts of indirect prejudice (such as rumors and stereotypes) to acts of prejudice (such as avoidance) to acts of discrimination (excluding persons from the targeted group from employment, housing, and educational opportunities) to acts of violence (such as assault, vandalism, and riots), culminating in life-threatening acts (such as lynching, assassination, and genocide).

The Southern Poverty Law Center (1999) in Montgomery, Alabama, has outlined ten interventions to end racism: (1) act and do something, or apathy will be interpreted by hate activists as acceptance; (2) unite and organize a group of allies from churches, schools, clubs, and other civic sources; (3) support the victims of hate crime and let them know that you care; (4) research the hate crimes and deliver the accurate information to the community; (5) hold a unity rally or parade to create a hate-free zone; (6) speak up to expose and denounce hate crimes; (7) lobby politicians, business, and community leaders to take a stand against hate; (8) look long-range and hold annual events such as a parade or culture fair to celebrate diversity and harmony in the community; (9) teach tolerance workshops in the schools, the workplace, and community centers; and (10) dig deeper into economic inequality, stereotypes, immigration, and the targeting of same-sex couples.

Moreover, the Declaration of Schlaining (Mader 1995, 7) calls upon "all of humanity, regardless of sex, occupation, social standing, or age to act jointly in solidarity against racism, violence, and discrimination." It is the responsibility of all citizens to work to promote human rights, nonviolence, conflict transformation, tolerance, democracy, and peace education within a multicultural context. In 1996, the late Jim Ward retired as director of Human Resources for Miami-Dade County in southern Florida. He formed a "Love Your Neighbor" NGO to promote a tolerant multicultural community and in the process founded a local newspaper, *Love Your Neighbor Good News*, that reports positive stories of constructive community building in southern Florida.

The next chapter outlines some of the causes of corporate violence, and abusive violence in the workplace and some of the intervention measures that can prevent such violence.

## Websites Related to Hate Crime

California Association of Human Relations Organizations, http://www.cahro.org/html/hate_crimes.html

Centre for Preventing Hate, http://www.preventinghate.org/

Hate Crime, http://www.hatecrime.net

Let's Kick Racism Out of Football http://www.kickitout.org/

Matthew Shepard Foundation, http://www.matthewshepard.org

National Coalition for the Homeless, http://www.nationalhomeless.org/hatecrimes/

Political Research Associates, http://www.publiceye.org

Southern Poverty Law Center, http://www.splcenter.org/

Teaching Tolerance, A Project of the Southern Poverty Law Center, http://www.teachingtolerance.org

## Suggested Questions for Further Discussion

1. How can a global network of connections transform perceptions of the Other and eradicate hate crime at the same time?

2. How effective are national and international laws and regulations concerning hate crime? What can be done to enhance the effectiveness of these laws and of the overall performance and influence of the legal system, the police, NGOs, and international institutions in the prevention of hate crimes?

3. How can society intervene to prevent acts of prejudice, discrimination, and violence and life-threatening acts against people because of their race, religion, ethnicity, sexual orientation, age, class, or gender?

4. How can tolerance networks and policy makers work together to prevent hate crimes and environmental racism and to promote tolerance? How is the legitimacy or illegitimacy of violence established through narratives in civil society?

5. What are the contributing factors that lead to the perpetuation of violence against GLBT people? Why are young white men responsible for most of the violence committed against GLBT people? What must be done to stop these injustices?

6. Is it possible to use storytelling to remember and affirm past tragedies and achievements across divides without perpetuating a sense of victimization or triumphalism that exacerbates hate violence? If so, how?

7. Why do neo-Fascists, skinheads, and soccer hooligans bash people of color, GLBT people, and the homeless?

# 6

## Understanding and Preventing Corporate Violence and Abusive Behavior in the Workplace

Enron, under the leadership of Kenneth Lay, developed into an enormous trading firm in electricity and natural gas, among other commodities. *Fortune Magazine* listed Enron seventh out of five hundred of the largest corporations in the United States valued by the stock market at over $50 billion. Enron was under pressure to deliver even more wealth for its shareholders. The firm applied aggressive accounting strategies to achieve the desired effect. Enron's failure in 2001 to disclose detailed information of its inflated share earnings and partnership transactions with Merrill Lynch, Arthur Andersen, Citibank, and JP Morgan Chase led to its collapse. Enron went bankrupt, with debts of $31.8 billion and leaving more than four thousand people jobless. The courts and shareholders accused Lay of hiding billions of dollars of losses and of lying about the state of the energy-trading firm (Salter 2008).

This chapter focuses on violence by corporations and violence in the workplace. Our global ecology is devastated daily by a myriad of environmental problems caused by multinational corporations. Even as China develops into a formidable economic power, international corporations in the Special Economic Zones (SEZs) dump industrial waste deposits into the Yangtze River, polluting the water and decimating the fish population (Homer-Dixon 2007). Air pollution from corporations using fossil fuels creates acid rain, which is destroying large tracts of forests in Canada and in the Black Forest in Germany (Klare 2002). Corporations also restrict development in developing countries that are dependent on the corporations for manufacturing investment and technology; the global South is forced to cut down its forests to repay foreign debt, which results in deforestation and hunger (Klare 2008). Countries in the global South also depend on the development of a few products in a global marketplace, which creates economic vulnerability for poorer countries (Jeong 2005). Corporations mold public opinion through advertising campaigns and hide information from the public (Clinard and Yeager 1990; Mokhiber 1989). In the United States, the tobacco industry blocked numerous attempts by the government and the public to ban the marketing of tobacco.

Corporations also sell unsafe pharmaceutical products and contaminated foodstuffs to developing countries in which legal remedies banning such goods are lax (Homer-Dixon 2001). Local communities have organized to resist the power of the corporations. Baldemar Valásquez founded the Farm Labor Organizing Committee to organize migrant workers in the United States to nonviolently protest against agribusiness for fair wages and improved working conditions. César Chávez created the United Farm Workers union to inform the American public that pollutant weed killers were poisoning consumers as well as the migrant grape pickers (Reza and Barger 1994). Violence against the environment is also reflected in the lack of environmental laws in the global South that permits developed countries to cheaply sell garbage and radioactive material to corrupt governments, poison water supplies with pharmaceuticals from factories, and sell antipersonnel mines that kill and maim children, women, and the elderly (Klare 2008).

Corporate violence is also directed against the worker so that unsafe working conditions and a competitive work environment promote violence in the workplace (Mokhiber 1989). Sexual harassment and workplace bullying are grave issues that impair the health of employees (Gill, Fisher, and Bowie 2002). Discriminatory employment practices exclude certain groups such as same-sex couples and veterans from health and pension benefits (Keashly, Trott, and MacLean 1994). Moreover, the recent global economic recession was fueled in part by greedy banks and Ponzi schemes that have brought countries to their knees. Violence in the workplace costs the global economy billions of dollars every year (Gill, Fisher, and Bowie 2002).

This chapter outlines some of the underlying causes and results of corporate violence and violence in the workplace and examines an intervention system that explores the range of interventions needed to address corporate violence and workplace violence.

## Corporate Violence and Violence in the Workplace

Clinard and Yeager (1980) argue that corporate violence inflicts air and water pollution on the health of the public and workers as a result of unsafe and defective appliances, drugs, and food. Plant workers are injured on the job by toxic chemicals without adequate safeguards to protect them (Clinard and Yeager 1980, 9). Corporate and other white-collar crime committed by elites are more damaging to society than street crime in terms of both economic costs and physical injury (Mokhiber 1989; J. Coleman 1994; Salter 2008; Simon 1996). Corporate violence can take the form of willful negligence toward employees, consumers, or the public at large. Not all corporate violence is against the law (Mokhiber 1989, 4). Some corporation's lobby to have laws passed that will be in their interests; in those instances, "corporate lawbreakers double as corporate lawmakers" (Mokhiber 1989, 5). This speaks to the power of the corporate perpetrator: street criminals are not so able to influence legal policy, and corporations are insulated against the stigma and effectiveness of criminal sanctions (Mokhiber 1989; Perkins 2007). The 1890 Sherman Anti-Trust Act created a "two-track prosecution system" in the United States in which corporate criminals are tried in a "civil court behind closed doors so that a corporation does not admit to or deny the allegations" against it (Mokhiber 1989, 58). Business persons therefore do not conform to the stereotype of the criminal in the public's perception (Mokhiber 1989).

The media does not draw attention to corporate violence. Jean Kilbourne (1995) argues that magazines will not write honest, critical reports regarding their advertisers such as cigarette companies. The clients of magazines are not the readers; rather, the clients are the advertisers, and the product that the magazine sells is its readers (Kilbourne 1995). The so-called liberal media is a myth; the media, in effect, is owned by corporations (see video documentaries produced by the Media Education Foundation in Northampton, Massachusetts, such as *Mickey Mouse Monopoly: Disney, Childhood and Corporate Power; Captive Audience: Advertising Invades the Classroom;* and *Class Dismissed: How TV Frames the Working Class*).

In the United States, the meatpacking industry is the nation's most dangerous occupation (Kinney 1992; Stromquist and Bergman 1997; Wilson 2006). More than "one out of three meatpacking workers suffer an injury or a work-related illness" (Schlosser 2001a, 172). It is estimated that about forty thousand men and women are injured annually. These estimates likely reflect underreporting, because workers are discouraged from reporting injuries (Schlosser 2001b, 2); "thousands of additional injuries and illnesses may go unreported" (Schlosser 2001a, 172). Injured workers are put "back on the job quickly" to reduce the number of lost workdays recorded (Schlosser 2001b, 2). "The rate of these cumulative traumas in the meatpacking industry" is almost thirty-five times higher than the national average in the industry (Schlosser 2001a, 173).

Changes have emerged in the industry. In the past, the powerful union lobby ensured that employers provided an excellent salary and benefits to meatpackers (Schlosser 2001a, 153). "There were waiting lists for these jobs," which were dangerous but offered dignity and "a middle-class lifestyle" to the workers (Schlosser 2001b, 3). Beginning in the 1960s, the Iowa Beef Packers (IPB) revolutionized the industry (Schlosser 2001a), "opening plants in rural areas" that were isolated from the trade unions while "recruiting immigrant workers from Mexico" (Schlosser 2001b, 3). The IPB created "a new division of labor that eliminated the need for skilled butchers and intensively battled the trade unions" (3).

Because the IPB's strategies increased its profits, by the 1980s other meatpacking companies were forced to adopt the IPB's strategies to stay in business (Schlosser 2001a, 155; Schlosser 2001b, 3). Wages fell dramatically, and today the meatpacking occupation is among those jobs with the lowest pay and the highest turnover rate (Schlosser 2001a, 160; Schlosser 2001b, 3). Shortages of workers have increased the workload, with the result that "these jobs are even more dangerous," and the "meatpacking industry has become highly centralized and concentrated" (Schlosser 2001b, 3). A few agribusinesses (IBP, ConAgra, Excel, and National Beef) control most of the market in North America and abroad (Schlosser 2001a, 158; Schlosser 2001b, 3). Trade unions have become much weaker.

Danger and profitability are correlated in the demand for increased speed in the production line (Schlosser 2001a, 178); the most dangerous plants are those where cattle are slaughtered (Schlosser 2001b, 3). Schlosser (2001a, 173) reports that technological advances have increased line speeds to "four hundred cattle per hour." All sorts of accidents that involve conveyor belts, knives, saws, and falling carcasses become more likely because the chain moves so fast and fails to stop for an injured worker (Schlosser 20001a, 172; Schlosser 2001b, 4).

Weak trade unions and the exploitation of migrant workers remain key issues to be addressed in the meatpacking industry (Schlosser 2001b, 3). Meatpacking companies resist trade unions, and a high employee turnover rate weakens trade union membership (Schlosser 2001a, 174; Schlosser 2001b, 3). In addition, there are limits placed on workers' compensation claims by injured workers. "The ability of meatpacking firms to delay payment discourages many injured workers from ever filing workers' comp claims" (Schlosser 2001a, 185).

Pressure by supervisors within the company negatively impacts workers injured on the job (Schlosser 2001a, 175), as the company's organization develops "a culture that discourages reporting of injuries" and/or seeking compensation for injuries (Schlosser 2001b, 6).

The supervisors "discourage workers from reporting their injuries," encouraging them to quit (Schlosser 2001a, 175; Schlosser 2001b, 6). "Far from being a liability, a high turnover rate in the meatpacking industry, as in the fast food industry, also helps to maintain a workforce that is harder to unionize and much easier to control" (Schlosser 2001a, 161).

Is violence in the workplace a symptom of the pressures resulting from other social issues and corporate trends? In the words of Schell (2003, 359), "no one is safe from becoming a target of aggression in the workplace." In the United States, approximately 750 workers are victims of homicides annually, and 75 percent of these incidents were fistfights and physical assaults, while 67 percent were employee-to-employee or employee-to-supervisor violence (Paludi, Nydegger, and Paludi 2006). The average financial cost to an employer is $250,000 per incident, while workplace violence is costing American employers an estimated $4.2 billion annually (Philbrick, Sparks, Hass, and Arsenault 2003, 84). Negligent hiring and negligent supervision and retention are more recent legal issues.

In a survey by Chappell and Di Martino (2001), more than half the health care personnel from developed and developing countries reported incidents of physical and psychological violence in the year prior to the study. A total of 61 percent of the sample in South Africa, 54 percent in Thailand, 60 percent in Portugal, 37 percent in Bulgaria, and 41 percent in Lebanon reported incidents of verbal or physical violence (Chappell and Di Martino 2001). A 1996 European Union survey of 15,800 people from fifteen member states found that 6 million workers reported physical violence, 3 million workers were subjected to sexual harassment, and 12 million workers experienced intimidation and bullying (Chappell and Di Martino 2001). In the United Kingdom, a 1995 British Retail Consortium conducted a survey of crime in the retail sector and found that during 1994–95, 11,000 retail staff workers were victims of physical violence, while 350,000 suffered threats and verbal abuse (Chappell and Di Martino 2001). In a study conducted in the United States during 1993–99, the National Crime Victimization Survey (NCVS) found that more than 1.7 million American workers were victims of workplace violence (Duhart 2001).

## Table 6.1. Average annual number, rate, and percent of workplace victimization by type of crime, 1993–1999

| Percent of Crime Category | Average Annual Workplace Victimization | Rate per 1,000 Persons in the Workforce | Workplace Victimization |
|---|---|---|---|
| All violent crime | 1,744,300 | 12.5 | 100% |
| Homicide | 900 | 0.01 | 0.1% |
| Rape/Sexual assault | 36,500 | 0.3 | 2.1% |
| Robbery | 70,100 | 0.5 | 4.0% |
| Aggravated assault | 325,000 | 2.3 | 18.6% |
| Simple assault | 1,311,700 | 9.4 | 75.2% |

Sources: Homicide data are obtained from the Bureau of Labor Statistics Census of Fatal Occupational Injuries. Rape and sexual assault, robbery, aggravated assault, and simple assault data are from the NCVS (Duhart 2001, 2).

Table 6.1 highlights that during this time approximately 36,500 rapes and sexual assaults occurred; in 80 percent of these incidents, the victim was female (Duhart 2001).

Except for rape and sexual assault, males experienced all categories of workplace violent crime at higher rates and percentages than did females (table 6.2).

Conflict between management and labor unions, domestic violence seeping into the workplace, and changes in an organization's cultural system seriously impact the health, morale, and safety of people in the workplace (Denenberg and Braverman 2001). Management must be more sensitive to the needs of women in volatile domestic violence situations (Brownell and Roberts 2002, 415). These types of

# Table 6.2. Average annual rate and percentage of workplace crime by gender, race, and crime category, 1993–1999

## Violent Victimizations in the Workplace

| Characteristic of Victim | Rape and Sexual Assault Rate | Rape and Sexual Assault Percent | Robbery Rate | Robbery Percent | Aggravated Assault Rate | Aggravated Assault Percent | Simple Assault Rate | Simple Assault Percent |
|---|---|---|---|---|---|---|---|---|
| **Gender** | | 100% | | 100% | | 100% | | 100% |
| Male | 0.1 | 20.0 | 0.7 | 70.2 | 3.1 | 71.4 | 11.2 | 64.1 |
| Female | 0.5 | 80.0 | 0.3 | 29.8 | 1.5 | 28.6 | 7.3 | 35.9 |
| **Race** | | 100% | | 100% | | 100% | | 100% |
| White | 0.3 | 88.4 | 0.5 | 80.7 | 2.4 | 85.6 | 9.9 | 89.0 |
| Black | 0.2* | 9.0* | 0.7 | 16.0 | 2.1 | 10.4 | 7.4 | 8.9 |
| Other | 0.2* | 2.6* | 0.4* | 3.3* | 2.5 | 4.0 | 5.1 | 2.0 |

Note: Detail may not add to total shown because of rounding.

Percentages are of total workplace victimization; rates are per 1,000 persons in the workforce.

*Estimate based on 10 or fewer sample cases (Duhart 2001, 3).

violence cost organizations from $3 billion to $4 billion annually in lost time, higher health care premiums, and lower productivity (416).

Organizations are "crisis-prone or crisis-prepared" to deal with large-scale disasters such as the Exxon *Valdez* oil spill or the racial discrimination suit filed against Texaco (Braverman 1999, 9). The ability to take direct action is the difference between "reactive and proactive crisis management" (11). Crisis-prepared organizations use a systems thinking approach to deal with early-warning indicators of possible conflict situations such as domestic violence, downsizing, and threats erupting into violence (Braverman 1999; Turner and Gelles 2003). A systems thinking approach examines faulty systems for communication, prevention, and decision making that often create a crisis-prone milieu (Braverman 1999).

Who is the violent employee in the workplace? Braverman (1999) argues that focusing on individuals who may be at risk for violence on the basis of lists of characteristics is not useful as a predictive tool. Instead of profiling, employers should consider personality issues in conjunction with other stresses on the person, the context in which a threat is made, and the escalating situation (Braverman 1999). People who feel insufferable stress or disempowerment in the workplace are at risk for violent behavior. For example, Braverman (1999, 4) has noted that "Anyone who has ever had to manage crises concerning human behavior in the workplace knows that the causes of violence lie as much in our systems as they do in the people themselves." As Jack Howard (2002, 61) proposes, there is a continuous interaction involving the person, the situation, and the context within the workplace as the perpetrator commits calculated acts that provide indications of her or his intentions.

Inappropriate antisocial or deviant behavior can cause severe psychological stress to the person being harassed, resulting in threats and/or lost productivity and creating an abusive work environment for that person that damages workforce morale (Sommers, Schell, and Vodanovich 2002, 211). Aggressive high-risk behavior can escalate to direct physical assault, including homicide and sexual assault (Golden, Johnson, and Lopez 2002). Sexual harassment is a serious problem in the workplace; results of a survey of a stratified random sample of 23,964 federal workers in 1982 by the U.S. Merit Systems Protection Board found that 42 percent of all female respondents reported experiences of sexual harassment in the workplace (Fitzgerald and Shullman 1993; Tangri, Burt, and Johnson 1982). Sexual harassment is a function of organizational structural and cultural characteristics and job context that affects job performance and the person's health (Fitzgerald, Drasgow, Hulin, Gelfand, and Magley 1997; Fitzgerald and Shullman 1993).

Workplace bullying is the intentional implementation of a hostile work milieu upon a person by a coworker that combines nonverbal and verbal behaviors in which stresses are manipulated to frustrate the person's basic human needs (Vickers 2001, 207). Workplace bullies use rumors, threats, and other malevolent actions to stir up fellow employees, creating a hostile work milieu to marginalize or to force the person to leave the workplace (213). At work, a victim is vulnerable because the perpetrator is frequently successful in attempts to get that person fired (Reeves 2004, 116). Vickers (2001, 206) reported that sociopathic predators use their power and influence to bully successful colleagues and undermine their confidence.

Bullies are unlikely to change their behavior, and their sociopathic behavior must be stopped (Vickers 2001, 215). Litigation sometimes must take place if all other options have been depleted. Bullying behavior evolves in the workplace because it often provides rich terrain where it can flourish (Randall 1997; Vickers 2001, 216). All perpetrators pass through three stages, according to Wodarski and Dulmus (2002, 362). Stage 1 acts include objectifying and dehumanizing others, starting and spreading untruths about others, verbal abuse, and sexual harassment. Stage 2 behaviors include physical confrontations, displaying weapons, and committing assault. Stage 3 is committing an act of violence.

Violence is just as likely to arise from without as from within the workplace, as an external and enraged client is apt to direct violence at the employee who is providing a service to the perpetrator (Griffin and O'Leary-Kelly 2004). On September 11, 2001, airline crews in the United States were overpowered, and the airplanes that were hijacked were crashed into the Twin Towers of the World Trade Center and into the Pentagon. The fourth hijacked plane, United Airlines Flight 93, crashed into a field near Shanksville, Pennsylvania, as passengers tried to regain control of the aircraft. In other cases, university professors are shot by irate students over grades. Housing officers are placed in cages in Glasgow to protect them from irate customers. More direct contact with the public places women at more risk for workplace violence (Fisher and Gunnison 2001, 152). Proportionately, females are spending less time than males at work but are experiencing one-third of violent incidents (152).

Random acts of violence in the workplace have become almost an accepted part of everyday life, or a so-called acceptable level of violence. The media's expression for work rage—"going postal"—has become an accepted part of our language (Keashly and Harvey 2006). Corporations and workplaces in general are scrambling to find solutions to these tragic interactions between a violence-prone individual and a system that provokes the violence (Denenberg and Braverman 2001). What can be done to prevent corporate violence and violence in the workplace?

### Corporate Violence and Workplace Violence Interventions Strategies

Fines do not deter corporate violence; they merely become "the cost of doing business" (Mokhiber 1989, 29). Economic penalties ignore the role of corrupt individuals who run risks for profit and who can be replaced by like-minded managers (Jeong 2000a; Mokhiber 1989). Russell Mokhiber (1989, 1–65) proposes five intervention tracks to end corporate crime. First, corporations can transform their behavior by re-arranging their "standard operating procedures" and by setting up conflict resolution processes that change workplace behavior and practices (64). Corporations could also use the media to inform the public of any illegal activities (34). "Adverse publicity would deter corporations from illegal misdeeds" that would hurt profit margins from public boycotts (59). Corporations would support their public policy opponents by providing economic resources to these watchdog agencies (37).

Second, citizens need to be empowered to act against corporate violent behavior. Individual survivors of corporate violence can pool their resources in "class-action lawsuits to seek compensation from corporate wrongdoing" (59). Grassroots citizens can set up "neighborhood watch committees" to monitor corporate activities (46). A corporation can enact regulations that protect employees who report illegal activities. "Governments must curtail the advertising power of corporations by limiting their control over the media" (61). Citizens can work with corporations to frame a set of ethics to which corporations would be held accountable.

Third, "white-collar crime needs to be equated with criminal behavior" (59). "Fines and prison sentences must be severe" to deter executives from criminal behavior (58). Corporations that break the law could be "put on probation" and be made to make restitution to their victims and do community work (56). Corporations that violate the law can create educational programs on corporate crime for the public. Corporations would have to take out "an advertisement in the newspaper to inform the public" about their illegal activities (60).

Fourth, governments can give "free media time to politicians" so that they do not have to depend on corporations for substantial contributions during elections (62). Governments can prohibit contracts going to corporations that break the law. Internal security agencies such as the Federal Bureau of Investigation (FBI) in the United States can create "a corporate crime index" to monitor corporations that break the law (41). The public can disinvest in corporations that flout the law and commit crimes. Each country's "attorney general's office can also prosecute corporations" that deliberately misinform the public about their activities (62). Executives and employees should have mandatory conflict resolution and business ethics training that educate them about corporate violence and how to resolve conflict in the workplace.

Fifth, in the United States, Mokhiber (1989) suggests that "a Corporate Crime Task Force" (CCTF) should be created across the policing agencies—the Occupational Safety and Health Administration (OSHA), the Food and Drug Administration (FDA), and the Environmental Protection Agency (EPA)—to monitor and prosecute corporate wrongdoers (44). "Toll-free hotlines" can be provided for citizens to report corporate violations (44). The CCTF can train local citizens on how to effectively monitor and report illegal corporate activity in their neighborhoods. "Interpol can also be empowered to monitor and prosecute corporations" that dump hazardous waste in developing countries and otherwise behave illegally (48).

The causes of workplace violence lie in both the systems that are constructed to deal with a myriad of human issues that arise at work and in the people who are at risk and those who implement those systems, policies, and procedures (Braverman 1999). Tolerance often takes second place to abuses of intimidation, workplace bullying, and fostering morale in a team-oriented workplace (Doi 2001, 136). Under each country's legal system, employers have a duty of due diligence to create a zero-tolerance policy regarding workplace violence and harassment, to provide a safe work milieu to protect the human dignity of each employee, and to correct unprofessional behavior in the workplace (Braverman 1999). As Doi (2001, 137) has noted, an episode of workplace violence that is attributable to negligent hiring, retention, supervision, or training leaves that organization liable to the targeted employee and survivor of workplace bullying.

Human resource managers must pay particular attention to health, labor relations, safety, and policy changes. Organizational structure and supervisor-subordinate interactions are strongly related to aggression in the workplace (Arway 2002; Keashly, Trott, and MacLean 1994). In the words of Tobin (2001, 100), "aggressive acts are a hostile invasion of a person's dignity and self-esteem." Human resource managers have to clue into stressors and early warning signs to proactively minimize potential stressors and to intervene immediately to prevent the escalation of conflict into violence (McFarlin, Fals-Stewart, Major, and Justice 2001).

An employer can be negligent in retaining a high-risk employee when the employer does not demonstrate a clear awareness of the situation or does not attempt to discipline, supervise, or discharge the employee when needed (Philbrick, Sparks, Hass, and Arsenault 2003, 87). If an employer is concerned that the safety of the company will deteriorate as a result of releasing a violent or mentally unstable employee, the employer can also refer the troubled employee to employee assistance programs (Philbrick, Sparks, Hass, and Arsenault 2003, 88). If these measures are ineffective, termination is the only viable option for securing the safety of others.

Mark Braverman (1999) argues that it is important to balance personal rights with privacy and the safety of others so that all interventions are within the scope of fair and equitable policies and procedures in regard to all of the factors involved in the violent context. Braverman (1999, 124–35) outlines seven necessary steps to create a violence-prevention program in the workplace that is preventive and not emergency reactive: (1) get support from top management to appoint a team and to change the organization's culture; (2) create a team of key stakeholders who will design and develop policy; (3) perform a workplace violence risk analysis about past experience, current exposure, and possible warning signs; (4) develop simple and sensible policies and procedures; (5) conduct training in the new policies and procedures to ensure implementation and wide support; (6) arrange for easy nonpunitive access to medical and mental health professionals to ensure that all employees feel comfortable in the process and that employers have access to information; and (7) have timely, clear, and accurate policies and procedures for termination and layoffs, including continuous communication, an organizational transition team, and safety nets.

Managers and supervisors must change the organization's culture by modeling professional behavior and by providing strong leadership in creating a violence prevention and intervention plan to prepare for crisis situations and in recognizing and responding to high-risk situations by taking appropriate action (Bowie, Fisher, and Cooper 2005; Denenberg and Braverman 2001). Thus, it is important to create an indigenous violence prevention and intervention strategy that can be incorporated into an effective risk assessment and violence prevention multitrack zero-tolerance policy to create a harmonious violence-free and productive workplace milieu based on mutual respect and transparency (Keashly and Harvey 2006; Leather, Cox, and Farnsworth 1990; Schell 2003). Training supervisors in the policy is also important so that they can protect all of the employees and create a safe and productive work milieu (Howard 2002; Wodarski and Dulmus 2002). Employees should also receive conflict analysis and resolution training so that they are empowered to recognize high-risk behaviors (C. Anderson 2001; Harper 2004). A proactive rapid response multidimensional violence prevention and intervention team comprised of people from across the workplace (e.g., from counseling, human resources, public relations, and trade unions) can also carry out a thorough analysis of an event and address volatile situations before they escalate and explode into violence (Braverman 1999; Burton 1997; Rogers and Chappell 2003). Conflict analysis and resolution (e.g., the Thomas Kilmann Test: avoider, accommodator, compromiser, competitor, and collaborator) training can also educate employees about violence and assist them in settling disputes in a nonviolent way with a win-win outcome (Harper 2004). Employees, supervisors, and management would then model cooperation instead of aggressive competition in the plethora of relationships that exist in the workplace (Paludi, Nydegger, and Paludi 2006). Having an intervention policy clearly indicates an organization's proactive efforts to create and maintain good relations among and between employers, supervisors, and employees and to prevent violence in the workplace (Burton 1997; Kennedy, Homant, and Homant 2004; Kenny, 2002).

## Conclusion

The workplace is a crucible of competition that can push employees against each other so that the workplace becomes a place of desperation, conflict, and isolation (Braverman 1999, 6). The threat of direct violence or psychological abuse is an important source of stress in the work lives of employees (Keashly and Harvey 2006). Preventing violence in the workplace becomes a question of the quality and sanctity of life. Management needs a thorough multidimensional analysis of the underlying complex causes of violence to create a harmonious work milieu in which the work and dignity of employees are valued (Leather, Cox, and Farnsworth 1990). A conspiracy of silence and bystander apathy in which management and other employees blame the victim creates a toxic work milieu (Harper 2004).

Employers and employees must work collaboratively to prevent workplace violence. A zero-tolerance policy as well as a multitrack violence intervention and prevention systems approach must be in place in the workplace to protect the physical and psychological well-being of each employee. Otherwise, when the perpetrator detonates, management will face the consequences of inaction (Braverman 1999; Landau, Landau, and Landau 2001).

Violence in the workplace is a symptom of the pressures resulting from other social issues and corporate trends. The malpractices of corporations acting on the global stage do have a profound effect on the health and quality of life of all citizens as well as all life forms on Earth (Perkins 2007). In today's global society, citizens and governments must become empowered to act to prevent corporations from abusing the resources and the longevity of all life forms on this planet.

The next chapter outlines some of the causes of ethnopolitical violence and a multitrack intervention approach to preventing ethnic violence.

## Websites Related to Corporate Violence and Violence in the Workplace

Canadian Initiative on Workplace Violence, http://www.workplaceviolence.ca

Centers for Disease Control and Prevention (NIOSH), http://www.cdc.gov/niosh/docs/2006-144/

Centre for Conflict Resolution International, http://www.conflictatwork.com

International Labor Organization, http://www.ilo.org

National Crime Prevention Council, http://www.ncpc.org/

National Institute for the Prevention of Workplace Violence, http://www.workplaceviolence911.com/

The People Bottomline, http://www.worktrauma.org/

Workplace Bullying Institute, http://bullyinginstitute.org/

Workplace Violence News, http://workplaceviolencenews.com/
World Health Organization Violence Prevention Alliance, http://www
.who.int/violenceprevention/en/

## Suggested Questions for Further Discussion

1. Is it important to use a crisis context to understand workplace violence? Why should organizations incorporate a systemic violence prevention early-warning policy rather than profiling potential violent employees?

2. Why are harassment, sexual harassment, and bullying at epidemic proportions in the workplace? Why is a bullying employee directly liable for an unlawful employment practice? Why is the employer vicariously liable for the bullying employee's behavior? How can organizations create a harassment-free zone in their workplaces?

3. Why is it important to appoint a violence prevention and intervention team that includes employee assistance program counselors, physicians, trade unionists, judges, local police, psychologists, and management?

4. Why are most corporations crisis-prone rather than crisis-prepared organizations? Should harassment of any type be brought to litigation or mediated or arbitrated in private?

5. Does economic development need to trump human rights in order to become established in the global South?

6. In what ways could employees themselves be more involved in establishing and maintaining a safe workplace? Why is it important for an organization to enhance connectedness and trust among employees?

7. How do we hold corporations accountable for their actions and their senior executives who cause violence against consumers, the environment, and the global South?

# 7

## Ethnopolitical Conflict

### Causes, Intervention, and Prevention

Today Moamer Hasonovic is a thirty-nine-year-old man living on the outskirts of Sarajevo. He was studying electrical engineering at the University of Sarajevo when the war broke out. Suddenly on April 5, 1992, during the siege of Sarajevo, Moamer and his classmates were thrown into the defense of their city against the surrounding Serbian forces. He served in the same squad with his six friends, sharing two AK-47 rifles among ten soldiers. When the siege lifted on February 29, 1996, four of his friends had perished in the war. Moamer is not bitter about the war, just about the loss of his friends who had so much to live for. He pays tribute to and honors the memory of his Croat, Serb, and Bosniak friends who died together defending their homes, families, and fellow citizens of Sarajevo. Sarajevo was and is a multicultural city whose residents live as cosmopolitan citizens in an exciting and eclectic cross-cultural milieu. Moamer successfully earned his master's degree in electrical engineering at Syracuse University. He is very positive and has great hope for the future of his city, whose young citizens rebuild their lives in a positive transcultural environment (Moamer Hasonovic, personal communication, July 1996).

Ted Robert Gurr (1993) argues that the analysis of intergroup and ethnopolitical conflicts considers the role of relative deprivation and group mobilization as well as primordialist, constructionist, and instrumentalist interpretations of ethnicity. The end of the Cold War witnessed a realignment of power in intrastate conflicts along ethnopolitical lines (Gurr 1993). Ethnic nationalism became a mechanism of belonging, recognition, and revenge as ethnopolitical groups mobilized against state dominance (Wallensteen 2002; Wolff 2006). Ethnic cleansing in Kosovo, Sierra Leone, Rwanda, Burundi, and Bosnia demonstrated the role of revenge by ethnopolitical elites bent on the genocide of rival ethnopolitical groups (Paris 2004; Sekulic 1997). Ethnically divisive strategies provoked ethnic warfare (Carment and James 1998). Because of stalemate or war weariness, ethnopolitical groups must take advantage of ripe moments to negotiate, especially when they perceive that they cannot win (Zartman 1995). A third-party intermediary can assist in negotiating an end to the conflict and in settling substantive issues (Pearson 2001).

Consequently, in the postaccord peace-building phase, efforts are needed to promote contact at the grassroots so that bridges are built between people (Oberschall 2008). In combination with elite agreements, nongovernmental organizations (NGOs) and international NGOs (INGOs) can assist by encouraging communication and confidence building among grassroots people to change attitudes and perceptions and to build common goals (Miall, Woodhouse, and Ramsbotham 1999). Critical spaces have to be created in which people can get to know each other across the ethnopolitical divide and to build trust and respect for each other (Bose 2007). Track II diplomacy (or citizen diplomacy), expressed through problem-solving workshops and dialogue groups, rehumanize the enemy (Fisher 1997; Rothman 1997). Reconciliation and cooperative relationships can also assist in embedding changes at the personal, relational, and structural levels to fulfill people's basic human needs (Lederach 1997).

The infrastructure of the postaccord society also must be rebuilt to nurture capacity building and sustainable economic development (Byrne et al. 2000). External international agencies as well as private sector investment are crucial to building the peace dividend in postagreement societies (Byrne and Irvin 2002). Peace-making skills can also be taught through workshops in the workplace. In Northern Ireland, cultural-traditions training, antisectarian training, communications, and problem-solving skills have been relatively successful in empowering Protestant and Catholic workers from the Unionist and Nationalist communities (Fitzduff 1996).

Analysis and intervention in the postaccord peace-building phase involves a continuous interaction of six social forces—historical, psychocultural, religious, political, economic, and demographic—over time and space (Byrne and Carter 1996; Byrne, Carter, and Senehi 2003). Moreover, policy makers and conflict resolution practitioners need to examine the increase in the range of interventions in the postagreement peace-building phase to accommodate the intricate web of individuals, groups, and organizations with their own approaches and resources (Byrne and Keashly 2000). Coordinated action across the levels of intervention is necessary to prevent duplication and to ensure that the tangible and intangible conditions are met to build the peace process (Diamond and McDonald 2000).

This chapter uses the social cubism analytical model to outline some of the underlying micro and macro causes of ethnopolitical conflict, examines the multitrack intervention system that explores the range of actors and interventions needed at multiple points in the conflict to build the peace dividend, and outlines an INGO to coordinate the multilevel and multimodal interventions in the conflict in building cross-community ties. The chapter also proposes a model to both analyze the underlying causes of ethnopolitical conflict and design a conflict systems multitrack model to build peace organically in the postagreement society. This chapter is based on empirical findings in the literature that show that the grassroots and multitrack approaches are necessary or sufficient for peace.

## Ethnopolitical Conflict and Six Social Forces:
## A Multidimensional Force Field Analysis

During involvement in a complex ethnopolitical conflict situation, ongoing assessment of the actors, issues, and other dynamics is essential to develop an effective strategy and make wise conflict-intervention choices (Laue and Cormick 1978). Broad participation in an analysis and assessment of grievances by the ethnopolitical groups and outside interveners will assist in building a shared perspective on the problem and in identifying the steps necessary to move forward (Lederach 2005). Indeed, joint analysis is often a key step in bringing the ethnopolitical groups to the table (Sislin and Pearson 2001) (table 7.1).

The social cubism structure provides such a framework to examine six interrelated social forces at work in ethnopolitical conflicts in Northern Ireland and Quebec (Byrne and Carter 1996) (figure 7.1). Similar to the Rubik's Cube puzzle of getting each side to one color by understanding the interconnectedness of all sides and the arts-based cubist movement of Pablo Picasso and Georges Braque rendering three-dimensional subjects in two dimensions, the social cube of group conflict escalation illustrates that six social forces—demographics (e.g., double minority–double majority, space), economics (e.g., poverty, internal colonialism), history (e.g., golden age, events), politics (e.g., nationalism, populism), psychoculture, (e.g., identity, fear, symbols), and religion (e.g., true believers, sectarianism)—interactively and simultaneously combine to produce multiple relationships and patterns of ethnopolitical intergroup behavior through time and context, emphasizing the complexity of conflict (Carter and Byrne 2000). Social cubism is a qualitative approach that provides a multidimensional analytical model that considers how the relationships among the six social forces or factors are important in the understanding of the complex dynamics that fuel and drive ethnopolitical conflicts if a constructive, lasting peace is to be built (Byrne, Carter, and Senehi 2003).

Between 1960 and 1974, Greece and Turkey were locked in the Cyprus conflict in a dependent relationship, with Greek and Turkish

**Table 7.1. How ethnic conflict evolves, transforms, and ends**

| Variable | Evolves | Transforms/Ends |
|---|---|---|
| **Psychological** | Identity<br>Esteem<br>Fear<br>Anger | Grieving and trauma work<br>Healing groups |
| **Political** | Exclusion from power<br>Minority scapegoating<br>Paramilitaries | Increase justice<br>Nonviolent protest<br>Power sharing<br>Systemic change |
| **Economic** | No access to resources<br>Internal-colonialism | Sustainable economic development<br>Appropriate local technology<br>Superordinate goals<br>Interdependence |
| **Historical** | Independent and negative<br>Exclusion of minorities | Common historical experience<br>New history books |
| **Cultural** | Flags and events<br>Anthems<br>Segregated housing and schools | Restoration of common identity<br>Cross-cultural training in workplace<br>Consciousness raising in integrated schools<br>Build Trust |

Table 7.1. How ethnic conflict evolves, transforms, and ends (cont't)

| | | |
|---|---|---|
| **Religion** | In-group–out-group<br>Fundamentalist<br>Intragroup conflict | Ecumenical meetings<br>Compassion and forgiveness (Desmond Tutu's Truth and Reconciliation Commission)<br>Apologize to the victims (Sorry Day in Australia) |
| **Language/Race** | Subject-object | Give equal status to all languages (Belgium)<br>Problem-solving workshops<br>Empowerment of the colonized |
| **Gender** | Women are excluded or killed (Rapes in Bosnia, East Timor and Rwanda) | Participation and respect |
| **Social** | Divided communities | Create mutual interdependent processes<br>Storytelling<br>Dialogue groups |
| **Outside Forces**<br>(Large and small states, NGOs, IGOs, MNCs) | Power and alliances<br>Economic resources<br>War and political violence<br>Divide and rule<br>Escalate tensions and mirror imagining | Diplomacy and negotiation<br>Humanitarian and economic aid<br>Mediation and arbitration<br>International law and human rights<br>Sustainable economic development<br>Media attention forces parties to negotiate with each other<br>Prenegotiation, peacekeepers |

## Figure 7.1. Early-warning contingency social cube escalators/de-escalators

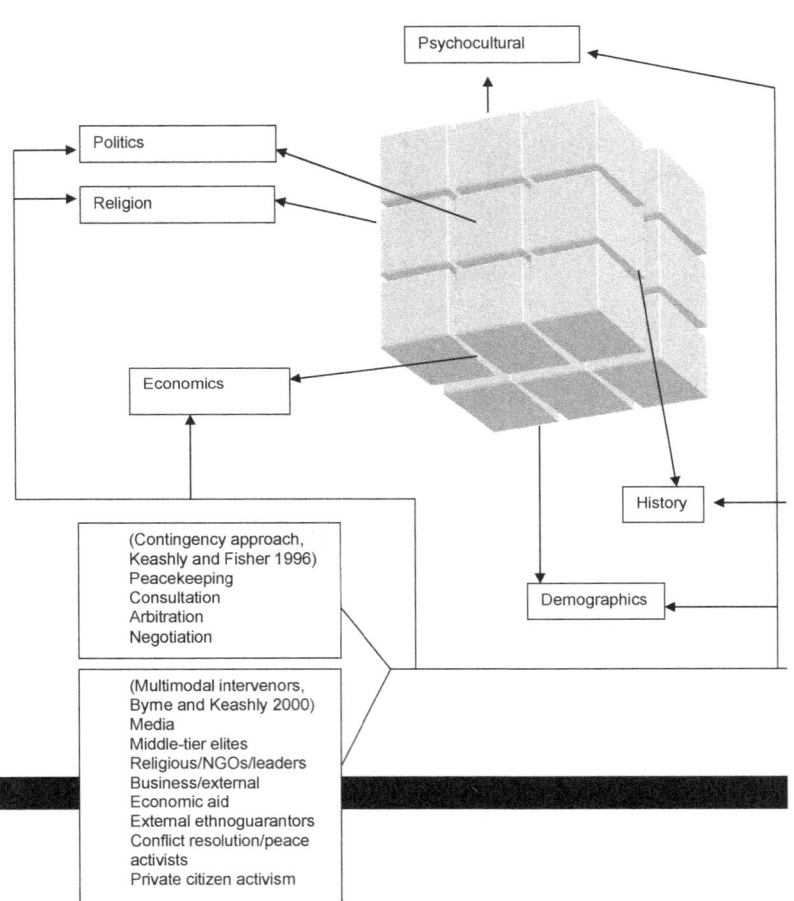

Source: Batista, Byrne, Jenkins, Posadas, Rozlivkova, and Superville, 2001, p. 240.

Cypriots using the external support to retaliate against each other (Pollis 1996), which led to a zero-sum confrontation between both "external ethnoguarantors" (Greece and Turkey) (Byrne 2007, 150). Greek Cypriots recently voted against the unification of Cyprus, while Turkish Cypriots voted in favor of union and membership in the European Union (EU). Tassos Papadopoulos and Rauf Denktash, the rival Greek and Turkish Cypriot leaders, used an "ethnocentric intranational and exclusionist nationalism" to rally support against a unified Cyprus, appealing to extremists in Greece and Turkey to support their positions (Anastasiou 2009, 42). Finally, in 1974 Turkish troops invaded and divided the island. This illustrates that what happens politically on the island of Cyprus was and is influenced by political events on mainland Greece and Turkey.

### Historical Factors

Ethnopolitical conflicts are historic and deep-rooted conflicts that go back centuries. Often there is nostalgia to rediscover an "authentic past golden age," and intellectuals create a genuine "ethnohistory" for the people whereby "their culture is purified and the other is excluded" (Smith 1996, 447). Cities such as Jerusalem or Derry become enshrined in the collective memory of the groups (Arthur 2009). The "historic homeland's boundaries" are significant for the sufferings and celebrations of the ethnopolitical group so that a picture is created of a natural ethnopolitical "territorial homeland or ethnoscape" based on events from the ethnic past (Smith 1996, 449). Colonialism privileged certain, often minority, groups over others to divide and conquer (Horowitz 2000).

Elites devise destructive stories of past events to perpetuate new myths and group history that becomes enshrined in the collective memories of ethnopolitical groups (Senehi 2002, 2009a, 2009b). "Time collapse," in which past and present become one, keeps the conflict from moving into a future mode of resolution (Volkan 1998, 11). Conflicts are dynamic, crossing historical timelines (Lederach 1997). The out-group feels deprived, dehumanized, and not accommodated by the dominant group. This history of mistrust, composed of myth and reality, is passed orally from one generation to the next through grandparents, schools, churches, and the media (Adekanye 1998). A victim mentality unites the group and justifies the victimization of other ethnopolitical groups as ethnopolitical leaders seize power to avenge the past and make sure that their group is never again victimized (Volkan 1992).

If the dominant ethnopolitical group has used violence in the past to suppress the minority ethnopolitical group or vice versa, then the relationship is embedded in violence (Carter, Irani, and Volkan 2009; Zariski 1989). Franco's violence against the Basques during and after the Spanish Civil War continues to define the relationship between the Basques and the Spanish government to this day (Irvin 1999). Afrikaner nationalism represented all class alliances and a supremacist ideology in South Africa (Byrne 1999). Afrikaners believed that they were a civilizing force with a clear national and cultural identity symbolized in historical events such as the Great Trek (Hirschsohn 1996). The 1948 race laws turned blacks, Asians, and coloreds (South Africans of mixed ancestry) into nonpersons. In the 1960s, the implanted colonization structure awakened African armed resistance through the African National Congress (ANC), Spear of the Nation, and Pan African Congress (PAC) movements (Byrne 2002) as well as a competing Zulu Inkatha movement, which the government sought to manipulate. As a result of South Africa's pariah status, an international economic and political boycott, and war weariness, the minority whites were forced to negotiate with the ANC, PAC, and Inkatha to end apartheid and establish a nonracial political system (Lieberfeld 1999; Minow 1998).

Colonialism also shaped group relations by creating new functions for groups to fulfill, recruiting some of the ethnopolitical groups into new roles, and simplifying preexisting political arrangements to administer the groups (Horowitz 2000). The colonial administration strengthened ethnic allegiances by using traditional ethnopolitical leaders to enforce policy and by employing and protecting certain ethnopolitical groups ahead of others (Horowitz 2000). The "civilized" and racially superior colonial power saw all of the ethnic groups as inferior (Fanon 1965). The ethnopolitical groups were encouraged to be like the European colonies, and some groups sought to emulate the

Europeans by civilizing other ethnopolitical groups (Horowitz 2000). In Rwanda, Belgium created differences to manipulate the Tutsis and Hutus and stripped the Hutus of their power over the land while using the Tutsi elite to enforce its policies.

### Psychocultural Factors

Polylinguistics, cultural differences, and cultural discrimination can also escalate ethnopolitical conflict (Ross 2007; Zariski 1989). Unequal access to education and legal and political restraints regarding minority cultural issues can be sources of ethnopolitical conflict (Finlayson 1998). Subjective perceptions lead to ethnocentrism in which stereotypes and prejudicial attitudes form to demonize the out-group (Sandole 1998, 2003; Ross 1998, 2007). Language, dress, customs, and dialect make ethnopolitical communities different from one another (Bostock 1997; Smith 1996). In a cultural region, moderates within the in-group are inclusive of members of the other community, while extremists see the other ethnopolitical group as inferior (Ross 1993, 2007). The symbolic trappings of culture such as flags and national anthems promote an in-group identity to the exclusion of other ethnopolitical groups. The ethnicization of the post-1948 Sri Lankan state placed Sinhalese within the bureaucracy and the army and excluded the Tamils, who became separatists (de Silva 1997). Extremist militant leaders such as Radovan Karadžić, Ratko Mladić, and Slobodan Milošević riled up Serbian public opinion in Bosnia that saw a shift from the spirit of Sarajevo to the slaughter of Sarajevo (Sekulic 1997).

Fear of the other ethnopolitical group can escalate intergroup misperceptions, insecurity, and frustration in which the use of stereotypes structures relationships (Avruch 1998). Lack of contact expressed through voluntary segregation and a low mixed-marriage rate ensures each group's cultural isolation, with the result that ethnic identity becomes more salient (Lederach 1995). But intermarriage does not guarantee peace. Each of the ethnopolitical groups may perceive that its culture is better than the other. In the conflict in the former Yugoslavia, the Serbs perceived that their cultural group was superior to all others, and a war of urbicide saw rural Serbs attack urban Muslims and Croats in Bosnia (Beriker-Atiyas 1995; Volkan 1992). In the Holy Land, ethnopolitical groups have different perceptions of the conflict: Palestinians believe that foreigners invaded and occupied the land and dispossessed them, while Israelis feel that they gathered their exiles to redeem the land and fought a war of independence against hostile aggressors (Rouhana and Korper 1996; Smith 1996). Israelis and Palestinians hold mirror images of each other, each believing that it is the indigenous group and that the other is the invader who has no legitimacy (Lieberfeld 1999; Smith 1996). Both groups have a history of victimization in which they feel persecuted and present themselves as victims of the other side (Smith 1996). The ethnic family provides the psychological needs of the individual group member in the same way that myths and symbols of a common ethnic ancestry provide a powerful vision of the nation-state (Smith 1996; Volkan 1998). "The ethnically defined nation" replaces the "emotional security of the family," as ethnopolitical elites provide economic security, political order, and "cultural purification" (Smith 1996, 453). Ethnopolitical conflict then becomes a struggle for group worth as the groups compete and compare themselves to other groups (Brown 1998; Byrne 2001).

### Religious Factors

Different religious leaders often fuel ethnic hatred and ethnopolitical war (Abu-Nimer 2003). The religious elite mobilizes around religious symbols. In Sri Lanka, the Sinhalese mobilized initially around language and then around the symbols of Buddhism (Little 1994). Radical Buddhist monks supported the Sri Lankan Freedom Party (SLFP) in the late 1950s because it opposed a multiethnic and multicultural society. The Buddhist monks led by Dharmapala argued that religion could not be separated from politics and that the Tamil's Hindu religion was intolerant of Buddhism (de Silva 1997; Little 1994). In 1956 the monks supported the Sinhala Only Campaign that opposed the equality of the Tamil language. Tamils could not be part of that religious tradition, since religion became a metaphor for nation (Little 1994). Thus, religion became a badge of ethnonational identity and was at the center of culture and language in Sri Lankan Buddhism (Little 1994). Buddhism is open to all Sri Lankan Buddhists despite their class or caste and was used by the monks to "save" and "protect" the motherland from Tamil separatism (Sahadevan 1997). Political elites manipulated religious differences within the fulcrum of nationalist and identity separatism (Little 1994).

A sectarian wall prevents contact as extremists escalate tensions (Harris 1972). In Northern Ireland, both ethnoreligious groups voluntarily live in segregated neighborhoods and attend separate schools. The society is further polarized by the low rate of intermarriage. Enclaving has become a way of life for Protestants and Catholics who live in a besieged milieu (Byrne 1995). The different denominations within Protestantism (Church of Ireland, Methodist, Presbytarian, and Free Presbytarian) reflect the heterogeneity of Protestant beliefs. Protestants band around the concept of conditional loyalty (Miller 1978) to resist perceived British government disloyalty toward the Protestants of Northern Ireland (Byrne 2009b). The British government is perceived as pushing loyal Protestants into an all-Ireland Catholic state, that is, of being intolerant of their belief system (Dixon 2000, 2007). The Nationalist Catholic community feels and acts as an estranged minority discriminated against in the past by sectarian policies in housing, employment, voting, and education (Irvin 1999). British government policies of crisis management such as internment, criminalization, the Prevention Against the Terrorism Act (PTA), and a shoot-to-kill policy intensified polarization and sectarianism (O'Leary and McGarry 1993, 1997).

### Political Factors

If dominant ethnopolitical groups control political institutions and exclude minority ethnic group representation, a struggle for political power can ensue (Zariski 1989). The human rights of the minority group can be put in jeopardy. How the dominant group responds to the political demands of an ethnopolitical group can also cause political violence (Zariski 1989). If the dominant group does not negotiate directly or if "it yields too readily," then the conflict can spiral out of control (Zariski 1989, 264). The reduction of grievances by the dominant ethnopolitical group is also a tactic to deter the rebels from continuing the conflict (Zartman 1995).

Internal conflict in the ethnopolitical group between moderates and extremists also escalates tension within the ethnopolitical group.

Consociationalism is a form of government that includes guaranteed group representation in a power-sharing arrangement (Byrne 2001; McGarry and O'Leary 1995). Political elites can manipulate consociational power-sharing arrangements that stall the political process and inflame relationships (Byrne 2001). The Turkish Cypriot political leadership used the power of veto to prevent policy making in the Cypriot Parliament in the late 1960s and early 1970s because it anticipated that its ethnoguarantor, Turkey, fifty miles away, would intervene on its behalf (Byrne 2000, 2007).

Furthermore, ethnonational ideology can lead to conflict. Group outsiders are treated with suspicion and mistrust as intragroup conflict escalates between inclusive moderates and exclusive extremists. Group norms regulate the behavior of group members and treat harshly those who are seen as betraying group loyalty (Brown 1998). Perceived traitors are boycotted, beaten, and shot. An insular-looking group identity is used to separate groups.

The stronger the ethnic and communal ties, the easier it is to mobilize the ethnopolitical group into collective action for self-determination or to redress grievances (Gurr 1993). An overseas diaspora can also provide material, political, and moral support to sustain a level of political violence (Guelke 1988). A critical dimension of political extremism involves the levels of violence used to achieve one group's political goals (Zariski 1989). Ethnopolitical groups can choose to use bombs and political assassinations if the dominant ethnopolitical group blocks its political aspirations, such as the Provisional Irish Republican Army's (PIRAs) armalite and ballot box approach in Northern Ireland to demand outright secession from the state (McGarry and O'Leary 1995). The PIRA used political violence as a tool to both attract media attention and force the British government to use further repression against the Nationalist community (O'Leary and McGarry 1993; Zariski 1989).

### Economic Factors

A discriminatory economic system, in which there is no equitable distribution of resources for minority ethnopolitical elites who want to enhance their status and privileges, can escalate conflict (Horowitz

2000). The upward mobility of these elites is blocked, and they become alienated because their professional experience and education are not used, especially when benefits decline and their expectations rise (Jeong 2000a, 2000b; Zariski 1989). They become politicized and mobilize for action to get access to economic resources (Pieterse 1997). Ethnic identity becomes a mechanism to get access to economic resources. Socioeconomic and political institutions distort the history and culture and enhance the nationalism of its own group (Byrne, Thiessen, and Fissuh 2007). Economic gaps in wealth distribution and economic downturns as well as provisional or regional differences in a country can be manipulated by rival political elites to foment conflict (MacGinty and Williams 2009).

Consequently, in the internal colonialism economic development and modernization model, the economically developed core exploits the poorer periphery, and the resulting uneven development of the region creates ethnic competition and hostility (Hechter 1975). The dominant elites create a cultural division of labor around cultural identity and a reactive ethnonationalism (Zariski 1989). The French government modernized the coastal regions of Corsica from which outsiders from mainland France benefited to the detriment of the Corsicans (Zariski 1989). Hence, economic competition from outsiders in an underdeveloped region such as Corsica or developed regions such as Croatia or the Basque region can mobilize the local ethnopolitical population (Glenn 1997; Zariski 1989). The other ethnopolitical group perceives a concession to one group as a loss as the minority group revolts against economic and cultural marginalization (Zariski 1989). Uneducated youths in the urban Bantu in South Africa have turned to petty crime as the political authority of the state continues to erode (Byrne 2002). The expectations of the poor were raised when the new ANC government came into power. However, basic human needs aimed at new jobs and housing and land for the poor have not yet been met (McGarry 1998).

Sanctions can cause tremendous hardship for the population of a country (Cortright and Lopez 2000). The thirteen-year economic sanctions against Saddam Hussein's regime in Iraq strengthened his economic and political position. All goods entering and leaving Iraq went through Hussein's office as he built palaces to show the global community that Iraq was not cowering to the effects of the sanctions and as hundreds of thousands of children perished (Schwartz 2008). The international community had banned dual-use equipment, which could be used for military as well as health care purposes, from entering Iraq. Statistics on the number of civilian deaths as a result of the sanctions were distributed by Hussein to antisanction NGOs to embarrass the United States and Britain (Bilmes and Stiglitz 2008).

## Demographic Factors

The modern state and nationalism have sometimes excluded and denied the political aspirations of ethnopolitical groups, leading to intractable conflicts between rival ethnopolitical groups whose security becomes threatened (Boudreau 2009). At the same time, ethnopolitical groups "reimagine their communities" to create a sense of identity in which deep fears and threats to the group's self-esteem, "existence, and legitimization are acted out" against the rival ethnopolitical group (Smith 1996, 448). There is anxiety about perceived threats emanating from other ethnopolitical groups that reflect demographic and geographic insecurity (Paris 2004). This fear of extinction flows from an exaggeration of danger that provides extreme reactions to modest threats, and prejudice allows a discharge of hostility to reduce anxiety (Horowitz 2000; Smith 1996). Israelis and Northern Irish Protestants feel besieged, fearing extermination by Arabs and Catholics, respectively. In Bosnia and Croatia, Serbs came to believe that they were surrounded by blood enemies (White 1996) as fanatics such as Željko Ražnatović ("Arkan") and Chetnik forces carried out mass killings in a deliberate policy of ethnic cleansing (Beriker-Atiyas 1995).

The most protracted conflict is when two or more ethnopolitical groups with separate identities compete for the same territory in which one group constitutes the majority and the other constitutes the minority in a geographical context (Byrne 2000). This issue becomes more prevalent when the majority/minority status of the group changes as the territorial border changes. John Whyte (1990) describes this phenomenon in Northern Ireland as a "double minority–double majority" situation. Within the geopolitical context of Northern Ireland, Unionist Protestants are a majority, and Nationalist Catholics are a minority. Within an all-Ireland context, Unionists become a minority, and Nationalists become a majority. The group that is in the minority often feels that it is a besieged community whose very physical existence is threatened by a perceived hostile Other (Byrne 2009a).

Moreover, within ethnopolitical groups, men and women are often socialized into the assumption that strong male patriots are needed to defend the ethnic homeland and its women and children (Enloe 2001; Smith 1996). Men's experiences may be included and valued, while women's experiences are ignored in the construction of the ethnic worldview (Smith 1996; Wilmer 2002). Gender differences are socially constructed, as the male warrior's courage and toughness are often idolized in the defense of the ethnopolitical group (Enloe 2000). During the 1990s women in Bosnia and Rwanda were raped, and their bodies became the site of battle between male-dominated paramilitary units (Allen 1996). Thus, male domination and patriarchy may reinforce oppressive structures within the ethnopolitical community, and women's experiences and voices may be marginalized (Tickner 2001). Women are also strong ethnonationalists and can contribute to the tension by the values they pass onto their children such as distrust of the Other or revulsion of intermarriage (Kaufman 2001). As further evidence of gender-biased socialization, women's actions actually are supportive of men in the armed struggle. For example, Northern Irish Nationalist Catholic women within the PIRA acted as couriers and smuggled weapons but rarely took part in the political violence of Active Service Units.

## Multitrack Diplomacy:
### The Range of Actors and Interventions

Multitrack diplomacy, or multimodal and multilevel intervention, is a multidisciplinary systems approach to peace building (Diamond and McDonald 2000; Byrne and Keashly 2000). This systems intervention approach ensures that individuals and organizations are more effective working together in complex ethnopolitical conflicts that involve a broad array of factors and parties (Byrne and Keashly 2000). Each of the tracks requires its own perspective, approach, and resources to build strong intergroup relationships and to change the power asymmetry (Diamond and McDonald 2000). The greatest resource for sustaining peace in the long term is rooted in the local people and their culture (Lederach 1997, 2005). The multitrack approach is not a panacea for an immediate solution to the ethnopolitical conflict; local people must own the peace (MacGinty 2006).

### Political Elites

Political elites must work together to forge "functional and democratic" intergroup rapprochement (Anastasiou 2009, 42). Ethnopolitical leaders must make sure that their group members are part of a process that constructs a new paradigm of thinking so as to create a vision of peace that includes the Others (Boudreau 2003). Dialogue groups between Palestinians and Israelis seek to change conflict beliefs to new beliefs that facilitate constructive interaction that legitimizes the Others (Kaufmann and Hassassian 2009; Kelman 1997). Political elites can institutionalize the peace-building process by ensuring equal access to jobs and resources and fair and free elections (Paris 2004). Minority ethnopolitical groups can express their cultural heritages by having access to their own radio and television programs and education system (Zariski 1989). A process of mutual political accommodation ensures that the ethnopolitical elites can reciprocate with each other and agree on policy (O'Leary and McGarry 1993). Elites have the opportunity to work together in a consociational power-sharing system to forge democratic institutions that actively protect the cultural, political, economic, and human rights of all citizens (McGarry and O'Leary 1995). A just political process must address the dignity and respect of each group, or the seeds will be sown for intense conflict in the future.

Middle-tier elites also have a specific location in the conflict and are vital actors in creating an infrastructure for achieving and sustaining peace (Lederach 1997). Problem-solving workshops provide middle-tier elites a space in which to develop relationships, look at shared problems and solutions, and influence both the grassroots and key elite decision makers (Rothman 1992). These middle-tier leaders from business, education, health care, religious, humanitarian organizations, and academia assist in developing peace-building approaches that anchor issues within a set of relationships and subsystems (Lederach 1997).

### Citizen Diplomats

People in the grassroots become involved in the peace-building process because they want to make a difference (Lederach 2005). Individuals can empower themselves by joining advocacy, cross-cultural, or conflict resolution groups that create formal and informal dialogue across the ethnopolitical divide. Mohammed Abu-Nimer, Nadim Rouhana, Julia Chaitlin, Simona Sharoni, Herbert Kelman, and Jay Rothman's problem-solving workshops between Palestinians and Israelis and Loraleigh Keashly, Ron Fisher, Benjamin Broome, and Harry Anastasiou's interactive workshops between Greek and Turkish Cypriots have attempted to build trusting relationships with middle-tier elites from opposite ethnopolitical groups over time that may have been important to the welfare of both peace processes. However, little evaluative research has been done to truly explore the success rate of these initiatives (Anastasiou 2009).

Citizen diplomats work to provide critical spaces for proactive involvement in conflict transformation by building from resources within the postviolence setting (Senehi 2009b). They can use their culture's approach to handling conflict as the foundation for building a transformational framework (Lederach 1995). Natural networks of village elders, known and trusted by the ethnopolitical communities, were used in the past in Bosnia to resolve conflict at the local level (Zagar 2000). These insider-partial peacemakers, as opposed to outsider-neutral peacemakers, know the setting, the parties, and the conflict and remain present and available within the conflict context and setting (Kriesberg 1998; Lederach 1995). But Olson-Lounsbery and Pearson (2009) show that insider-partial intermediaries are not always effective.

The term "citizen diplomat" was coined by Joseph Montville (1981) while he worked at the U.S. Department of State. Citizen diplomats are persons who are concerned about world and local affairs in their own countries. They are activists who want to make a difference. The input of leaders such as former presidents Jimmy Carter and Bill Clinton is not always welcome by the authorities. The elder citizen diplomat wishes to share accumulated wisdom and serve as a political agent for social change (Ross 2002, 2007). Citizen diplomats are reformers, organizers, advocates, innovators, mediators, members of NGOs, collaborators, empowered grassroots peacemakers, and peace managers (Montville 1981; Ross 2002).

These are men and women who, as private individuals, have assumed a responsibility to serve as conduits to improve conditions for peace, nonviolence, the environment, and the development of national and international relationships (Ross 2002). They also have worked for the pursuit of intergenerational programs, human rights issues, matters of legal aid and political freedom, election monitoring, and the improvement of educational opportunities for the poor (E. Boulding 1990, 2000). Furthermore, some of their ranks were active in the global campaign against apartheid and in defusing the Cold War (Ross 2002).

Citizen diplomats represent middle-level and semielite citizenry who seek to create and sustain peaceful relationships with neighbors and nations, advocating nonviolent solutions to global problems (Lederach 1995; Byrne and Keashly 2000). Citizen diplomats seek to engage in meaningful dialogue in their nongovernmental diplomatic deliberations (Ross 2002). Citizen diplomats may be accepted as intermediaries by conflict parties in conditions of stalemate or simply to avoid government pressure (Bercovitch 1984, 1996). In the process of any negotiation, they place emphasis on developing human relationships for trust and mutual benefit (Saunders 1999). Their developed sense of priorities and experience in political matters has given them an ability to build bridges between diverse organizations and individuals (Ross 2003). Citizen diplomats provide lines of communication during dangerous periods when official discourse is close to nonexistent (Ross 2002). They seek to be alert to the cross-cultural challenges facing all global societies in ethnic, religious, civic, and socioeconomic matters (Lederach 1995).

Elders, as citizen diplomats in this so-called era of longevity are aware that they can be leaders in building a culture of peace, developing new ties of friendship with their global counterparts, and generating creative solutions for economic opportunities instead of spending enormous sums on war (Ross 2003). Serving as a citizen diplomat—being an empowering, nonjudgmental participant—is a form of mentoring people to help them move into the future, into peace (Ross 2002). Citizen diplomats as Track II diplomats may have more success at the grassroots level rather than with Track I political elites (Sampson and Lederach 2000).

### Educators

Conflict resolution trainers, teachers, and academics can educate citizens on the theories, skills, and processes of conflict resolution and peacemaking. Educators can change how people analyze and resolve conflict by giving them the knowledge to work creatively for justice and peace (Bekerman 2009). Mediation centers at the grassroots level can psychologically empower people by teaching them peacemaking skills that build self-esteem and self-efficacy, can socially empower them by creating the space to work with like-minded individuals, and can politically empower them to be critical thinkers who critically analyze and deconstruct political issues (Schwerin 1995). Mediation Northern Ireland and the Community Relations Council have been relatively successful in delivering conciliation, reconciliation, facilitation, mediation, negotiation, and socioeconomic and community development in Northern Ireland (Byrne 2009a).

Academics and teachers can impart knowledge to inform the public about structural and cultural violence, basic human needs, and the tools of peace making. Integrated schools in Northern Ireland provide a shared curriculum and are safe spaces for Catholic and Protestant students to develop a shared identity; in the process, students change their perceptions of each other (Byrne 1997a, 1997b).

Educators can also assist the parties to reframe the conflict using reconciliation (truth, mercy, justice, and peace) to restore relationships, which are the centerpiece of the peace-building system (Lederach 1997). Telling constructive stories that focus on "we" rather than "us/them" can transform the moral landscape to create a serendipitous scaffold by breaking down barriers in nonthreatening ways (Senehi

1996, 2000, 2002, 2009a, 2009b). People on the ground need to work their way through a throng of symbols and rituals so that they can understand each other (Schirch 2004). Constructive story sharing is both inclusive and relationship-based and empowers the grassroots so that the people can tell new stories, retell the destructive stories, and develop a common story of sameness, putting a communal identity before ethnopolitical identities and, in the process, forging a shared national narrative (Senehi and Hawranik 2009).

### Nongovernmental Organizations

NGOs work generally at the grassroots level to explore the root causes of conflict, to transform relationships, and to design processes to resolve conflict (Aall 2001). NGOs are important in restoring and rebuilding relationships through the use of problem-solving workshops, dialogue groups, and training for people in the grassroots (Aall 2001). People can imagine and build a shared future by actively participating and working within NGOs to build capacity and relationships in the society (Boulding 2000). International funding agencies and NGOs can categorize funds related to peace building and conflict transformation. For example, the International Fund for Ireland (IFI) and the EU Peace II Fund work with local NGOs that are working for peace in the grassroots (Byrne 2009a).

NGOs can also act effectively to influence the transformation of ethnopolitical politics in the new civic culture, sharing their hopes, fears, and needs (Rothman 1997). In 1978 Peace Now encouraged the Israeli government to make peace with Egypt after Anwar Sadat's trip to Jerusalem. Israeli prime minister Menachen Begin said at the time that "If this is possible then nothing is impossible" (Princen 1991).

The 1995 Truth and Reconciliation Commission (TRC) in South Africa, authorized by a governmental agreement with the ANC, gave voice and reparations to survivors of apartheid violence and granted amnesty to perpetrators who told the truth about their involvement in the culture of violence (Minow 1998). The TRC's goal was to build lasting reconciliation on social justice. There are limitations to such approaches, however. In South Africa, whites reportedly felt that they were targets of the TRC, while some blacks felt that justice has not been done because old wounds that were opened up have not been healed (Edelstein 2002).

## Public and Private Sector Investment

Public and private sector investment is critical not only in rebuilding the economic infrastructure after violence but also in addressing underlying poverty issues that lead to conflict (Byrne, Irvin, and Fissuh 2009). Multinational corporations (MNCs) need peace to be able to run successful business ventures in postviolent societies. MNCs need to protect their investments by improving the quality-of-life conditions for their workers, by employing a diverse workforce, and by training their workforce in cross-cultural conflict resolution (Haufler 2001). Business leaders can also convey to the political elites ideas and suggestions about ethnic pluralism in economic policy making. Ethnopolitical group leaders must be sensitive to the needs of subordinate groups and must also be sensitive in educating the grassroots about the reality of economic development. Nelson Mandela defended the economic rights of the white minority because he recognized the socioeconomic costs of continued conflict in South Africa (Byrne 2002).

In addition, external economic aid from international agencies can create opportunities for people in the grassroots to empower themselves to start up indigenous businesses. External economic assistance and security guarantees are important for capacity building and in building the peace dividend (Byrne and Irvin 2001, 2002; Olson-Lounsbery and Pearson 2009). Economic aid is an important component of constructive conflict resolution because it also promotes partnerships involving local communities, NGOs, and governments. In addition, economic aid foments a creative new way of thinking about economic recovery after the war and promotes responsibility and accountability for action (Byrne 2009b; Matic, Byrne, and Ghebretsadik 2007). The EU Peace and Reconciliation Fund and the IFI have channeled economic aid to impoverished regions in Northern Ireland and the border counties to encourage capacity building, grassroots entrepreneurs, and reconciliation and to actively promote the peace dividend (Byrne and Ayulo 1998). However, economic aid is not a panacea; a political solution is needed to transform the conflict (MacGinty 2006; Ryan 2007).

### Journalists and Media

In a postviolent multicultural society, the media can work to create awareness of socioeconomic and cultural practices of all the ethnopolitical communities (Webel and Galtung 2007). The media could focus on new tolerant heroes who are attractive to young people; Johan Galtung and his colleagues at Transcend argue that peace journalism must seek out different voices and articulate the range of interests in any given conflict situation (Galtung 2009; Galtung, Jacobsen, and Brand-Jacobsen 2002). Peace journalism courses through the Transcend peace network are empowering journalists to examine the deeper roots of conflict and bring the truth into the open (Webel and Galtung 2007).

The media's so-called CNN effect can influence a government's policies by putting critical issues on the agenda (Strobel 2001). The information that the international media provides can challenge the use of propaganda to heighten ethnopolitical tensions of an indigenous media that is working to escalate ethnopolitical conflict (Strobel 2001). Hate radio was used in Rwanda by the Hutu-controlled government to exploit fears and ethnic hatreds that resulted in the deaths of one million innocent people (Strobel 2001). The media is a pervasive and dynamic instrument that can be used as a proactive mechanism of conflict prevention and reconciliation (Strobel 2001). The media is central to the creation of a just and peaceful society and can draw attention to building cross-community ties rather than playing a large role in the escalation of ethnopolitical conflict.

### Religious Leaders

Because of their leadership position within their communities, religious leaders can initiate a reconciliation dialogue with contending ethnopolitical groups by having a certain amount of credibility in the inhuman situation in which they are imprisoned at that moment in the conflict (Appleby 2000). "The use of rituals and symbols, scriptures and text allows for a deeper and more meaningful engagement" by religious leaders through interfaith dialogue groups to nonviolently "promote understanding and reconciliation," compassion, and tolerance, to improve, repair, and restore relationships (Smock 2002, 128). Religious leaders can prod participants in these groups to compromise by realizing the disastrous consequences of ongoing conflict and the fact that swords must be beaten into plowshares if the conflict is not to reignite into violence (Funk and Said 2008).

Religious leaders can also work together to create tolerance and coexistence, which promotes a culture of forgiveness. The TRC in South Africa, chaired by the Anglican bishop Desmond Tutu, allowed people to take responsibility for their actions through the concept of *ubuntu*, or forgiveness, to heal from the trauma of violence and empathize with all of the victims of political violence (Adam and Moodley 1997; Minow 1998). Religious leaders have also facilitated cease-fires during the troubles in Northern Ireland, while the ecumenical movement has brought Christians together to build a deeper understanding of where they are coming from (Byrne 2001). Of course, religious leaders can have the opposite effects as well. During the late 1960s in Northern Ireland, the fiery rhetoric of the Reverend Dr. Ian Paisley escalated the mobilization of Protestant Loyalists to prevent the implementation of civil rights for Catholic Nationalists.

### External Actors

External third parties play an increasingly critical intervention role in postviolent peace building (Bercovitch 1996). Humanitarian relief agencies assisted Kosovar refugees fleeing the ethnic violence to get to neighboring countries (Aall 2001). NGOs intervene to promote socioeconomic development, human rights, and peace by joining people across conflict lines, promoting shared values, and distributing resources in ways that encourage cooperation and interdependence (Aall 2001). NGOs need to be careful that mandate blinders and aid-on-our-terms-only approaches can exacerbate tensions by favoring certain groups for assistance and in the process alienating others from the peace process (M. Anderson 2001).

External powers can cooperate together using their political and military power, muscle, motivation, and resources to enforce agreements between ethnopolitical groups to make a conflict tractable (Bercovitch 1996). In Northern Ireland, the British and Irish governments—external ethnoguarantors—have worked success-fully to impose a peace settlement on the Unionist Protestant and Nationalist Catholic communities embroiled in conflict (Byrne 2000). This is in contrast to the Cyprus conflict in which the politi-cal actions of Greece and Turkey sabotaged agreements between the Greek and Turkish Cypriots, making the conflict intractable (Byrne 2007). Studies show that embargoes and sanctions can also impact relationships in ethnopolitical conflicts (Cortright and Lopez 2000).

### Military Peacekeepers

Soldiers on the ground need to keep the peace and do nation building when a state lacks the capacity to govern. As the military begins to restructure physically and philosophically to face the broader security challenges of the new century, robust peacekeeping will ensure that soldiers will have the choice to take the combat track or the peace track, or both, where they will be trained in conflict resolution and peace-building processes and skills (Byrne, Fergusson, Ben-Ari, and Michael 2006). The peace soldier will help to create a long-term peace process that changes patterns and norms of citizens by promoting and protecting good government structures and securing human rights and human needs as well as rebuilding the infrastructure of post-agreement society (Byrne, Fergusson, Ben-Ari, and Michael 2006). The peace soldiers will create integrated conflict resolution systems within the cultural context, intervening at multiple levels. Some of the obstacles to successful peacekeeping remain, such as effective funding, force contingent insufficiencies, mission definition, political bickering, and troop misbehavior (Byrne, Fergusson, Ben-Ari, and Michael 2006).

## Coordination of the Peace System

An infrastructure providing clear channels of communication and links between the multilevel systems of interventions can provide a cross-fertilization of ideas and expertise to connect the activities of internal and external actors to prevent duplication (Lederach 1997). A nation-building or peacekeeping council at the United Nations or the creation of an INGO called EthnoWatch could provide the umbrella to coordinate all of the activities of both the internal and external actors (Byrne and Keashly 2000). EthnoWatch could create an early warning system to forecast the escalation and de-escalation of ethnopolitical conflicts using a Delphi methodology so that local communities and NGO and INGO workers on the ground could provide important information to aid in violence prevention and intervention (Byrne and Keashly 2000); for example, see Doug and Joe Bond's PANDA early warning system. EthnoWatch could coordinate the actors from the various tracks or intervention modes by centralizing the functions of different groups, becoming an information network for NGOs on the ground, and becoming a clearinghouse for all of the external and internal actors by organizing and bringing together their efforts to build the peace dividend (Byrne and Keashly 2000).

## Conclusion

Practitioners and protagonists must be included in the postaccord peace-building stage following ethnopolitical conflict (Kaufman 2001). Coordination of multimodal and multilevel intervention at multiple levels in an organic peace-building system could promote sustainable human development and human security. Citizens must have the opportunity to get together in critical spaces to share stories and to build trust, forgiveness, and reciprocation and repair relationships rather than to tie their destructive stories to the past, to atrocities and to grievances (Senehi 2009b). It is important to be sensitive to the cultural context of ethnopolitical groups (Lederach 1995). There must be a combination of indigenous peacemaking with Western conflict-resolution processes so that peace-building systems are true to their cultural roots (Byrne and Keashly 2000; Byrne and Senehi 2009; MacGinty 2006). A critical link between the activities of local and external actors working in the postconflict peace-building phase also needs to be coordinated (Carter, Irani, and Volkan 2009).

The next chapter outlines some of the causes of war and discusses a multitrack intervention approach to build global peace.

## Websites Related to Ethnopolitical Violence

Centre for the Study of Civil War, Peace Research Institute of Oslo, Norway, http://www.prio.no/CSCW/

European Centre for Minority Issues, http://www.ecmi.de/

International Alert, London, http://www.international-alert.org/

International Conflict Research Institute, Magee College, University of Ulster, Derry, http://www.incore.ulst.ac.uk/

Minorities At Risk Project, http://www.cidcm.umd.edu/mar/

Peacemakers Trust, http://www.peacemakers.ca

Protocol for the Analysis of Nonviolent Direct Action (PANDA), http://vranet.com/papers.html

United Nations Research Institute for Social Development, http://www.unrisd.org/

United States Institute of Peace, http://www.usip.org

## Suggested Questions for Further Discussion

1. Has economic integration eroded ethnopolitical and national divisions or led to greater conflicts in the United States, between the United States and Canada, or between the United States and Mexico? How does economic growth mitigate ethnopolitical conflicts?

2. How can third parties intervene to affect conflicts? How could they use a social cubism analytical perspective?

3. How does history shape people living within ethnic conflict environments? How do psychocultural and structural factors interact with both of these dimensions, economic factors, and the international milieu?

4. What effect does the existence of a state-of-emergency regime have on community relations in ethnopolitical conflicts?

5. How do regional actors influence and shape intergroup relations and the dynamics of ethnopolitical conflict milieus?

6. How do ethnopolitical conflicts change over time? Is de-escalation simply escalation in reverse, or are different mechanisms at play? Is self-determination a human right?

7. What factors encourage external powerful third parties to become engaged in peace-building processes?

# 8

## War

### Causes, Intervention, and Prevention

Robert Lavers was a sixteen-year-old boy with starry eyes when he arrived in 1916 on the green fields of Flanders with the Lancashire Fusiliers as they prepared for the Battle of the Somme. The trenches were full of water, and a lot of the frontline veterans suffered from foot rot. Rats as big as dogs greedily devoured the remains of dead British soldiers that lay half-buried in no-man's-land. The adventure and excitement gone, Lavers began to think, "How am I going to survive this mess?" On July 1 the attack on Beaumont Hamel commenced. Lavers emerged over the top of his trench as his comrades dropped left and right in the withering fire of German machine guns; bullets and shells went through the British troops like a scythe. A German sniper took aim. Lavers was shot through the jaw by a Mauser rifle, and he was ferried to the rear by the stretcher-bearers. There was no going home for him. After spending time recuperating from his wounds, he rejoined his company in December 1916. He would go onto fight at Ypres, Cambria, and Macedonia. Lavers survived World War I and was captured at Dunkirk in 1940. He would always say that "war was hell" (Robert Lavers, personal communication, July 1979).

The philosophy of political realism stems from an understanding that human nature is, as Thomas Hobbes (1904, 84) said, "solitary, poor, nasty, brutish and short." Realism was a theoretical school that arose in reaction to the horrors of twentieth-century war and genocide (Power 2007). While recognizing that there are different streams in realist thought, this chapter discusses the overall key assumptions in the tradition. The realist tradition in international relations posits that states are unitary, rational, and coherent units and are the dominant actors on the world stage (Kegley and Wittkopf 2006). States struggle in a semianarchic international milieu to secure national interests where force is an effective instrument of foreign policy (Kegley and Wittkopf 2006). States are independent, autonomous, and sovereign. There is a hierarchy of issues in the international system, but military or hard power is the most important (Wartenberg 1990). A balance-of-power system is used to maintain order, secure alliances, and deter aggressors in an armed self-help international anarchical system in which there is no peace; war is almost inevitable, though not in every instance (Blalock 1989; Diehl and Lepgold 2003). In an amoral world, insecurity breeds mistrust and fear, leading to an arms race as states amass power and capabilities to arm for deterrence and yet confront a security dilemma of diminishing returns (Pearson and Rochester 1992). Machiavelli (1977, 55) advised the prince that the end justifies the means: "A Prince who wants to keep his state, is often bound to do what is not good." Applying this logic, the assumption could be made that the U.S. intervention in Iraq was conceived to protect the vital interests of the United States: crude oil, control, and security. Some critics have argued that by discussing the world in terms of violence and war and then providing advice to state leaders about how they should act, realists are justifying one particular conception of global politics (Enloe 2000).

Feminist critics of realism argue that military power as the dominant discourse is deeply embedded within the value systems and social institutions of society (Enloe 2000). Sovereignty and nationalism are at the very core of the dominant discourse, although sovereignty itself as a defining principle of international order (live and let live) emerged from the chaos of war among rival princes and religions in the Peace of Westphalia in 1648 (Tickner 1992). The identity of the individual and the state is constructed along a patriarchal warlike culture (Goldstein 2003; Sylvester 2002). The prevailing hegemonic discourse is based on coercion, manipulation, and a power-over system in which "dissent and nonconformity are concealed by the structural and cultural violence of the prevailing patriarchy" (Tickner 2001, 23). Feminists argue that new possibilities of security not based on hegemonic masculinity are needed to promote gender justice (Sylvester 2002; Tickner 1992). The "militarization of masculinity" ensures that in general women "accept particular assumptions about mothering, marriage, femininity, and unskilled work, while public policy is used to limit women's ability to act" (Enloe 1993, 257). Militarism has created a misogynist masculinity that serves the state's interests even as large numbers of women soldiers serve in the armed forces, and male dominance ensures that women and men are objectified by patriarchy (Enloe 1993, 2001; Tickner 1992; Wilmer 2002). The objectification of male prisoners at Abu Ghraib prison in Baghdad by female guards is also a case in point.

Feminists also argue that the "demilitarization of masculinity" in society would remove an "important ingredient of patriarchal culture" that builds on "assumptions based on masculine behavior," including a "Eurocentric state system that has promoted colonialism, anarchy in terms of security, a world capitalist system, and two world wars" (Tickner 1992, 128–29). New possibilities not based on hegemonic masculinity are needed to promote justice, transformation, and gender equality (Snyder 2003). As Tickner (1992) argues, it is critical to forge an interdependent world that is relationship- and community-focused rather than state-focused. Elise Boulding (1990, 2000), David Burrowes (1996), and John Paul Lederach (1997, 2005) clearly articulate that we need to imagine a new society by changing our hearts, building our relationships, and developing a critical consciousness that empowers the individual to deconstruct the dominant discourse and to get involved as part of the solution. Yet some feminists see everything through the lens of gender, ignoring the intersection of other important causes of war such as power, class, nationalism, and global systems (hooks 1990).

Pluralists contend that nonstate actors are important entities in global politics and cannot be ignored. Given the increasingly interdependent global economy, international governmental organizations (IGOs) and multinational corporations (MNCs) can be capable of circumventing a state's authority (Keohane and Nye 1989). The state is not a unitary actor but instead comprises interest groups, individual bureaucracies, and individual leaders who attempt to influence foreign policy; the competition, conflict, and compromise between transnational state and nonstate actors illustrates the complexity of interdependent relations (Allison 1999; Janis 1972; Jervis 1976). Decision making is rational as coalitions of groups negotiate and compromise with each other (Byrne 2003). The global political agenda is extensive, with socioeconomic, health, and environmental issues, among others, dominating military and security issues (Kegley and Wittkopf 2008). Critics argue that pluralists are utopian. Pluralists underplay the security issue and the role of anarchy in world politics, which places limitations on all states' actions (Bull 1977).

Globalists contend that we need to pay attention to the global context within which states and other actors interact and to how the structure of the global system conditions them to behave (Amin 1997; Escobar 1995; Gunder Frank 1971). Globalists also argue that it is critical to perceive global politics from a historical perspective to understand the current milieu and the impact of capitalism on states (Agnew and Corbridge 1994). The world capitalist system conditions and constrains the global North and the global South, creating dependent relations between the global North and the global South as the latter provides cheap labor and resources for the former (Wallerstein 2004). The global South is underdeveloped because it is poorly integrated into the world capitalist system (Wallerstein 2004). The global political economy keeps the global South underdeveloped and dependent on the rich global North, which uses international organizations such as the World Bank and the International Monetary Fund (IMF) to maintain its privileged position and domination (Agnew 2005). Critics of globalism question whether there are noneconomic explanations of imperialism, such as strategic military motives (Skocpol 1979; Kegley and Wittkopf 2006).

This chapter examines system, state, and individual levels analyses of the causes of war and explores a multilevel approach to building a global peace.

## Causes of War

The nature of war as an institution has not changed, but the enhanced killing power of modern armies has moved from knights on horses to tanks and nuclear weapons (Darby 2001; Geller and Singer 1998). State nationalism and technological development have ensured that interstate wars have moved from local contests between two armies fighting each other in local theaters to global catastrophes (Stoessinger 1990). The targeting of civilians as part of a scorched-earth policy and the plight of refugees in World War II and the Holocaust and during protracted civil wars of the twentieth century are intrinsic elements of modern warfare. However, ecowarfare, transnational terrorist organizations, ethnic cleansing, and rape warfare are part of the so-called new war as the complexity of political violence has changed since the Cold War (Kaldor 2007).

During the Cold War era, the rival superpowers armed their allies and competed with each other in what came to be termed low-intensity warfare (or counterinsurgency) and other covert and overt politico-military operations. The West and the Soviet Union supported internal death squads that carried out counterinsurgency tactics against rival factions to combat revolutionary guerrillas who had a deadly effect on local populations in Angola, El Salvador, and Nicaragua (Kegley and Wittkopf 2006). The superpowers carried out their war by proxy, sometimes using proinsurgency methods and other times backing rather untenable regimes and testing weapons at the same time (Wittkopf 1994). In 1979 the United States sent Stinger missiles and other sophisticated munitions to the mujahideen in its internal struggle in Afghanistan against the occupying Soviet military, only to find these weapons and insurgents opposing the American presence in the region just a few years later.

The costs of war are unimaginable. New methods of ecowarfare, such as Sadaam Hussein's firing of the oil wells in Kuwait in 1991, has impacted the environment (Klare 2002, 2008). The arms race is a drain on economies. Most of the gross national product of the global south goes into buying arms (Jeong 2000a). During 1900–90 more than 75 percent of deaths in the world were estimated to have been caused by war, representing more than 111 million people (Eckhardt 1992). The escalation of wars around the globe necessitates more interventions by the international community such that the costs for peacekeeping and humanitarian aid have skyrocketed.

Recently, military interventions by the United States in Afghanistan and Iraq have raised the possibility of the escalation of war in the West and the Central Asian region, along with the question of whether both wars are legitimate and just (Rogers 2008). Since the global community now feels threatened by violence from the Al Qaeda and Taliban networks, many Western states and other members of the international community, despite popular opposition, have been willing to demonstrate a show of force against transnational terror groups (Rogers 2008).

This chapter draws on the analytic framework set forth by neorealist Kenneth Waltz's *Man, the State, and War* (1957), which suggests analysis at the individual, state, and global levels (table 8.1). It is best to think of the levels as occurring along a scale from the general (systems-level analysis) to the specific (individual-level analysis).

### Systems-Level Analysis

Are the causes of war to be found in the nature of the international system of states? The concern with this level of analysis is with the distribution of power among states (Waltz 1957). In a period of power changeover, uncertainty and fear can lead to misperceptions and can escalate conflict between states (Wrong 1995). Fear and an arms race were partly responsible for the outbreak of World War I, a war that had little by way of coherent policy rationales. In a unipolar world, the United States came under attack on September 11, 2001, by a

*Table 8.1. The structure of international relations*
**Systems-level Analysis/Structural Explanation of World War II**

Global external events beyond the control of anyone
Power
Balance of power (multipolar world)
Failure of the League of Nations (world government)
Appeasement (utopian idealism)
Warfare changes (blitzkreig and the Battle of Britain)
Alliances (Britain's lack of support for allies; lack of loyalty)
Appeasement (Weak and misguided)
Collective security
Defensive mentality
British ten-year plan
Isolationism (Britain and the United States)
No strategic thinkers (Failure of the British and French to act; they
   were psychologically disarmed)
Fear of the Soviet Union (Hitler exploited this factor)
Irrationality (British and French overestimate the military power
   of Germany)

**State-level Analysis of World War II**

Sovereignty and power of the state
Realist (Hitler)
German rearmament
Radical nationalism (hurt pride, anger, and self-esteem in Germany)
Fascist type of government (built on war)
Use of propaganda (power of the media and press)
Decline of the Weimar Republic (reparations and a fledgling democracy)
Power (revenge for the Treaty of Versailles)
Authoritarian system (nationalist, antiliberal, antiparliament,
   antibourgeois, anti-Semitic)
Strategy of terror (willingness to use violence)
Guilt clause (Britain and the United States felt shame for the way
   Germany had been treated)

Lack of foresight and complacency (if British and French leaders had
   read Mein Kampf, they would have seen that Hitler wanted war)
Ideology (concessions of British; hate of the Germans)
Appearance of cowardice (British and French appeared weak;
   spurred on Hitler)

### Individual-level of Analysis/Rational Choice Explanation of World War II

Misperceptions and calculations of individual leaders
Hitler (quest for power; fear of Soviet attack; policy of living space
   and racism; will power; ambition and self-determination)
Chamberlain (Fear of war; policy of appeasement and rearmament;
   fear of the future; conciliation; goodwill; fear; influence)
Daladier (French paralysis and inaction; Maignot mentality; despair;
   ambition)
Groupthink (Hitler and Chamberlain surrounded themselves with
   people who thought like themselves)

---

transnational violent organization. A perceived power vacuum can also lead to an unequal power distribution in the international system (Ziegler 2001). In the post–World War I period, the United States went into a period of so-called splendid isolationism (though it maintained financial and other interests abroad), which encouraged aggressor powers such as Germany, Italy, and Japan to escalate conflict because there were fewer strong powers to challenge their aggression (Kaldor 2007).

To this argument Robert Gilpin (1983) adds the assertion that war results because of ascending-descending hegemons. As one power is stretched militarily, economically, and politically, a rival ascending hegemon challenges the descending hegemon's power. War results as the declining hegemon uses its military power in an attempt to save its hegemonic position. The great sea powers of Portugal and Spain were challenged by the British naval power of Sir Walter Raleigh and Sir

Francis Drake in the sixteenth century, resulting in the decline of Iberian naval superiority in Latin America toward the end of the century.

The scramble for new markets by imperial powers in Africa and Asia led to economic competition that fueled an arms race at the outset of World War I. Lenin (1969) argued that as the imperial powers dried up the markets of their colonies, they could only expand new markets at the expense of rival colonial powers; this meant that rival colonial powers such as Britain and Germany finally went to war against each other, despite defusing prior crises during "Iron Chancellor" Otto von Bismarck's Concert of Europe period that preserved the peace among European powers.

In the international system there is no world government, though there are forms of order in cooperative arrangements such as alliances, IGOs, laws, and norms of expected behavior (Jeong 2000b). The survival of the fittest, however, means that military power rather than international law is usually relied upon to protect the interests of the sovereign state (Bull 1977). The global South demanded a new international economic order (NIEO) in the latter part of the twentieth century because of the unequal distribution of resources between the global South and the global North (Kegley and Wittkopf 2006). When these demands fell on mainly deaf ears and when guarantees against hostile interventions were not available, some states, such as North Korea and Iran, moved toward developing nuclear devices to impact this conflict between the developed and developing worlds (Rogers 2008).

The Cold War bipolar alliance system played a role in providing a balance of power and stability in the international system that remained frozen in a nuclear standoff between rival superpowers, whereas a multipolar system, such as the one that some see developing in the twenty-first century, might be unstable, leading to misperception, fear, and an arms race (Morgenthau 1948; Kwan Koon 2003; see also Singer 1962; Deutsch 1957; Waltz 1957; and Organski 1958).

In 1914 the Triple Alliance (Germany, Austria-Hungary, and Turkey) and the Entente Cordiale (Britain, France, and Russia) went to war because once one country declared war on another, each feared that if it refrained from the fight it or its allies would be attacked next. An international crisis can also escalate tensions and lead to war between rival blocs (Bercovitch 1996). During the 1960 Cuban missile crisis, the Soviet Union put short-range nuclear weapons into Cuba both to balance against American weapons in Europe and to protect (by proxy) Cuba's Fidel Castro regime, which had been attacked by Washington-trained insurgents the prior year (Byrne 2003). The superpowers went to the brink of a nuclear war before a deal was ultimately struck. Similarly, the 1948 Berlin Blockade created tensions between the West and the Soviet Union that could have sparked a major confrontation; it was avoided by an American airlift of supplies to Berlin and Russia's acceptance of the face-saving arrangement. Thus, crisis management is a key aspect of preserving peace.

Societal revolutions can also escalate tensions within the international system (Goldstone, Gurr, and Moshiri 1992). The 1979 Iranian Revolution against the U.S.-backed shah Reza Pahlavi escalated the conflict between Iran and the United States when sixty-six diplomatic hostages were taken from the American embassy in Tehran. Ultimately it was the successful intervention by Algeria as a third-party mediator and the successful release of the remaining fifty-two hostages with the signing of the Algiers Accords that relieved the immediate tension (Bercovitch 1996; Princen 1991). Despite the long-term freezing of Iran's assets in American banks and a freeze in U.S.-Iran relations, a member of President Reagan's staff, Colonel Oliver North, engineered the ill-fated Iran-Contra Scandal in which funds from the sale of weapons to Tehran in exchange for Iran's help in securing the release of American intelligence agents held hostage in Lebanon were diverted to insurgents in Central America (Fisk 2005). In another case, General Douglas MacArthur's determination to push the Korean War close to the Chinese border brought more than three hundred thousand Chinese soldiers into the conflict and escalated tensions between the United States and China (Pearson and Rochester 1992). Thus, in delicately balanced or even in hegemonic and dominated international systems, dangers of local conflict escalating to major war cannot be ignored.

Are the causes of war to be found in the nature of states and societies? The concern with this level of analysis is with the characteristics of an individual country and the impact of those traits on the country's behavior (Waltz 1957). For example, Machiavelli (1977) has argued that war exists as a result of human nature, for human beings are inherently evil. The inevitable ensuing struggle for power leads to anarchy and necessitates militarism to protect the interests of the state (Bull 1977). States can teach their citizens to kill, and war becomes ingrained within societal norms (Pearson and Rochester 1992). However, anthropologists have shown that some cultures express aggression differently and that war does not exist in some societies (Fry 2006; Ross 1993, 2007).

Domestic tensions can also lead to a state creating an external enemy against whom to go to war (Bueno de Mesquita 1981). States use nationalist ideology to unify the nation against the constructed other. The military junta in Argentina invaded the Falklands-Malvinas Islands because of the economic recession and nationalist ideology besetting Argentina in the early 1980s. This act resulted in a war between Argentina and Britain over the sovereignty of the islands. Similarly, Anwar Sadat used the 1973 Yom Kippur War against Israel to quell riots by students in Egypt who were protesting unemployment. Wars can thus unify disputing groups and populations, but war also risks the unraveling of states. Nationalism also can lead to liberation from occupation and repression, as when states struggle against foreign occupiers or when colonies mount independence movements (Kriesberg 1998).

A clash between economic systems can lead to war. This was the stated goal of the Marxist Soviet Union to destroy the capitalist states in the West, though because of power calculations direct war between them was averted (Jeong 2000b). Communism sought to destroy and transcend private property to create the necessary conditions for a transition to a new form of socialist society. The Soviet Union supported international communist movements globally as independence movements in Asia, Africa, and Latin America embraced revolutionary socialism to overthrow oppressive structures and abolish the division of labor and private property (Kaldor 2007). Socialist revolutions in Cuba, Vietnam, Mozambique, Nicaragua, and Angola, among others, also challenged the hegemony of the West, which went on the offensive in a proxy war against the Soviet Union and the People's Republic of China (PRC) in the developing world (Pearson and Rochester 1992). The United States feared that the domino effect of communism in developing countries would spread, challenging its global power and interests (Pearson and Rochester 1992). Interestingly, though, Marxist states themselves, such as the Soviet Union, the PRC, and Vietnam, often disagreed even to the point of open warfare (border conflicts in the 1970s and 1980s), indicating that power and control of territory tend to trump ideology as a cause of conflict (Vasquez 1993).

Nationalism has also led to xenophobia and was a catalyst to war in the twentieth century as religion, language, history, and territory were merged to promote citizens' loyalty to the state (K. Boulding 1990). The outbreak of civil war in the former Yugoslavia demonstrates how nationalism is used as a tool to create the Other and to re-create the in-group and thus facilitates the viciousness and atrocities of one nation against another. Rwanda illustrates such destructive ideological campaigns on the group level. Neonationalism has witnessed the challenge of ethnic groups wishing to secede from the state, such as the Muslims in Kosovo (Paris 2004). Internal civil wars have escalated between rival ethnic factions in newly independent states in developing countries (Gurr 1993; Olson-Lounsbery and Pearson 2009).

Economic and political factors are calculated by a state as an expected utility under conditions of uncertainty or risk of deciding to go to war (Bueno de Mesquita 1981). In 1991 Iraq calculated that if it invaded Kuwait to gain access to Kuwaiti oil wells and a port, then the rest of the global community would not intervene (Fisk 2005; Klare 2002). Saddam Hussein believed that in a meeting with April Glaspie, the American ambassador to Iraq, she had given him the green light to press ahead with his plan to invade Kuwait (Kegley and Wittkopf 2006). As in many warlike situations, calculation was miscalculation. The international community rallied to Kuwait's cause, fearing erosion of the sovereignty and nonintervention principles of international law

(Kegley and Wittkopf 2006). In 1973 Sadat decided to go to war with Israel in part to force action on the long-frozen conflict and territorial claims between Egypt and Israel as well as to quell the domestic unrest in Egypt referred to above (Kriesberg 1998).

Rising expectations can also lead to war or a collapse of the state if a government cannot fulfill its promises to the people (Goldstone, Gurr, and Moshiri 1992). The 1917 Russian Revolution resulted in part because the tsar had promised that the war would be over by Christmas. Despite nationalist appeals, as the war dragged on the general population became ever more disenchanted with the tsar and the royal family, thus paving the road for a Bolshevik revolution and Lenin's slogan of "bread and peace" (Sharp 2005). In 1990 the Soviet Union collapsed because Mikhail Gorbachev could not deliver promised reforms fast enough to satisfy the people's demands for change (Kegley and Wittkopf 2006). The resulting coup by hard-line Communists was resisted by Boris Yeltsin and his supporters, which led to the eventual collapse of the Soviet Union and the birth of a protodemocratic Russia (Kegley and Wittkopf 2006). The democratic peace theory suggests that democratic societies rarely go to war with each other (see the debate between its proponents and critics in Brown 1996; MacGinty 2006; and MacGinty and Williams 2009).

The literature has shown that types of government in a state, or pairs of states, can lead toward or away from war. Fascism was built around a war economy (Carsten 1969; Walzer 1995). Nazi Germany built a world-dominance ideology and a strong military machine with pocket battleships, tiger tanks, the V1 and V2 rockets, fast fighter planes such as the Messerschmitt 109-E and the Fokker Wolfe, and the blitzkrieg (lightning war) strategy of fast-moving tanks and mechanized infantry supported by Stuka dive-bombers (Kagan 1995). Japan decided that bombing the American pacific fleet at Pearl Harbor in 1941 was better than taking the chance that the United States would turn its Seventh Fleet against the imperial Japanese navy as Japan's oil supplies ran dangerously low under a Western blockade because of Tokyo's invasion of China in the 1930s (Ferguson 2006).

## Individual-Level Analysis

Is the cause of war to be found in the nature of individuals; that is, are humans innately aggressive? The focus of this level of analysis is on the behavior of individual leaders (Waltz 1957). Foreign policy decision-making scholars are now studying the role of personality in world leaders from Adolf Hitler to Saddam Hussein in order to understand their drive for power (Hermann 2008). Personality, health, ambition, personal history, family background, or a national crisis can impact a leader's decision to act (Hermann 2008). Perceptions also can distort how a decision maker observes reality. The Argentinean junta figured that Britain was more than six thousand miles away and would not be interested in sending a task force to oust Argentina from the Falkland-Malvinas Islands (de Mesquita 1981).

The aggression of nations' leaders can stem from witnessing a humiliating defeat (Ferguson 2006). The German homeland was never occupied by the victorious Allies in 1918, which allowed the myth that it was the German politicians who surrendered Germany when the German military was just months away from a victory over the British, French, and American forces (Kagan 1995). When Germany defeated France in 1940, Hitler made the defeated French Vichy government sign the surrender in the same train car in which German politicians in 1919 had signed Germany's surrender to the victorious Allied powers. The 1919 Treaty of Versailles imposed a war-guilt clause and heavy reparation burdens on a defeated Germany that sowed the seeds of revenge of the Nazi Party and its public followers (Kagan 1995).

Cognitive factors and a confusing anarchic international milieu that breeds mistrust and suspicion can result in poor foreign policy decisions (Jervis 1976). Each decision maker has a particular image of the world that is shaped by her or his interpretation of historic events such as revolutions and wars. Jervis (1976) emphasizes that history lessons combined with personal experiences contributes to an individual's belief schemata about how the global environment works and influences how that person makes decisions. Cognitive consistency entails that information that clashes with a decision maker's political imagery will be ignored and dismissed (Jervis 1976).

## Preventing War and Building Peace

Elise Boulding (1990) asks how world peace can be imagined. How can we create an emancipatory society that is based on participation, empathy, recognition, justice, equality, and the transformation of structural constraints? It is critical to move away from the war culture's coercive power-over model to a new empowerment paradigm based on a power-with model, or shared power model, to create a positive peace (Galtung 1996) (table 8.2). The following are some pragmatic steps in a multitrack system to build peace in the global milieu.

### Interdependence

Liberal theorists pose the prospect that mutual international transactions such as the flow of money, goods, and technology across states creates peaceful relations (Keohane and Nye 1989). States recognize that they are linked together in a so-called global village, that they are affected by activities in other states, so that "the severing of the functional relationship" can damage another state (Keohane and Nye 1989, 11). Still, wars have erupted between close trading partners, such as the United States and Japan in 1941, so interaction is no guarantee of peace. In 1989 the Soviet Union kept oil from Lithuania because the Baltic state was advocating for its independence. "Less vulnerable states will try to use asymmetrical interdependence in particular groups of issues as sources of power" (Keohane and Nye 1989, 32). Ironically, during the Cold War nuclear weapons made the superpowers interdependent because of the fear of a nuclear Armageddon (Pearson and Rochester 1992).

In any event, people in the global village are cognizant of what is happening in other societies (Kegley and Wittkopf 2006). CNN's coverage of the 1989 collapse of the Berlin Wall, the atrocities committed by Serbian militia in the former Yugoslavia, and the tragic events on September 11, 2001, in the United States were broadcast around the world by the media, promoting propeace sentiment and responses worldwide (Strobel 2001).

"Vulnerability and sensitivity interdependence" within the international system also constrains behavior, which can lead to cooperation

**Table 8.2. Alternative images of international conflict resolution and their underlying assumptions**

| Theories | Realism | Pluralism | Globalism | Humanism/PACS | Feminism |
|---|---|---|---|---|---|
| Analytic units | State is the principal actor | State and nonstate actors are important | Classes, states, societies, and nonstate actors operate as part of world capitalist system | People, states, societies, and nonstate actors operate as part of an ecological world system | Individuals, states, societies, and nonstate actors operate as part of an ecological world system |
| View of actors | State is unitary actor | State disaggregated into components, some of which may operate transnationally | International relations viewed from historical perspective, especially the continuous development of world capitalism | International relations viewed from the perspective that relationships need to be transformed to create a positive peace | International relations viewed from the perspective that relationships need to be transformed to create a shared power |
| Behavioral dynamic | State is rational actor seeking to maximize its own interest or national objectives in foreign policy | Foreign policymaking and transnational processes involve conflict, bargaining, coalition, and compromise, not necessarily resulting in optimal outcomes | Focus is on patterns of dominance within and among societies | Focus is on the transformation of patterns of dominance within and among individuals and societies | Focus is on transforming the patriarchal war structure within and between societies |
| Issues | National security issues are most important | Multiple agenda with socioeconomic or welfare issues as or more important than national security questions | Economic factors are most important | Agency of the individual and the creation of a just society for everyone | Gender issues are most important |

Adapted from: Talentino, 2005, 5.

or conflict (Keohane and Nye 1989, 12). The international community boycotted the Republic of South Africa because of its apartheid system before the Convention for a Democratic South Africa (CODESA) negotiations between the African National Congress (ANC) and the National Party in the 1990s. South Africa's membership in the United Nations (UN) was suspended, and its athletes could not compete at the international level. Embargoes are not always effective (see Cortright and Lopez 2000), but given certain dependencies such as the South African business community's ties to international financial centers, they can be rather decisive in changing minds and policies.

Internal government policies are connected to the policies of other states, as "changes in one country" can lead to "costly changes in another" (Keohane and Nye 1989, 12). The 1973 war between Israel and Egypt led to the 1974 Organization of Petroleum Exporting Countries (OPEC) oil crisis as the petroleum nations from the Middle East retaliated against the global North's support for Israel during that short war (Keohane and Nye 1989). Rising oil prices and contrived shortages pressured Western states to take or avoid taking positions on the war.

Global issues also weaken the authority of states (Keohane and Nye 1989). The spillover of refugees from the ethnic conflicts in Rwanda and Kosovo destabilized neighboring countries, while the 1985 Chernobyl and 2011 Japanese nuclear reactor meltdowns impacted the global climate and brought more citizens out to support the environmental global movement (Rogers 2008). The AIDS epidemic has ripped through central Africa and Asia, infecting people with the HIV virus and greatly compounding public health dilemmas and burdens for governments (Kegley and Wittkopf 2006). The 2003 AIDS conference in South Africa brought together health experts from around the world to formulate health policy and antiretroviral treatment ideas to address this global health issue.

"Technological change and increases in economic interdependence will make existing international regimes obsolete" (Keohane and Nye 1989, 40). Domestic and international politics interact due to complex issues and actor interdependencies and tensions, while conflict is resolved by international regimes (29–37). "The very complexity of relationships, and the multiplicity of contacts between societies can contribute a considerable mutual adjustment of policy even when conflict exists and formal rules cannot be developed" (233). "Interdependent relations will always involve costs since interdependence restricts the autonomy of states" and prevents war, as states have to figure out the "cost of giving up the benefit" (9).

States are also sensitive to the fact that "sensitivity interdependence can be social or political as well as economic" (Keohane and Nye 1989, 12). Hong Kong's return to China in 1997 impacted the Association of Southeast Asian Nations (ASEAN) trading bloc. Taiwan, Japan, and South Korea feared a projection of China's military and economic power in the region. States are also "vulnerable" to the international system because they can suffer from "costs imposed by outside actions" (14). The 1929 Wall Street crash in the United States and a similar crash in 2008 impacted economies across the world. The 1929 crash hastened war fever in the 1930s in Europe and Japan. International institutions provide order in the international system, outlining the "network of rules and norms" to avoid conflict and uncertainty (19). International institutions such as the UN and the European Union (EU), among others, help governments pursue their interests through cooperation because "specific sets of rules and procedures have been developed to guide states and transnational actors in a wide variety of areas" (20). Prospective EU membership has even proven to be an incentive for states for resolving some of their conflicts and improve their human rights records, as in the peace accords in Northern Ireland and similar attempts on the divided island of Cyprus (Byrne 2007). Heads of states hold "beliefs and values" in common and want to collaborate with each other for "joint gains" (Keohane and Nye 1989, 229).

### Functionalism and Integration

States also form supranational authorities so that they can cooperate, especially in less overtly political areas such as science and economics (Haas 1976). The European Coal and Steel Community (ECSC) was formed in 1948 to pool coal and steel reserves and trade to prevent future war between France and Germany after World War II. The ECSC became the European Economic Community with the 1956 Treaty of

Rome and developed into the EU in 1992 with the Maastricht Treaty. The EU has been relatively successful at achieving political unity by integrating one sector at a time, and the organization has delegated decision making to new institutions such as the European Commission, the European Parliament, the Council of Ministers, and the European Court.

Even though they have not completely merged (some states resist using the euro currency, for example), why have the people of Europe shifted from one political center to another? European states did so because of joint rewards and benefits, such as the free flow of persons and goods across borders, the elimination of tariffs in trade, a common agricultural policy, and a common monetary unit, the euro (Pearson and Rochester 1992). Today the EU is expanding its membership to include states from the former Eastern bloc to form a Europe stretching from the Atlantic to the Urals as General Charles de Gaulle foresaw, though not without squabbles and conflict (eg. the current economic bailout of Greece) (Rogers 2008). The formation of the EU-created cooperation and a "habit of interaction" to build common values, creating a "working peace system" for limiting nationalism and leading to the "withering away" of parts of the state system (Mitrany 1966, 63). The EU has become a working system of collective bargaining and creative conflict management (Kegley and Wittkopf 2006).

Elites in the EU countries collaborate to increase their own welfare (Haas 1976). Increasing transactions in trade and communication "spill over" into other aspects of politics (Mitrany 1966, 84). Thus, the elites are socialized into cooperating with each other (Haas 1976). The process of referendum allows the people of each state to vote on a single issue. The referenda protects the unity and the diversity of each state. It is a creative mechanism of conflict management, because as new issues arise, shifting coalitions of interest groups develop around those issues (Pearson and Rochester 1992).

### New Social Movements

Melucci, Keane, and Mier (1989) discuss the role of new social movements clustering around issues once considered private in the civic culture. The social base of these organizations are the elderly, immigrants, the unemployed, youths, and women who feel alienated and unrepresented by the mainstream political parties that are organized around issues of class and who are not in touch with new issues.

These evolving interest groups demand a new way of life that is both universal and humanistic (Melucci, Keabe, and Mier 1989). The values of these new social movements generally revolve around dignity, equality, and peace. The global village has witnessed the explosion of the Green movement for the environment. The Green Party has become a significant political entity in many countries and has formed solid alliances with other partners for quality of life changes (Porritt and Winner 1988). The feminist movement has also influenced theory, practice, policy making, and laws to free women and men from structural violence and gender inequality (de Lauretis 1987). In addition, the peace movement focuses on human rights violations, peace education, and antinuclear issues (Gallant 2009).

### International Security

Nonviolence has been attempted by states through the practice of civilian-based defense (Sharp 2005). Civilian-based defense empowers the citizens of an occupied country to use creative nonviolent mechanisms such as boycotts, sick days, and slowdowns in direct action to challenge the power of the occupying force (Sharp 2005). Costa Rica does not have a formal standing army (though it does have a defense force) and could use the process of noncompliance with an invading army to resist nonviolently. During World War II, Denmark and Norway refused to give up their Jewish citizens to the invading Nazis. In Denmark, every Danish citizen wore the Star of David in protest of genocidal laws (Sharp 2005). Groups such as the Quakers, the Church of the Brethern, the Mennonites, and the Baha'i as well as conscientious objectors have protested to abolish war and work to promote disarmament, tolerance, understanding, and human security (Axworthy 2003).

Institutions such as the International Peace Bureau (IPB) and International Lawyers Against Nuclear Weapons (ILANA) are part of a network of NGOs in Geneva working to end the proliferation of nuclear weapons (Leatherman and Griffin 2009). Partly as a result of work by the IPB, ILANA, and other NGOs, the Nuclear Non-Proliferation Treaty was extended indefinitely in 1995 as South Africa, Argentina, and Brazil dismantled their nuclear programs and as Belarus, Kazakhstan, and Ukraine returned their nuclear weapons to Russia. Nuclear-free zones (NFZs) have been enunciated in Latin America and elsewhere, binding states not to acquire such weapons and nuclear states not to threaten their use in the NFZs (Kegley and Wittkopf 2006).

Realist approaches to security also include limited self-defense. A limited self-defense strategy limits the size of the arsenal that a state may own and also reduces the number of weapons that states now have (K. Boulding 1990). Unlimited self-defense necessitates a balance of terror to preserve the peace in a dangerous world (K. Boulding 1990). Limited self-defense enables states to develop defensive capabilities such as fortifications (e.g., the Maiginot Mentality). In 1992 the United States and Russia signed the Strategic Arms Reduction Talks I (START) treaty to reduce the number of nuclear weapons that each side possessed, and in 1993 they signed START II to eliminate biological and chemical weapons (Kaldor 2007). Broad international consensus, since somewhat threatened, emerged as well for the Nuclear Non-Proliferation Treaty and the Limited Nuclear Test Ban accords. Unlimited self-defense cautions states about abandoning arms that are necessary to deter rogue states and terrorist organizations from going to war (Kaldor 2007). On the other hand, war abolitionists argue that the world needs to disarm, that is, that states need to beat swords into plowshares to achieve at least negative peace.

UN blue-helmeted peacekeepers identify hot spots and deploy troops to prevent conflict from reigniting and to deter aggression. The peacekeepers' role has changed as the missions and challenges of recurrent civil and international wars have become more complex (Byrne, Fergusson, Ben-Ari, and Michael 2006). These missions range from observation of armistices and cease-fires to the separation of belligerent forces and enforcement action to provide humanitarian aid, train local police, monitor elections and human rights, and restore government and civil administration in postaccord societies (Doyle 2001). The UN Security Council has a limited budget for UN peacekeepers. The Security Council needs to provide better and more comprehensive training, and provide a clear mandate and a command and control policy for field commanders on the ground who need to address human security issues, including human rights, hunger, ethnic cleansing, and rape (Alger 2005). The timeliness of peacekeeping must also be improved to avoid coming to war zones after the fact.

State sovereignty is a fundamental premise but also a substantial barrier to the enforcement of international law (Pearson and Rochester 1992). However, there is growing support for multilateral institutions such as the International Criminal Court (ICC), whose rulings define and advance international law (Schabas 2001). The ICC, situated at The Hague, prosecuted war criminals from the conflict in the former Yugoslavia, including Slobodan Milošević, Ratko Mladic, and Radovan Karadžić. A number of policy makers now state that if individuals are accountable for gross violations of human rights, then sovereignty resides in the person, not the state, and human security should then hold precedence over state sovereignty when there is a violation of citizens' human rights and dignity (Axworthy 2003). Certain key states that frequently use military force, however, such as the United States, have clung to sovereignty notions in refusing to recognize the International Court of Justice (ICJ's) jurisdiction (Rogers 2008).

### Resource and Income Redistribution

The global South has sought an NIEO to stabilize markets in order to repay their heavy international debt and increase international funding from both the IMF and the World Bank. The NIEO also proposed allowing the global South better control of its own resources and providing economic aid to all global South countries (Jeong 2000b). Global South joint actions include OPEC reducing its production in 1974, allowing oil companies to deliver fuel to their favored customers but creating a world recession; OPEC still accounts for most of the world's oil production (Kegley and Wittkopf 2006). The global South has also nationalized foreign MNCs and protected their home industries, such as China's five Special Economic Zones, though global institutions such as the General Agreement on Tariffs and Trade (GATT) and the World Trade Organization (WTO) pledge members to opening up world trade markets.

## Responsible Development

Responsible development is evidenced by a plethora of new industries being developed in the global North and the global South that are creating environmentally safe products such as electric cars, windmills, solar power, and expanded recycling. As a result of this new politics, class issues in the global North have declined in importance, with new focuses on quality of life issues such as human rights, conservation, and environmental protection (Melucci, Keane, and Mier 1989).

States also confront a global population problem that is influencing the human and responsible development global debate. Some states, such as Japan and Sweden, have an aging population and an uncertain economic future unless new measures such as immigration are implemented (Kegley and Wittkopf 2006). On the other hand, in China couples are required by law to limit families to only one child. The UN Economic Scientific and Cultural Organization (UNESCO) works to improve the status of women globally (Kegley and Wittkopf 2006).

The UN and other IGOs slowly create cooperative norms of behavior and interaction and are often better than states at promoting international cooperation (Uvin 2004). IGOs provide a safety valve by which states can negotiate and air their differences (Pearson and Rochester 1992). IGOs also promote quality of life for people in the global South. The WHO is a major player, along with some NGOs such as Rotary International, in global campaigns against diseases such as polio.

## International Law

International law is another means of preventing war and effecting peace. Forms of international law include The Hague Conventions of 1899 and 1907 to ban war as an instrument of statecraft as well as multilateral and bilateral treaties and customary law (Lentz 1976). International organizations, such as the ICJ in The Hague, and NGOs also focus on implementing international law. Amnesty International centers its efforts on international human rights law, whereas Greenpeace works to ensure that states comply with international environmental law.

National leaders also follow international law, such as the extensive Law of the Seas Treaty. In 1990 the emir of Kuwait invoked international law after his country was invaded by Iraq. The late Colonel Muammar Gadaffi invoked international law when Libya was bombed in 1986 by the United States. Furthermore, world opinion is an integral component of international law (Jeong 2000a). World opinion condemned Libya's brutal treatment of opposition prisoners of war during the 2011 Libyan civil war, and the new government over the flagrant execution of Gadaffi and his son, and both Israel and the Palestinians accuse each other of violating legal principles against attacking civilians. (eg., the recent Gaza war).

International law is most effective in areas of low politics (everyday transactions), such as trade and technological cooperation, but is least successful in high politics, such as protecting the state's security and national interests (Gallant 2009). However, global citizens are outraged by unacceptable norms of behavior, such as the apartheid system in South Africa and the condemnation and enforcement of sanctions against Serbian aggression in Bosnia and Kosovo (Axworthy 2003). The laws against human trafficking are meant to reinforce norms against slavery, child labor, and sexual abuse. CNN images of suffering and death in Rwanda, Egypt, Syria, and Kosovo and the death of civilians in the civil wars in Libya, Syria, Sudan, and Sri Lanka emphasize that the immorality of inhuman actions is unacceptable to the international community (MacGinty and Williams 2009).

### International Organizations

A concern for humanity and a rejection of war have fostered the growth of international organizations (Pearson and Rochester 1992). Increased international contact through travel and communication, transnational movements such as Greenpeace, and successful regional models such as the EU and the North American Free Trade Agreement have created successful models to emulate for future world government (Saunders 1999). IGOs cooperate to build trust, mediate disputes, counsel states, create norms of behavior, and forge treaties (Covey, Oziedic, and Hawley 2005). The barriers to world government include state sovereignty and nationalism.

The UN, which is open to all nations that adhere to the principles of the UN Charter, encourages states to cooperate on issues and pursue their national interests peacefully (Doyle 2001). South Africa was also suspended from the UN between 1974 and 1991 because of its continuation of its racist apartheid system. The UN provides collective security for all of its members, sending its rapid deployment force to hot spots around the world (Pearson and Rochester 1992). The UN secretary-general has acted as an intermediary to end the 1980–88 war between Iran and Iraq (Bercovitch 1996; Boudreau 1991).

## Conclusion

The consequences of World War I were evidenced in the collapse of empires, the birth of new nations, the deaths of more than ten million soldiers and civilians, the creation of the League of Nations, and the development of a new world order based on idealism and a revulsion to war (Ferguson 2006). However, the humiliation of Germany as a result of the 1919 Treaty of Versailles, a fledgling German Weimar Republic, the appeasement policies of the British and the French American isolationism, the collapse of the international economic system, and the failure of the League of Nations to halt the rise of fascism all sowed the seeds of World War II (Kagan 1995). World War II resulted in the deaths of more than fifty million people, including during the Holocaust, and the creation of the Iron Curtain dividing Europe into pro-West and pro-Soviet blocs. In the midst of this global turbulence, the UN was established in 1945 to keep the peace in a bipolar world with the growing threat of a nuclear Armageddon.

The Cold War struggle between the United States and the Soviet Union resulted in the 1947 Truman Doctrine to contain communism, as evidenced by both the Korean War and the Vietnam War (Kegley and Wittkopf 2006). During 1963–78, a period of détente witnessed the development of interdependent relations between the United States and the Soviets that ended with the 1979 Soviet invasion of Afghanistan. In 1985 Mikhail Gorbachev opened up the Soviet Union with policies of glasnost and perestroika that soon resulted in the collapse of the Berlin Wall and the Warsaw Pact and the creation of at least a temporary unipolar world order with the United States as the dominant hegemon (Kegley and Wittkopf 2006).

But as the twentieth century drew to an end, this era of the United States as the leader of the so-called New World Order also witnessed an explosion of vicious protracted ethnopolitical conflicts in Chechnya, Darfur, Georgia, and Somalia as the Pandora's box of genocide decimated entire generations in these conflicts (Kaufman 2001; Power 2007). The wars of the twenty-first century may have their roots in the dismantling of the bipolar Cold War system that kept a lid on the proliferation of micronationalist conflicts (Kaldor 2007). Transnational terrorist organizations such as Al Qaeda have demonstrated their capacity to strike at the heart of the Western world, bombing targets in Indonesia, Spain, Britain, India, and the United States (Rogers 2007). Warfare in the twenty-first century has taken on a new face and threatens the security of the global North as the violence is taken to the streets of New York, Washington, London, Madrid, Bali, and Bombay.

War does not solve conflict; rather, war reflects and constructs views of irrational and aggressive opponents who need to be controlled and dominated (Olson-Lounsbery and Pearson 2009). Consequently, the practices of peace building (rebuilding relationships and structures) and conflict transformation seek to mobilize people to become critical thinkers and deconstruct the dominant patriarchal or hegemonic war discourse (realism), which involves making a paradigm shift away from the power-over philosophy of realism to a power-with philosophy (peace building) to transform unjust structures and relationships (Lederach 1997, 2005; Ryan 2007). We have cited tentative indicators that despite the continued national feelings of insecurity and rivalry that drive wars, evolving patterns of collaboration and cross-national networking are under way that might produce such transformations as the centuries progress, if indeed we preserve Earth and humanity so that they can progress (MacGinty and Williams 2009). Our very foundations of conflict knowledge influence how we frame and analyze conflicts, how we intervene in conflicts, and ultimately how we think and act in conflict within the dominant macrostructure.

The next chapter outlines how the Peace and Conflict Studies (PACS) field can assist in the process of transforming violence.

## Websites Related to War

Crisis State Research Centre, London School of Economics, http://www.crisisstates.com/

Doctors Without Borders, http://www.doctorswithoutborders.org/

Institute for International Assistance and Solidarity, http://www.ifias.eu

International Committee of the Red Cross, http://www.icrc.org/

Montreal Institute for Genocide and Human Rights, Concordia University, http://migs.concordia.ca/

Political Economy Research Institue, University of Masachusetts at Amherst, http://www.peri.umass.edu/dpe/

Quaker United Nations Office, http://www.quno.org

United Nations Human Rights, Office of the High Commissioner for Human Rights, http://www.ohchr.org/

## Suggested Questions for Further Discussion

1. The globalization and fragmentation going on in world affairs today might seem to be the opposite more than complementary. How can they be related to one another? Why is this useful to the student of war?

2. It is popular to think of war as invoking ancient hatreds. Why would this chapter suggest that this is not at all adequate as a way of thinking about war?

3. War has not been a historical constant of the past two hundred years. Rather, war occurs in spurts. What does this tell us about why it occurs?

4. In dealing with wars, to what extent are we prisoners of history and to what extent can we successfully innovate historical patterns of cooperation to build a common constructive narrative among nation-states?

5. What is the relationship between leaders and masses in wars? Have peace movements been successful in the prevention and abolition of war? Why or why not?

6. What role do countries external to a war play in the search for peace or in escalating the war?

7. Which processes in democracy do you think democratic peace theorists believe will lead to the erosion of war? Why?

# 9

## Peace and Conflict Studies

### Nonviolence, Social Justice, Human Rights, and Social Change

On February 7, 1986, Florida's Haitian radio, Radio 2020, reported that Jean-Claude "Baby Doc" Duvalier, Haiti's ousted president, had fled to the French Riviera. Radio 2020, an important source of information for Florida's growing Haitian community, called on all of Florida's Haitian community to come to the radio station in Davie, Florida, near Ft. Lauderdale to celebrate the fall of Baby Doc. The Klu Klux Klan on hearing that a large group of black people were gathered at the radio station decided to go to Radio 2020. They surrounded the celebrating Haitians gathered at Radio 2020 with the intent of forcing the black people out of the radio station and out of Davie. The Haitians gathered in front of the station spoke little English and knew nothing of the Klu Klux Klan and its sordid history. When the Klu Klux Klan arrived the Haitians applauded, thinking that they were supporting them. The Haitians went up to the Klan members present and tried to embrace them, saying "my friend thank you for coming and helping us to celebrate the fall of Baby Doc Duvalier." The local media was covering the event, and the Klu Klux Klan did not react to the efforts of the overjoyous Haitians to hug them. However, the Klu Klux Klan asked the

Haitians to leave the premises, and they did so peacefully (Margaret Armand, personal communication, June 2000).

Over the past several decades, influential thinkers from a variety of disciplines have more or less explicitly challenged the relationship between knowledge and power. In 1942 Carl Rogers developed the idea of client-centered therapy, which placed power not in the mind of the therapist but rather in the client. Rogers (1942, 28) argued that the aim of the intervention was to assist the individual to grow rather than to solve a problem so that the person can cope with present and later problems in an integrated fashion. The role of the therapist is to facilitate, through dialogue, the client's efforts to make sense of her or his own experience and determine her or his future direction. This process must occur in the context of a therapeutic relationship characterized by unconditional positive regard that allows the client to feel safe and valued and to trust her or his own knowledge.

In *Pedagogy of the Oppressed*, Brazilian educator Paulo Freire (1999) argued that the education system served as an instrument of oppression by creating a culture of silence. He reframed the teacher-student relationship as interdependent and intersubjective. Students bring important knowledge to the educational process. Education should provide opportunities for teachers and students to work together through a dialogic process to critically examine and better their social situations and their lives. In this kind of an educational process, persons do not have the world explained to them but instead become more able to interpret the world themselves. Freire believed that for the human being to exist, she or he must be empowered to not only name the world but also to change it.

Michel Foucault (1979, 1993) also challenged the authority of experts when he persuasively argued that knowledge is not discovered but rather is produced by powerful technologies. Some discourses are seen as more legitimate or politically powerful: mass media versus what has a lesser audience or no audience, discourses from within academia versus from without, and what the literary canon includes rather than omits. These privileged discourses, however, may not represent or may even misrepresent the experience of many social groups, including communities of women, groups from the global South, or the global North's poor (e.g., Gugelberger and Kearney 1991; Randall 1991).

In sociology, symbolic interactionists strive to understand how individuals and groups make sense of their lives and world (Blumer 1969). Feminist methodologists emphasize the needs of disempowered groups when they ask who research is for (Harding 1987). In the field of sustainable development, appropriate technology is the idea that those being helped are partners in designing and implementing solutions to their problems (Escobar 1995).

It is arguable that the discipline that is the least touched by these ideas is the one most explicitly concerned with power: political science. Increasingly, however, the traditional concepts of high politics—state power, state interests, and interstate diplomacy—are gradually accommodating more complex and more dynamic paradigms, emphasizing the role of a diversity of actors including not only states but also transnational organizations, nongovernmental organizations (NGOs), regional groups, and individuals (Jeong 2008). An emerging subfield called transformational politics is seeking to develop a politics of participation by defining empowerment and examining the role of midlevel social organizations (Ryan 2007; Schwerin 1995).

Ultimately the goal of violence prevention is nonviolence and peace (Herman 2001). The classic readings in nonviolence represent a body of thinking that gave birth to Peace and Conflict Studies (PACS) as a conscious focus and a field of study by a group of scholars, practitioners, and activists from many different disciplines. If nonviolence and peace are the goal of violence prevention, it is important to give some thought up front as to what we mean by those terms. While these readings span several decades and a variety of professional, philosophical, and cultural backgrounds, there are some common themes that emerge very prominently. Specifically, we draw on theoretical ideas from the PACS literature to outline the socioeconomic and political problems that nonviolence addresses as well as to discuss implications for intervention.

## Interdependence

Interdependence refers to the idea that within communities, the well-being and fate of persons and families are inextricably interconnected. Interdependence also refers to the idea that the well-being and fate of different communities, different states, and even different hemispheres are inextricably linked. As storyteller Francis McMillan Parks put it, "I feel very strongly that we all have a vested interest in community, and that what I do has a consequence, but that what you do also has a consequence on my life" (personal communication, September 12, 1994). Interdependence suggests a relationship among all persons and groups whether or not those persons or groups want to recognize the existence of that relationship.

The idea of interdependence exists in every religious tradition. For example:

"Give and you shall receive" (Christian text, New Testament).
"They live in wisdom that see themselves in all and all in them, who have renounced every selfish desire" (Hindu text, *Bhagavad-Gita Gita*).
"If I am for myself only, what am I?" (Jewish theologian Hillel, *Chapters of the Fathers*).

The idea that what we do—for good or ill—will reverberate in society and will eventually similarly affect us also exists in all religions, including Wicca, indigenous, and Earth-based religions. This idea can also be seen as interdependence: What we do affects others and comes back to us because we are connected with others in a circle or web of relations (Kulchyski 2005). While there are power differences, relationships are not purely linear or hierarchical.

Not only are those issues grounded by moral considerations, but social and natural scientists increasingly argue that persons and groups are, in fact, interdependent. In political science and international relations, the paradigms of national interests, state diplomacy, coercion, and division are giving way to considerations of shared concerns over environmental degradation or the effects of a potential nuclear catastrophe (e.g., the Fukushima nuclear plant's breach in 2011 in Japan as a result of the tsunami); a diversity of political actors including not only states but also transnational organizations, NGOs, regional groups, and individuals; cooperation; and integration as a result of globalizing forces, such as the international economic system and mass communications (Enloe 2000). Also, natural scientists have increasingly examined the interrelatedness of all living things and the cooperation and integration that exist in nature. In *The Web of Life*, physicist Fritjof Capra (1996) states that ecological communities comprise all living creatures that are bound together in interdependent networks. A radical new system of ethics emerges and becomes an intrinsic part of our daily awareness when this deep ecological perception takes root (11). We are all a part of a web of social, political, economic, and biological relations (Burrowes 1996).

The significance of the concept of interdependence for the study of violence and the PACS field is that it suggests that the exercise of violence will generate more violence. As Martin Luther King Jr. (1958, 84) indicated in his book *Stride Toward Freedom*, bitterness is the aftermath of violence, while the creation of a beloved community is the aftermath of nonviolence. Both morally and strategically, violent actions and even violent interventions will come back to haunt us.

Importantly, interdependence refers to relationship. Ideally, that relationship should be one of shared power. Peace between and among persons and communities is not a static relationship but instead is a dynamic free flow of information that is possible in a context of a relationship characterized by trust and shared power (Curle 1971; Lederach 1997, 2005). A balance of power among parties that enables the collaborative development of shared knowledge and collaborate problem solving seems necessary for a peaceful relationship. Thus, peace researchers have examined the negative and positive aspects of power (e.g., E. Boulding 1990, 2000; Schwerin 1995; Herrman 1999).

Edward Schwerin (1995) has developed a definition and framework for the concept of empowerment as a necessary component of personal and political transformation and deep participatory democracy. He argues that empowerment is characterized by shared power (power with) and is an alternative paradigm to that of coercive power (power over). In his model, empowerment involves, at the level of the person, attitudes of self-esteem and self-efficacy and capabilities enhanced by knowledge, skills, and political awareness. At the level of community, empowerment involves social and political participation, which mediates between the individual and the community in the building of society.

Moreover, Jeffrey Sachs (2006) argues that survival in the global South depends on addressing challenges such as erratic rainfall, malaria and pandemic HIV/AIDS, nutrient-depleted soils, lack of adequate educational opportunities and access to safe drinking water and latrines, and the unmet need for basic transport, communication, cooking fuels, and electricity. He also contends that the poorest of the poor lack infrastructure as well as business, human, knowledge, and natural capital. Sachs also points to the Universal Declaration of Human Rights as well as the importance of reaching the goals of the United Nations (UN) Millennium Development Fund to overcome the global poverty gap so that economically developing countries can access vitally important basic human needs, all of which are a matter of human rights and social justice (251).

The concept of interdependence requires careful reflection: In what ways and to what degree are persons and/or groups interdependent? How does the nature and degree of interdependence between persons and/or groups depend on who is involved and the situation?

## Mutual Respect

Mutual respect and human rights are also a central concept to theories of nonviolence. Again, the value and worth of human life and personhood is taken as a basic universal assumption and premise. It is absolutely central to the ideas of Mohandas K. Gandhi, César Chávez,

Chief Oren Lyons of the Onondaga Nation, and the Reverend Martin Luther King Jr. During conflict, mutual respect involves regard for those with whom we are in conflict.

King (1992) advises us to hate murder but love the murderer. He represents this concept with the Greek word *agapé*, which refers to understanding and redeeming goodwill for all human beings. *Agapé* is a love that is creative, spontaneous, and from the heart. *Agapé* actively discovers the neighbor in every person, making no distinction between friend or enemy, as we are all embraced with the love of God (86–87).

Nonviolent interventions into violent conflict do not involve dehumanizing the enemy but instead involve humanizing the enemy or perhaps humanizing the self to the enemy by means of moral appeals to their conscience. A peaceful nonviolent community requires that people are free to define their identities and are not subject to forced assimilation (Galtung 1990). Persons are not punished by murder, expulsion, marginalization, or repression based on their identity (Galtung 1990). Alex Honneth (1995) and Honneth and Farrell (1997) argue that social conflict is characterized by an intersubjective struggle for mutual recognition. That is, recognition of the universal dignity of diverse persons and groups is a basic human need and is required for creating a peaceful society.

Moreover, Avishai Margalit (1996, 122–24) argues that a "decent society" involves freedom from the violence of humiliation. Humiliation is understood as rejection from the "human commonwealth" and is "a signal of existential rejection that is not symbolic at all" and "erodes the base on which respect is founded." Injuries of dismissal, disrespect, and dehumanization are forms of violence. While these injuries may be seen not to effect any real, material, or physical harm, Margalit argues that such social marginalization can have damaging psychological effects. Furthermore, as historical experience has demonstrated, the dehumanization of persons and groups is a prerequisite for and quickly facilitates direct violence of the cruelest kind (Galtung 1996). Marginalization from the center of power and humiliation are sustained by and entrench structural inequality (Pilisuk 2008).

Mutual recognition does not necessarily refer to a universalizing view in which one party embraces another party as essentially the same as itself. Claims of a common humanity can rationalize an assimilationist position that subordinates particularities to dominant prototypes (West 1990). The concept of mutual recognition instead encompasses the willingness of parties to engage in dialogue. This should include a struggle to articulate and examine differences (e.g., McLaughlin 1993; Rothman 1992). While developing understandings across boundaries of cultural difference may never be complete or unproblematic, it seems that trusting relationships require a desire on the part of all parties to recognize the dignity of the other (Senehi 2009b).

What signifies respect? What do you see as the role of mutual respect in violence prevention? Do you think that mutual respect is always possible? How do you frame the concept of mutual respect?

## Honesty and Openness

Often the perpetuation of inequality and violent social systems and relationships involves silence about what is going on. People do not speak up or speak out. This may be because they are frightened about giving up their privileges or are frightened about severe physical punishment if they speak up (Lederach 2005). Sometimes there is a genuine lack of knowledge or awareness among large groups of people about the exact ways in which social institutions, social systems, and cultural norms may be harmful (Pilisuk 2008). Because of a perception that things have always been this way, harmful systems may appear natural and unquestioned, and members of both dominant and subordinate groups may participate in systems of oppression in ways of which they are unaware.

Thus, processes of consciousness raising and advocacy must be part of the peace-building process (Lederach 1997). Developing political awareness or a critical consciousness is required for movement toward mutual recognition, empowerment, and peace (Ryan 2007). Peace involves the freedom for persons and groups to openly address issues important to them that otherwise may be suppressed from individual consciousness or public expression out of fear of repercussions. Developing a critical consciousness involves dialogue among all strata of society (Freire 1999). Secrecy breeds and sustains violence (Griffin 1992).

Consciousness-raising bridges the personal and political as well as the micro and macro levels of analysis (Senehi 2002). During the 1960s as the feminist movement began to take shape, through consciousness-raising—especially in small groups—women worked together to counter sexist socialization by developing increased self-awareness (Senehi and Hawranik 2009, 467). As discussed above, de Lauretis (1987, 25) describes this consciousness-raising process as a "critical method" because it "is the original critical instrument that women have developed toward such understanding, the analysis of social reality, and its critical revision."

Frantz Fanon (1965) and Albert Memmi (1967) described how colonialism operates as a system within which the colonized themselves, unknowingly and to their own detriment, participate. The authors argued that liberation for the colonized intellectual involved reaching a phase of consciousness where she or he is able to understand the exploitive nature of colonialism and rediscover connections with her or his native people. Paulo Freire (1999) described how education can encode and perpetuate oppression but can also encourage liberation through the development of a critical consciousness, or *conscientizaço* (see also Lederach 1995).

What keeps people from being honest or open? What are some things that we are not honest or open about in our society? Are there times when you feel that you must be silent about matters that are relevant to public welfare? How do we go about raising consciousness? How do we determine what is true? What is the relationship between knowledge and power? How do you consider the concepts of honesty and consciousness-raising?

## Nonviolence as Active Process

There is a continual emphasis by practitioners and scholars of nonviolence that nonviolence is not inactive, passive, or weak. Nonviolence is an ongoing process—such as with gardening—that involves continual and various efforts at nurturing the well-being of persons and communities (Barash 1991). Seen in this way, nonviolent interventions may take innumerable forms and require a diversity of talents and energies (Barash 1991). Gene Sharp (2005) describes nearly two hundred types of nonviolent political action.

It is easy to pick and choose historical examples of wars where might is right prevailed or media icons such as Rambo are used to exemplify the use of violence to solve conflict (Pilisuk 2008). It is more difficult to identify historical examples in which nonviolent action prevailed as a strategy to transform social relationships and structures. Gene Sharp (2005, 69–341), and David Barash (1991, 568–72) have highlighted the following eight nonviolent successes at forging social change. (1) In 1905 in St. Petersburg, nonviolent peasants on their way to hand a petition to the tsar were killed in their hundreds by the Cossacks. Bloody Sunday ensured that the regime lost legitimacy and helped to usher in the 1917 Bolshevik Revolution. (2) In 1943 in Denmark, the Danes smuggled 90 percent of Danish Jews to Sweden. All Danes wore the Star of David while government officials, religious figures, and trade unions opposed the Nazis. (3) In 1968 in Czechoslovakia, slowdowns and strikes during the Prague Spring caused Prime Minister Alexander Dubček to say that "We have socialism with a human face" (cited in Barash 1991, 569). (4) In 1989, prodemocracy demonstrations drove out the Communist government of Czechoslovakia. (5) In the 1970s in the United States, César Chávez fasted to support better working conditions for migrant farm laborers. (6) Between 1981 and 1989 in Poland, the Solidarity movement chose a nonviolent path of boycotts and strikes that were organized within Catholic churches to oust General Wojciech Jaruzelski from power. Lech Walesa, the Solidarity leader, said, "We did not break a single window" (cited in Barash 1991, 569). (7) In 1989 in China, the prodemocracy movement demonstrated that although people power was crushed in Tiananmen Square, the incident clearly indicated the brutality of the regime. The army should not have attacked the people, and the regime lost some of its support. (8) On October 20,

2000, a nonviolent Serbian grassroots movement ousted Slobodan Milošević from power.

Nonviolence is not cowardly. Being truthful in the face of powerful systems of denial takes courage. Nonviolent struggle, such as the movement for an independent India led by Gandhi, may demand the "courage to stand up nonviolently" and risk one's life in the face of extreme brutality (Barash 1991, 560). Nonviolent resistance is a spiritual approach to life as well as a practical technique for achieving social and political change (Burrowes 1996) and also involves courage, directness, honesty, and nonviolence.

Gandhi argued that Satyagraha, or active and nonviolent love, was the power of "adherence to the truth" so that one's "soul force and soul truth" meant the empowerment of the individual (Barash 1991, 558). It also meant the "voluntary suffering" of the individual who had to "suffer for the good of all" (561). Gandhi thought that self-restraint is assertive and that a person has the power to persuade the opponent through love and to empower oneself (Barash and Webel 2002). The idea was to resolve the source of conflict, not to defeat the opponent. Ahimsa, or truth, was Gandhi's idea of the respect for the other's humanity and meant the "noninjury by thought or deed" of another person (Barash 1991, 560). If one has love for another, it melts the heart; when the soul rules the body, it is free from fear so that "one's commitment is in favor of life with an absolute and unwavering firmness to the truth" (560). One seeks to convert the opponent to the truth, as the individual is responsible for "reforming the planet" (560). Gandhi also believed that suffering demonstrates one's devotion to justice (Webel and Galtung 2007); one has "to suffer so that one's commitment cannot be questioned," and one's "willingness to suffer demonstrates courage and power" (Barash 1991, 560). Thus, the person's willingness to accept beatings and death is also aimed at transforming and changing the evil policy. Gandhi did accept Christ's death on the Cross to save the souls of His children as an example upon which to model nonviolence. (Barash 1991)

Nonviolence also involves creativity. Sometimes nonviolent direct action takes tremendous ingenuity that is grounded in the specifics of a particular situation. John Paul Lederach (1999, 202) argues that as our global nonviolent movement cascades toward peace commitment, the concepts of creativity, dreaming, social imagination, and vision are critical in a world shrouded in famine, injustice, inequality, poverty, violence, and war.

Peace educators such as Elise Boulding (1990, 2000) argue that education is part of the process of creating new approaches to conflict resolution and envisioning the future. Imagining how things can be otherwise is an ongoing process that is crucial to peace building.

What is the role of creativity and imagination in violence prevention? How do powerful cultural images sustain violence or peace? How do you think about the nature of nonviolence?

## Personal Responsibility

Another central theme of the readings on nonviolence is the issue of personal responsibility. Power, or agency, has been a central problematic for all social theory. In an effort to expose the social dynamics of power, Karl Marx argued that the capitalist system traps the working-class person in a dehumanizing cycle of economic-based oppression (Tucker 1972). Marx argued that this exploitation exists whether or not the elite or working classes recognize it: the system leads to the development of a false consciousness within both class groups. Thus, while he attempts to theoretically arm those he sees as economically—and in other ways—oppressed, Marx denies persons the freedom to define their own experiences. If not defined by the social structure, the person is defined by the social theorist.

Symbolic interactionists attempt to recognize the power of individuals or groups to interpret their own life world. In his discussion of how persons make sense of their world, Herbert Blumer (1969) accounts not only for society's symbolic systems but also for a person's unique experience and ability to internally analyze this experience. Blumer in effect describes all persons as social theorists, since we each try to make sense of our experiences and make a multitude of choices on a daily basis. Still, while trying to empower ordinary persons by taking their accounts of their social lives seriously, Blumer and the symbolic interactionists may give short shrift to the economic, political, and cultural forces that shape us and our lives in ways that may be brutally limiting.

The Marxist and symbolic interactionist theories differently emphasize the macro and micro levels of analysis, but both are concerned with exposing the dynamics of power and see the social system and individual agency in a dynamic tension. Marx argues that through class consciousness-raising, the disempowered can become aware of their situation and fight together for change; thus, he recognizes the potential power of the oppressed (Tucker 1972). Studies using a symbolic interactionist framework show how individuals and marginalized groups protest and resist more dominant social structures and discourses. They recognize the power that social structure exerts over lives (e.g., Liebow 1967; Macleod 1995; Wiseman 1979).

The tension in social theory regarding how the world is determined has been reflected in the new interdisciplinary PACS field. Johan Galtung (1985, 1990, 1996), a parental figure in this field, emphasizes the social structural causes of conflict. He powerfully argues that social conflict is the result of structural inequalities, often encoded in culture, that limit persons' physical, social, and spiritual development in ways that promote death, regardless of whether or not there is overt warfare in the society. Galtung (1996) explicitly problematizes violence itself: he equates violence with all forms of social injustice whether or not there is physical combat. Both nonviolence and social justice are required for what he and others (e.g., Martin Luther King Jr.) term "positive peace." Thus, lasting peace likely requires broad and deep transformation of world cultural, economic, and political systems. Defined in this way, PACS seems to be an impossible and improbable task.

Yet to have a PACS field is to believe that there are coherent strategies for promoting peace and resolving conflicts. Gandhi (1992) arguably demonstrated that apparently powerless persons have the ability to effect desired nonviolent social change even in the face of powerful armies. Martin Luther King Jr. (1958, 1992) also argued for and demonstrated the possibilities of the disenfranchised struggling nonviolently to effect a new vision of society as he mobilized the civil rights movement in the United States in the 1960s.

The difficulty in bridging the micro and macro levels in the PACS field stems in part from the divergent disciplinary perspectives of PACS theorists, such as with international relations' macrolevel theory on the one hand and interpersonal communications' microlevel theory on the other (Byrne and Senehi 2009). Perhaps more fundamentally, this problem stems from the PACS theory's difficulty with accounting for culture and power (Scimecca 1991). To put it simply, the cause of conflict is typically blamed by social theorists on things outside the individual-structural inequality, needs deprivation, competing interests, and cultural/ideological contexts. This separates the people from the problem.

Nevertheless, according to PACS theory, the task of conflict resolution for our intergroup and interpersonal conflicts falls ultimately on our own shoulders (who else's?) and involves adopting certain principles and values (Gandhi 1992), acquiring new communication skills (e.g., Bolton 1986; Katz and Lawyer 1985), acquiring mediation and negotiation skills (e.g., Fisher and Ury 1981; Bercovitch 1984, 1996; Hocker and Wilmot 1995; Umbreit 1995), using creative problem solving (e.g., Kelman and Cohen 1976; Kelman 1991; Rothman 1992), and participating in social movements (King 1958, 1992). PACS asks us for personal adaptation and transformations, that is, changes in our consciousnesses.

Even if all were to accept Galtung's thesis that the deep structural and cultural roots of conflict require profound social and cultural change, there would be little agreement on how to make such change. All conflicts are unique, and broad social conflicts involve a complex intermeshing of psychocultural, historical, religious, demographic, economic, and political forces (Byrne and Carter 1996; Byrne, Carter, and Senehi 2003). PACS theory cannot provide blanket solutions, policies, or prescriptions. PACS theory attempts to develop ideas about how individuals and groups at odds can empower themselves and others to move effectively and in moral ways toward desired goals. While we may be personally awed by the immensity of the social world and our own smallness in the face of it, Gandhi urged that "It is possible for a single individual to defy the whole might of an unjust empire to save his honor, his religion, his soul, and lay the foundation for that empire's fall or its regeneration" (cited in Barash 1991, 560).

What is the role of personal responsibility in violence prevention? How can people and communities work from a local base to resist and alter patterns of violence at the level of interpersonal relations, family, community, society, and global relations? How do you consider the concept of the nature of nonviolence?

## Commitment to Work for Human Rights and Social Justice/Positive Peace

When we are exposed to the issues, we tend to see the world differently (figure 9.1). Young white college students in the 1960s were exposed to civil rights issues and joined the Freedom Riders, who formed to organize African Americans in the South to register to vote (Barash 1991, 666). Gandhi said that peace begins with the self and that everyone has a moral duty to work for peace (Barash 1991, 562). One needs to examine one's own life and beliefs and see if those beliefs reinforce patterns of oppression; "one needs to resist oppression to break out of oppression" (Barash 1991, 582). However, peace must also be made externally. Making one's own peace will not solve poverty and war in developing countries or political systems of oppression and alienation (Barash and Webel 2002). Peace must end with changes in the world such as the prevention of the destruction of the rain forests in Brazil and the end of racism, homophobia, and nuclear war (Barash 1991, 382). People's lack of awareness of problems such as environmental degradation and poverty in the global South also can mean that they will not get involved (Pilisuk 2008). However, the world is small, and one cannot be insulated from its effects, such as the terrorist attack on the World Trade Center and the Pentagon on September 11, 2001. Paulo Friere (1999) argues that people are empowered when there is consciousness-raising leading to personal and group awareness of injustice. The oppressed must perceive the "reality of oppression" if they are to recover their "lost humanity and dignity," which is a limiting situation that they can transform; the oppressed need a sense of "hope to be committed and to act" (Barash 1991, 384).

Barash (1991, 384–88) outlines seven motivating factors leading to personal transformation. (1) The decision to become involved in

# Figure 9.1. Peace and conflict studies framework

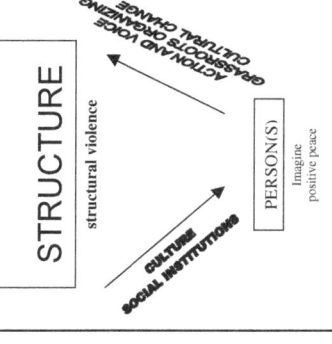

**RULER**
- Know yourself.
- Know your limits.
- Know your values.
- Understand your history.
- Respect yourself.
- Self-esteem.
- *EMPOWERMENT.*

**LOVER**
- Respect others.
- Value others even in the context of conflict.
- Seek to understand.
- Ahimsa (Gandhi).
- Agape (ML King).
- *UNDERSTANDING.*

**WARRIOR**
- Commit fully to principles.
- Seek knowledge.
- Learn to practice skills.
- Be aware.
- Power with / for.
- *INTERDEPENDENCE.*

**ALCHEMIST**
- Transformation.
- Turn lead into gold.
- Turn conflict into strong or renewed relationships and cooperatively solved problems.
- *OPTIMISM.*

*u n d e r s t a n d i n g*

**Assert**
- Make your own needs known.

**Listen**
- Seek first to understand.

**Problem-Solve**
- Work together for win/win.

**Conflict Resolution**
- Transformed relationships.

**Protest**
- Understand your interests/needs.
- Stand up for your needs.
- Value your heritage, history, and background.

**Love Your Neighbor**
- Seek understanding of other groups and marginalized.
- Learn about other cultures.
- Values differences.
- Believe in others.

**Problem-Solve**
- Involve all stakeholders.
- Participate at all levels possible.
- Nonviolence.
- Seek knowledge.
- Be aware.

**Social Change**
- Transformational politics.
- **IMAGINE POSITIVE PEACE**

**STRUCTURE**

structural violence

ACTION AND VOICE
GRASSROOTS ORGANIZING
CULTURAL CHANGE

CULTURE
SOCIAL INSTITUTIONS

**PERSON(S)**
Imagine positive peace

TRANSFORMATION

SILENCE → LANGUAGE → ACTION

DEATH → VOICE → LIFE

a social movement for change may involve one's religious persuasion. The scarlet pimpernel of the Vatican, the Irish monsignor Father Hugh O'Flaherty from Tralee, County Kerry, organized a successful underground in Rome during World War II that saved the lives of thousands of Italian Jews and escaped Allied prisoners of war. (2) "Outraged humanism" may open up one's eyes to social injustices. After Bud Deraps spoke with some Guatemalan refugees, he became involved in Veterans for Peace in St. Louis and its protest against the School of the Americas, which trained the officers commanding death squads in Central America and Latin America from the 1960s through the 1990s to keep the peasants quiescent. (3) One can get involved as a result of a "sudden insight that makes one see with clarity." Intellectuals from the colonized Third World such as Frantz Fanon, Albert Memmi, and Aimée Cesaire became mobilized when they saw how the colonial model was destroying their indigenous culture and people. (4) It can be "a slow and gradual realization" when the facts and personal experiences come together. Over time, Archbishop Oscar Romero saw how the dictatorship in El Salvador was torturing and killing his people and his priests, which prompted him to come out against the government. (5) People need to take "personal responsibility" and realize that we are "all victims of hidden oppression" or structural violence, such as malnutrition or environmental abuse; "it is empowering to work with others, and the load is lighter if it is shared with other people." (6) "Each one of us has a duty to contribute to world peace" because we are all on this spaceship Earth together. Dorothy Schneider, a retired nurse and a veteran of World War II living in St. Louis, Missouri, was so touched with that experience that she spent the next fifty years writing letters to all UN and world leaders to create a UN day. Her persistence paid off, and October 28 was officially established as United Nations Day in 1990. Archbishop Desmond Tutu's Truth and Reconciliation Commission brought together both perpetrators seeking amnesty and survivors seeking closure to tell their stories to the South African people so that the society could heal from the trauma of South Africa's apartheid past. (7) We need to appeal to a "sense of efficacy" if people are to "break through their crust of denial and indifference" so that it "is fun to work together for peace." People can make a difference but if people believe that "they are helpless, then they will act helplessly." Mother Teresa and the Irish nun Sister Cyril Mooney empowered the untouchables in their ministry in Calcutta, India. Dr. Martin Luther King Jr. empowered both black and white Americans during the civil rights era by mobilizing them to resist oppression in the South to work for transformational change within society.

According to Barash (1991, 386–87), for the realization of positive peace, three actions need to happen. (1) We need to "believe in the possibility of peace" and imagine or visualize peace as realistic and in terms of what it would be like. We need to reprogram our minds to achieve "positive images of desired change" and believe in the "possibility of peace," or efforts will be halfhearted. (2) Individuals need to believe in their personal power and effectiveness by "breaking out of the culture of silence." (3) In order for individuals to motivate themselves, "realistic goals must be set to change the way we think and act."

If social justice and positive peace are to be achieved, then structural violence—hunger, poverty, sectarianism, sexism, heterosexism, and racism—has no place in a new global society. In order to build positive peace, we need peace education and structural change to promote cooperation and respect for human dignity (Senehi 2009a, 2009b). We are observing the development of regional functional trading blocks such as NAFTA, the EU, and the ASEAN as well as the demands from the global South for a new international economic order and debt forgiveness.

Jeffrey Sachs (2006) notes that overcoming extreme poverty can be reached if the economically developed countries continue to commit .7 percent of their gross national product (GNP) to the countries of the global South. He insists on a global accord between rich and poor countries to end poverty and notes that poverty can be reduced by global level action needs that addresses the debt crisis, environmental stewardship, global trade policy, and science for development. Sachs understands that the debt held by the indebted poorest countries must be cancelled and that they will need trade plus aid. He makes the point that the United States is spending thirty times more on its military than on foreign assistance. Sachs recognizes that in order to secure the global well-being of all citizens, the global North must continue to commit .7 percent of their GNP to foreign aid.

We seek to generate diagnoses so that various bodies, agencies, and policy makers engaged in the funding and delivery of development programs might develop intervention strategies in partnership with parties in the global South and the Fourth World in the global North (Sachs 2006). It is crucial to identify and evaluate alternatives to the dominant paradigm of development and understand that new frameworks of governance and politics must be created to make development more democratic, equitable, just, and sustainable so that human security, human development, and social and gender equality can be achieved for the most exploited and vulnerable (Jeong 2005; MacGinty and Williams 2009). The traditional model of development thinking and practice has failed to deliver human security and socioeconomic development to the majority of the world's poorest people (MacGinty and Williams 2009; Sachs 2006). Because much conflict in the global South and the Fourth World in the global North is rooted in competition for scarce resources, a struggle for human dignity, women's rights, human rights, and empowerment of poor people, a reimagined and reenergized international development in terms of both funding and policy recommendations can obviously influence both economic and social development (MacGinty 2006; MacGinty and Williams 2009).

Socioeconomic development from international agencies can create opportunities for people in the grassroots to empower themselves to start up indigenous businesses (Byrne and Irvin 2001). This is important for capacity building and is a critical component of constructive conflict resolution because it also promotes partnerships involving local grassroots communities, NGOs, and governments (Byrne, Thiessen, and Fissuh 2007). An inclusive socioeconomic development strategy can foment a creative new way of thinking about economic recovery after ethnic wars and promote responsibility and accountability for action as well as shed new light on the impact of socioeconomic development in the postviolent peace-building process (Byrne 2009a). On the other hand, development aid can lead to corruption if it falls into the wrong hands, especially in the postviolent peace-building phase of ethnopolitical conflicts (Hoy 1998; MacGinty 2006; Ryan 2007).

In addition, personal empowerment demands social empowerment that enhances self-esteem and self-efficacy by providing skills that empower the individual (Woolpert, Slaton, and Schwerin 1998). Conflict resolution training, community organizing, and cross-cultural sensitivity training provide those skills. Personal empowerment also involves thinking critically about sociopolitical issues and asking questions about who is disempowered, what the future will be, and how we get there (Schwerin 1995). Personal empowerment that encourages people to participate in social and political activities such as mediation centers and sports clubs while voting and fundraising can also empower the individual to think critically and to act (Schwerin 1995). Getting involved in civil and human rights organizations teaches individuals to work within the system to transform it (Schwerin 1995). Individuals need to enhance and develop their access to psychological, social, and material resources, thereby developing grassroots empowerment and helping others to empower themselves (Schwerin 1995).

September 11, 2001 and the recent Arab Spring, has radically reshaped the way we teach, do research and service, and think about global and human security (Rogers 2007). Individuals, states, international governmental organizations (IGOs), NGOs and the global community have a responsibility to proactively promote individual liberty, socioeconomic and political rights, and indigenous people's collective rights. An agreed-upon set of principles and norms will protect the rights of indigenous peoples, women, children, and others in the face of seismic political, economic, technological, and cultural changes shaping our international milieu (Boudreau 2003). The knowledge and skills associated with the study and handling of human rights covers a wide variety of issues. We need to address critical issues such as child-soldiers, domestic violence, literacy, health care, trafficking of women and children, refugees, health care, the right to play and to have an education, war crimes, and humanitarian aid so that the dignity of each person is recognized. Indigenous people's human rights and justice resonate in other parts of the world around aboriginal people's rights (Kulchyski 2005; Rice 2011; Tuso 1997, 2011).

The study of human rights is an transdisciplinary endeavour in which learning, praxis, and theory building are best achieved through applied skills in people-to-people interactive contexts (Merry 2006). Legitimizing transnational rules and regulations for cultural, economic, political, social, and human rights is necessary for understanding people's basic human needs in order to intervene in multidimensional conflict milieus (Merry 2006). Human rights are also essential to the analysis and resolution of the deep roots of conflict because when human rights are breached, violent conflict follows suit (Kriesberg 1998). Resolutions reached on nonlevel playing fields do not promote long-term sustainable peace between disputants (Merry 2006). The denial of human rights works against the goals of peace and global security. The devastating costs of human rights abrogations necessitates finding creative methods of handling them (Stein et al., 2007).

Human rights knowledge must now expand. Students, academics, policy makers, and NGOs alike must conduct research into human rights so that we can prevent violations and protect the human dignity of every person (Stein et al., 2007). Countries around the world seek to design a form of healing for their citizens in the postviolent milieu. There are many variations on the use of storytelling in the healing and community-building process; one example is the South African Truth and Reconciliation Commission (Senehi 2000). Human rights and social justice studies deserve a place in the center of our undergraduate and graduate PACS curricula, with the approach focused on reflexive theory and praxis-practicum learning. Human rights are central to the creation of the whole cosmopolitan citizen, and training in human rights should begin in kindergarten well before a child begins her or his formal educational training (Axworthy 2003). Global education and citizenry in international civil society in the twenty-first century necessitates building a global network of relationships with respect for human dignity and human rights at the apex of humanity (Boudreau 2009).

# Conclusion

With the current turbulent turmoil in the Middle East, many people may feel that there is no hope for nonviolence in today's world. In North America it is perceived by some on the political Right as unpatriotic if a person supports the use of nonviolence, for the culture is built around the myth of toughness (e.g., Arnold Schwarzenegger, John Wayne) (Webel and Galtung 2007). The government argues that there is a need in our anarchic world to have a strong military or the United States will look weak to the rest of the world. Pacifists are seen by some of those on the political Right as a minority and as unimportant, as any successful nonviolent movement in the United States would need a charismatic leader to succeed (Barash 1991, 383). There is no such leader at the present time.

Yet people are working together to solve common problems to overcome economic inequity and poverty produced by global economic systems and destruction of the habitat and are also learning about the roots of militarism and violence within societies, the causes of peace, and the diversity of those citizens working to forge opportunities for participation (Alger 2005). Nonviolence is such an alternative to violence and can be used to transform a system based on violence and oppression, such as in South Africa. Civilian-based defense can be used to oppose war and the destruction of the environment (Sharp 2005). Nonviolence empowers people through love and truth, and nonviolence works for social justice (Cortright 2006). One has to suffer to transform one's life, and nonviolence represents a way of being and living in an interdependent world where care for self, Earth, animal life, and humankind is the meaning of life (Burrowes 1996). A new cosmology that recognizes the success of village life—whereby member's have knowledge of their history, culture, and bioregion—in meeting basic human needs will satisfy both human and planetary needs of ecological sustainability and economic self-reliance (Burrowes 1996, 147; Ziegler 1995, 46). Ecological security is centered in principles of traditional knowledge that value interconnectedness, the relationships between life and the land, and the cycles of life (Burrowes 1996, 148).

Citizen peace and justice actions and NGOs can become a key grassroots empowerment movement focusing on issues and people who otherwise become victims of institutional neglect (Pilisuk 2008). It is important to take multidisciplinary theory and apply its central tenets to a wide range of PACS issues to demonstrate how conflict analysis and resolution and peacemaking coupled with human security, local and global governance, and indigenous people's rights must address a new model of sustainable development to create a practitioner-generated set of policy guidelines.

In this chapter we discussed the merit of the PACS field in delivering new ideas and practices to nonviolently transform our world. The concluding chapter of this book focuses on some of the key findings to emerge from this study.

## Websites Related to Nonviolence and Social Justice

Centre for Social Justice, http://www.socialjustice.org/
Gandhi Institute for Nonviolence, http://www.gandhiinstitute.net/
Human Rights and Social Justice Research Institute, http://www
    .londonmet.ac.uk/research-units/hrsj/
Institute for the Study and Practice of Nonviolence, http://www.non
    violenceinstitute.org/
The International Centre for Research on Women, http://www.icrw
    .org
International Centre on Nonviolent Conflict, http://www.nonviolent
    conflict.org
The Martin Luther King Jr Research and Education Institute, Stanford University, http://www.stanford.edu/group/king/liberation
    _curriculum/resources/
Transcend International, http://www.transcend.org

# Suggested Questions for Further Discussion

1. How can we develop theoretical and practical ideas about the relationship between nonviolence and PACS? Is forgiveness possible without reconciliation?

2. How can nonviolence be a means of enhancing participatory democracy? To what extent is the state responsible for the existence of conditions of peace (social justice), and to what extent is the state to be held responsible when satisfactory levels of peace are not acquired?

3. What kinds of storytelling programs can you envision that could promote cross-cultural relations? How useful is storytelling in resolving ecological conflict involving indigenous peoples? Why is it important to legitimize indigenous knowledge and practice systems?

4. What would be involved in moving from the current international system of balance of power and collective security to a system of peace conversion involving the principles of nonviolence? Is it possible?

5. In what ways is identity politics important in understanding peace building? How do the justice ideals of community conflict intervention relate to the values of the liberation movements in Libya, Syria, Egypt, and South Africa?

6. How might the expansion of the definition of human rights for women possibly contribute to noncompliance or partial compliance by some governments? What are some of the dangers of working for peace in the developed world and in the developing world?

7. Why are our holistic visions of peace based on historical experiences and on social and cultural values? What are the complexities faced by those who would support ecological health in the global South while protecting the basic rights of local people?

# 10

## The Violence Prism

### Building Cultures of Peace to Make a Difference

Twelve-year-old Hannah Taylor is a student at St. John's Ravenscourt School in Winnipeg, Manitoba, Canada. She created the Ladybug Foundation when she was six years old to help the homeless because she believes that everyone deserves a home. When she was five, Hannah felt sad when she saw a man eating out of a garbage can. Later when Hannah was going to school, she saw a homeless woman; everything that the woman possessed was in one grocery cart. Hannah's mother encouraged her to do something constructive to address homelessness. Hannah raises money and people's awareness by collecting coffee cans and baby food jars and painting them to look like ladybugs to bring good luck to the homeless. Hannah also hosts Big Bosses lunches, where she meets the leaders of the business community to convince them to support the Ladybug Foundation. To date, the Ladybug Foundation has helped raise more than $1 million for the homeless. Corporations, schools, and nonprofit organizations from all over Canada have invited Hannah to speak to them about the Ladybug Foundation's programs to alleviate hunger and tend to homelessness. In 2007 she received Canada's Most Powerful Woman Award in the Future Leader's category as well as the BRICK award for community building (Hannah Taylor, personal communication, May 2009).

This book suggests that in order to build a culture of peace, we need to know the underlying causes of the various forms and ecologies of violence if we are to deconstruct violence and forge appropriate intervention and prevention strategies. The "web of violence" is expressed in the interrelationship among personal, collective, national, and global levels that link the personal to the global, which in turn frames the public discourse about what is violence and what can be done about it (Turpin and Kurtz 1997). "A peace-through-strength approach" ensures that "a legal coercive framework maintains the patriarchic war structure in which the best that can be hoped for at least in the short term is negative peace" (Enloe 1993, 256): the reduction or elimination of war, that is, a reduction or elimination of fighting and direct physical violence by governments or opposition groups (not to diminish the value of even such an achievement in many chaotic situations such as those in Libya and west African civil wars of recent vintage; see Barash and Webel 2002; Galtung 1996; Webel and Galtung 2007). Violence is both direct and indirect, and this distinction can be applied to the various forms of violence that we have explored in this book. Police brutality is direct violence, while failure to enforce occupational health and safety laws is conceived of as indirect structural violence.

Positive peace refers to the reduction or elimination of all forms of violence, especially structural and cultural violence (Galtung 1996) and generally entails the stage of peace building in which preconditions for constructive social relations are nurtured. Positive peace is identical to justice, and positive peace entails such factors as empathy, kindness, equity, social justice, inclusiveness, human rights, nonviolence, peace education, sustainability, and fairness (Galtung 1996). People often hear the phrase "just peace." To put it another way, positive peace is "related to overcoming oppression" (Barash 1997). The roots of war and the sources of conflict that lead to war are to be found in structural violence, that is, economic and social injustice (Galtung 1996). Most wars are traceable to political elites trying to retain and enhance illegitimate power and to oppressed groups rebelling against these elites (K. Boulding 1990; Gurr 1993). There are more global citizens killed by structural violence (lack of sanitation, food, water, health care, education, employment, shelter, etc.) than by civil, regional, or world wars (Barash and Webel 2002).

In contrast, the new and emerging Peace and Conflict Studies (PACS) field brings hope in the search for remedies to address the manifestations of violence at all levels (Byrne and Senehi 2009). PACS provides a framework of action on a wide basis that entails transformational conflict resolution, peace building, and imagining peace. Conflict analysis and resolution, conflict transformation, and peace and social justice have brought new theoretical notions and application for practice to the PACS field (Botes 2003). The new PACS field is critical to education about prevention and intervention in regard to the problem of violence and to the role of imaginative reframing in making a paradigm shift away from the power-over model to a power-with collaborative model that creates a new way of thinking and doing to transform and change conflict within our society constructively.

The chapter provides a general discussion of some important lessons from this study about violence and its many forms.

## Some Important Lessons from the Study of Violence

Conflict is complex and unavoidable, yet violence is avoidable but ironically difficult to define. Violence can have intricate dynamics ranging from controversies regarding genetic predisposition or programming to learned rationales, such as Adolf Eichmann's refrain "I was only following orders." If violence is justified, then it is made to seem desirable such as with capital punishment or war (Garbarino 1999), both of which sanction what otherwise would be treated as murder. Violence is therefore socially constructed and permeates through all of the dimensions and ecological forms of violence that this book has covered.

People commit and define violence; therefore, we need to unpack the different issues that make up violence. What people define as violence (e.g., spanking, abortion, forced circumcision, and human rights abuses) is hotly contested across cultures (Merry 2006). It is difficult to interpret or justify some of these cultural differences in terms of the conditions under which violence is acceptable. How has one learned to be violent? Moreover, violence prevention and intervention involves the complex systemic nature of different cultures and their interrelationships with natural environmental and human ecological relations and problems arising out of them as well as how ecosystems influence social systems, both of which are complex adaptive systems for shaping and influencing human culture (Marten 2004; Moran 2006; Rappaport 1999; Tsing 2005). We still too often do too little too late to prevent or limit violence from being reactive (crisis management) rather than proactive (preventative). Can we do better? Can we build propeace norms into our civic culture at all levels? What happens when international laws and treaties such as the inspiring Universal Declaration of Human Rights are not enforced or are rejected as culturally inappropriate by, for example, China, Sudan, Iran, Syria, or North Korea? How do we grapple with moral relativism and the reality and persistence of violent behavioral triggers, even in self-defense violence?

We need to recognize the breadth of violence in our global societies. Consequently, we need a keen analysis of these ecological forms or types of violence, ranging from police brutality to religious intolerance. What is the common thread that cuts across these forms of violence? We need detailed microspecific case study analysis to fundamentally grasp what is going on in the context of violence to find intentionality and to see how situations come to be violent (e.g., migrant workers) so that we can take responsibility and see our part in the violence (e.g., global warming) (Reza and Barger 1994; Foucault 1979; Steinberg 2002). Individuals reenact the violence to tell the story of what happened to them. Every August 12 and July 12 in Northern Ireland, Orangemen and the Apprentice Boys of Derry reenact the 1689 Siege of Londonderry and the victory of William of Orange in 1690 over the Catholic Jacobin forces, keeping the historic memory alive in the Northern Irish Protestant collective story (Senehi 2009b). Shi'a ceremonies of martyrdom, which inspired young Iranian soldiers during the 1980–88 Iran-Iraq War and Hezbollah guerrillas fighting in Lebanon during the 1980s and 1990s, may also inspire young jihadists and martyrdom operations in Afghanistan and Iraq today (Fisk 2005; Rogers 2008).

In addition, there is a need to work for a nonviolent paradigm shift to end proviolent attitudes and actions in the family, in schools, in places of worship, and in government and corporations (Kriesberg 1998). In overcoming nature-nurture debates, parents need to model affection rather than aggression, or children may develop pro-aggression values (Vestal 2001). Parents can be mentored by elders and parenting experts in their community on how to rear their children by minimizing sexism and physical abuse and refraining from spanking to change children's behavior (Ellison and Bartowski 1997). The school's culture can also be changed to empower the child's self-esteem and self-efficacy through learning problem-solving and mediation skills while negating bullying behavior (Brown 2000). Moreover, athletes, sports managers, and the media can influence fans to have a low tolerance for aggression and violence by rival fans or by athletes. Individuals need to feel empowered, not oppressed and silenced, in order to take personal responsibility for ending bystander apathy and to make important choices to create a more just, nonviolent, and peaceful society.

We also learn that peace begins with me. Everyone can make a difference. Institutions such as schools can also model an antibullying ethic. Gandhi was optimistic about human nature, believing that human beings were corrupt because their psychic makeup of untruths and secrets were out of sync with the heart, comprising love and truth (Burrowes 1996). Gandhi also recognized the need to use force in self-defense of the nation; however, if there was a choice, nonviolence was the better way (Barash and Webel 2002). If a person can renounce and overcome her or his selfish ego and thereby create an inner harmony, then that person can be peaceful (Burrowes 1996). In other words, a nonviolence practitioner must transcend and transform "selfish individualism, ego, and other troublesome attachments" (Barash 1991, 577). Anyone who reached that level of spiritual transformation would choose morally good actions free of violence, accepting suffering and working to create a society based on truth and political morality (Barash 1991; Webel and

Galtung 2007). Creating emancipatory peaceful language based on empathy, equality, and participation could create a zone of peace where social justice and peacemaking flourish (Brock-Utne 1985; Webel and Galtung 2007).

## Conclusion

In the twenty-first century, violence and the abuse of human rights plague the world. Terror presents a new and frightening face. Conflicts are complex. At the same time, the recent global financial meltdown, the impact of global climate change and the H1N1 pandemic, and the largely nonviolent Tahrir Square demonstrations that led to a peaceful transition of power in Egypt illustrate the collective need to collaborate to resolve violent conflict peacefully while promoting social justice for all. In this nuclear age, the future of the world could well depend on the ability to meet this need (e.g., the nuclear capabilities of North Korea, Iran, and Pakistan may threaten future world peace).

This book has highlighted some of the theoretical roots of modern scholarly approaches to violence perspectives as well as PACS prevention and intervention approaches. The primary objective of the book has been to become familiar with violence in its many forms and ecologies and how third-party practitioners can translate such identification into more informed and effective practice in numerous present-day violent and complex conflicts. The scholar-practitioner needs to learn to design a multidisciplinary theoretical approach, recognize and incorporate indigenous peace-building and methodological approaches, and understand the context that makes a multidisciplinary theoretical lens unique (Jeong 2009). There is a need to become familiar with how interpersonal, intergroup, and societal conflict are interconnected within Johan Galtung's (1996) framework of structural and cultural violence and positive peace: ending all forms of hidden violence in society, such as poverty, hunger, racism, heterosexism, sectarianism, sexism, and ethnocentrism as well as other forms of destructive prejudice.

A key point in peace building has to do with deep grassroots community empowerment that involves breaking down stereotypes, structuring interaction between communities, and establishing shared goals and hope (Jeong 2008). A first step to reducing violence is to understand what has produced it and what needs to be done to resolve, transform, and end it. We hope that this book contributes in some small way to that understanding.

## Websites Related to Peace and Conflict Studies

Association of Conflict Resolution, http://www.acresolution.org
The Carter Center, http://www.cartercenter.org
The Conflict Resolution Information Source, http://www.crinfo.org
Culture of Peace, United Nations Educational, Scientific and Cultural Organization, http://www3.unesco.org/iycp
Culture of Peace Initiative, http://www.cultureofpeace.org
Hague Appeal for Peace, http://www.haguepeace.org
Institute for Healing of Memories, South Africa, International Network for Peace, http://www.internationalnetworkforpeace.org/spip.php?rubrique94/
International Peace Research Association, http://www.iprafoundation.org/.
United for Peace and Justice, http://www.unitedforpeace.org

## Suggested Questions for Further Discussion

1. The deprivation of basic human needs appears to be a source of violent conflict. Think of as many violent conflicts as you can and write down the issues in the conflict to determine if they relate to human needs. Do these issues relate to human needs?

2. Does the destruction of the global commons or Earth's resources and biosphere present a convincing reason for private ownership of all lands and resources? In what ways could globalization have a positive impact on the environment?

3. Why are storytelling and the arts important mechanisms of grassroots peace building?

4. Does diffusion of the ethos of collaborative conflict resolution throughout civil society eventually dictate its pursuit within a country's legal and international sectors as well, or do successes of mediation in legal, labor, and international arenas pave the way for its applications in political life and civil society?

5. How is a multitrack intervention approach at multiple levels and at multiple points important in preventing conflict?

6. Why is peace education and the human dimension important in changing mind-sets about violence?

7. What are the implications in the difficulty of depoliticizing PACS research?

# References

Aall, Pamela. 2001. "What Do NGO's Bring to Peacemaking?" In *Turbulent Peace: The Challenges of Managing International Conflict,* edited by Chester Crocker, Fen Osler Hampson, and Pamela Aall, 365–84. Washington, DC: United States Institute of Peace Press.

Abernethy, Virginia. 1993. *Population Politics: The Choices That Shape Our Future.* Oklahoma City, OK: Insight Books.

Abu-Nimer, Mohammed. 2003. *Nonviolence and Peace Building in Islam: Theory and Practice.* Gainesville: University Press of Florida.

Adam, Herbert, and Kogila Moodley. 1997. "The Purchased Revolution in South Africa: Lessons for Democratic Transformation." *Nationalism and Ethnic Politics* 3(2): 113–27.

Adams, Gerry. 2003. *A Farther Shore: Ireland's Long Road to Peace.* London: Random House.

Adekanye, J. Bayo. 1998. "Power-Sharing in Multi-Ethnic Political Systems." *Security Dialogue* 29(1): 25–36.

Agnew, John. 2005. *Hegemony: The New Shape of Global Power.* Philadelphia: Temple University Press.

Agnew, John, and Stuart Corbridge. 1994. *Mastering Space: Hegemony, Territory and International Political Economy.* New York: Routledge.

Alger, Chadwick. 2005. *Future of the United Nations System: Potential for the Twenty-First Century.* Washington, DC: Brookings Institution Press.

Allen, Beverly. 1996. *Rape Warfare: The Hidden Genocide in Bosnia-Herzegovina and Croatia.* Duluth: University of Minnesota Press.

Allison, Graham. 1999. *Essence of Decision-Making: Explaining the Cuban Missile Crisis.* New York: Longmann.

Amin, Samir. 1997. *Capitalism in the Age of Globalization: The Management of Contemporary Society.* London: Zed Books.

Anastasiou, Harry. 2009. "Encountering Nationalism: The Contribution of Peace Studies and Conflict Resolution." In *Handbook of Conflict Analysis and Resolution,* edited by Dennis Sandole, Sean Byrne, Ingrid Sandole-Starosta, and Jessica Senehi, 30–42. London: Routledge.

Anderson, Craig A. 2001. "Heat and Violence." *Current Directions in Psychological Science* 10: 33–38.

Anderson, Elijah. 1999. *Code of the Street: Decency, Violence, and the Moral Life of the Inner City.* New York: Norton.

Anderson, Herbert, and Edward Foley. 1998. *Mighty Stories, Dangerous Rituals: Weaving Together the Human and the Divine.* San Francisco: Jossey-Bass.

Anderson, Mary. 2001. "Humanitarian NGO's in Conflict Intervention." In *Turbulent Peace: The Challenges of Managing International Conflict,* edited by Chester Crocker, Fen Osler Hampson, and Pamela Aall, 637–49. Washington, DC: United States Institute of Peace Press.

Anti-Defamation League. n.d. *Ten Year Comparison of FBI Hate Crime Statistics (2006–1997).* www.adl.org/international_affairs/osce_region_3.pdf.

Appleby, Scott. 2000. *The Ambivalence of the Sacred: Religion, Violence and Reconciliation.* Boulder, CO: Rowman and Littlefield.

Arendt, Hannah. 1994. *Eichmann in Jerusalem: A Report on the Banality of Evil.* New York: Penguin.

Arthur, Paul. 2009. "Memory Retrieval and Truth Recovery." In *Handbook of Conflict Analysis and Resolution,* edited by Dennis Sandole, Sean Byrne, Ingrid Sandole-Starosta, and Jessica Senehi, 367–80. London: Routledge.

Arway, Giles A. 2002. "Causal Factors of Violence in the Workplace: A Human Resource Professional's Perspective." In *Violence at Work,* edited by Bonnie Fisher, Vaughan Bowie, and Martin Gill, 41–58. Devon, UK: Willan Publishing.

Asch, Solomon. 1956. "Studies of Independence and Conformity: A Minority of One against a Unanimous Majority." *Psychological Monographs* 70(9): 1–70.

Avruch, Kevin. 1998. *Culture and Conflict Resolution.* Washington, DC: United States Institute of Peace Press.

Axworthy, Lloyd. 2003. *Navigating a New World: Canada's Global Future.* Toronto: Knopf.

Backstein, Karen. 1992. *The Blind Men and the Elephant*. Belair, CA: Cartwheel.

Bailey, Jane. 2003. "Private Regulation and Public Policy: Toward Effective Restriction of Internet Hate Propaganda." *McGill Law Journal* 49: 60–103.

Bales, Kevin. 1999. *Disposable People: New Slavery in the Global Economy*. Berkeley: University of California Press.

Bandura, Albert. 1977. *Social Learning Theory*. New York: Prentice Hall.

Bandyopadhyay, Mridula. 2003. "Missing Girls and Son Preference in Rural India: Looking beyond Popular Myth." *Health Care for Women International* 24(10): 910–26.

Barak, Greg. 1991. "Homelessness and the Case for Community Based Initiatives." In *Criminology as Peace-Making*, edited by Harold Pepinsky and Richard Quinney, 47–68. Bloomington: Indiana University Press.

Barash, David. 1991. *Introduction to Peace Studies*. Belmont, CA: Wadsworth.

Barash, David, and Charles Webel. 2002. *Peace and Conflict Studies*. Thousand Oaks, CA: Sage.

Barkun, Michael. 1996. *Religion and the Racist Right: The Origins of the Christian Identity Movement*. Raleigh: University of North Carolina Press.

———. 2003. *A Culture of Conspiracy: Apocalyptic Visions in Contemporary America*. Los Angeles: University of California Press.

Bar-On, Dan. 2008. *The Others within Us: Constructing Jewish-Israeli Identity*. Cambridge: Cambridge University Press.

Baron, Stephen. 2001. "Rough Justice: Street Youth and Violence." *Journal of Interpersonal Violence* 16(7): 662–78.

Bartos, Otomar, and Paul Wehr. 2002. *Using Conflict Theory*. Cambridge: Cambridge University Press.

Batista, Guilherme, Sean Byrne, Karen Jenkins, Gabriel Posados, Helena Rozlivkova, and Lieutenant Superville. Early Warning and Contingency Approaches: Shaping A Multi-dimensional Peace-building System Within Ethnic Conflicts. *Sir Lankan Journal of International Law* 13(1): 203–243.

Beah, Ishmael. 2007. *A Long Way Gone: Memoirs of a Boy Soldier*. New York: Farrar, Straus and Giroux.

Beckwith, Francis, and Todd Jones, eds. 1997. *Affirmative Action: Social Justice or Reverse Discrimination?* Amherst, NY: Prometheus.

Bekerman, Zvi. 2009. "The Ethnography of Peace Education: Some Lessons Learned from Palestinian-Jewish Integrated Education in Israel." In *Handbook of Conflict Analysis and Resolution*, edited by Dennis

Sandole, Sean Byrne, Ingrid Sandole-Starosta, and Jessica Senehi, 144–57. London: Routledge.

Belton, Neil. 1999. *The Good Listener: Helen Bamber, a Life against Cruelty.* New York: Pantheon.

Bemak, Fred, and Susan Keys. 2000. *Violent and Aggressive Youth: Intervention and Prevention Strategies for Changing Times.* Thousand Oaks, CA: Corwin.

Benda, Brent, and Robert Corwyn. 2002. "The Effect of Abuse in Childhood and in Adolescence on Violence among Adolescents." *Youth and Society* 33(3): 339–65.

Bercovitch, Jacob. 1984. *Social Conflicts and Third Parties: Strategies of Conflict Resolution.* Boulder, CO: Westview.

———, ed. 1996. *Resolving International Conflicts: The Theory and Practice of Mediation.* Boulder, CO: Lynne Rienner.

Bergeron, René. 2002. "Family Preservation: An Unidentified Approach in Elder Abuse Protection." *Families in Society: The Journal of Contemporary Human Services* 83(5/6): 547–56.

Beriker-Atiyas, Nimet. 1995. "Mediating Regional Conflicts and Negotiating Flexibility: Peace Efforts in Bosnia-Herzegovina." *Annals of the American Academy of Political and Social Science* 542: 185–201.

Bicksler, Harriet. 2002. "Teaching Peace to Children Who Play War." In *Peace Reader,* edited by E. Morris Sider and Luke Keefer Jr, 130–39. Nappanee, IN: Evangel Publishing House.

Bilmes, Linda, and Joseph Stiglitz. 2008. *The Three Trillion Dollar War: The True Cost of the Iraq Conflict.* New York: Norton.

Bjorkqvist, Kaj. 1997. "The Inevitability of Conflict but Not of Violence: Theoretical Considerations on Conflict and Aggression." In *Cultural Variations in Conflict Resolution: Alternatives to Violence,* edited by Douglas Fry and Kaj Bjorkqvist, 25–36. Mahwah, NJ: Lawrence Erlbaum.

Blalock, Hubert. 1989. *Power and Conflict: Toward a General Theory.* Newbury Park, CA: Sage.

Blumer, Herbert. 1969. *Symbolic Interactionism: Perspective and Method.* Englewood Cliffs, NJ: Prentice Hall.

Bolton, Robert. 1986. *People Skills: How to Assert Yourself, Listen to Others and Resolve Conflicts.* New York: Simon and Schuster.

Bondurant, Joan. 1988. *Conquest of Violence: The Gandhian Philosophy of Conflict.* Princeton, NJ: Princeton University Press.

Boose, Lynda E. 2002. "Crossing the River Drina: Bosnian Rape Camps, Turkish Impalement, and Serb Cultural Memory." *Signs: Journal of Women in Culture and Society* 1(28): 71–996.

Bose, Sumantra. 2007. *Contested Lands: Israel-Palestine, Kashmir, Bosnia, Cyprus, and Sri Lanka.* Cambridge: Cambridge University Press.

Bostock, William. 1997. "Language Grief: A Raw Material of Ethnic Conflict." *Nationalism and Ethnic Politics* 3(4): 94–112.

Botes, Johannes. 2003. "Conflict Transformation: A Debate over Semantics or a Crucial Shift in the Theory and Practice of Peace and Conflict Studies?" *International Journal of Peace Studies* 8(2): 1–28.

Boudreau, Tom. 1991. *Sheathing the Sword: The U.N. Secretary-General and the Prevention of International Conflict.* Santa Barbara, CA: Greenwood.

———. 2003. "Intergroup Reduction through Identity Affirmation: Overcoming the Image of the Ethnic or Enemy Other." *Peace and Conflict Studies* 10(1): 87–107.

———. 2009. "Human Agonistes: Interdisciplinary Inquiry into Ontological Agency and Human Conflict." In *Handbook of Conflict Analysis and Resolution,* edited by Dennis Sandole, Sean Byrne, Ingrid Sandole-Starosta, and Jessica Senehi, 129–41. London: Routledge.

Boulding, Elise. 1990. *Building a Global Civic Culture: Education for an Interdependent World.* Syracuse, NY: Syracuse University Press.

———. 2000. *Cultures of Peace: The Hidden Side of History.* Syracuse, NY: Syracuse University Press.

Boulding, Kenneth. 1990. *Three Faces of Power.* Newbury Park, CA: Sage.

Bowie, Vaughan, Bonnie Fisher, and Cary Cooper. 2005. *Workplace Violence: Issues, Trends, Strategies.* Devon, UK: Willan Publishing.

Bowling, Daniel, and David A. Hoffman. 2003. *Bringing Peace into the Room: How the Personal Qualities of the Mediator Impact the Process of Conflict Resolution.* San Francisco: Jossey-Bass.

Bradley, Rebekah, and Katrina Davino. 2002. "Women's Perceptions of the Prison Environment: When Prison Is 'the Safest Place I've Ever Been.'" *Psychology of Women Quarterly* 26: 351–59.

Brass, Paul R. 1997. *Theft of an Idol: Text and Context in the Representation of Collective Violence.* Princeton, NJ: Princeton University Press.

Braverman, Mark. 1999. *Preventing Workplace Violence: A Guide for Employers and Practitioners.* Thousand Oaks, CA: Sage.

Bregman, Randi. 1991. *Syracuse Area Domestic Violence: Coalition Resource Manual on Domestic Violence.* Syracuse, New York.

Brock-Utne, Birgit. 1985. *Educating for Peace: A Feminist Perspective.* New York: Pergamon.

———. 1997. "Linking the Micro and Macro in Peace and Development Studies." In *The Web of Violence: From Interpersonal to Global,* edited by Jennifer Turpin and Lester Kurtz, 149–60. Chicago: University of Illinois Press.

Bronfenbrenner, Urie. 1979. *The Ecology of Human Development*. Cambridge: Harvard University Press.

———. 1994. "Ecological Models of Human Development." In *International Encyclopedia of Education*, Vol. 3, 2nd ed., edited by Torsten Hussen and T. N. Postlethwaite. Oxford: Pergamon.

Brown, David. 1998. "Why Is the Nation-State So Vulnerable to Ethnic Nationalism?" *Nations and Nationalism* 4(1): 1–15.

Brown, Michael, ed. 1996. *The International Dimensions of Internal Conflict*. Cambridge, MA: MIT Press.

Brown, Warren. 2000. "School Children's Perceptions of Conflict: A View from the Urban Inner City." PhD dissertation, Department of Conflict Analysis and Resolution, Nova Southeastern University.

Brownell, Patricia, and Albert R. Roberts. 2002. "Domestic Violence in the workplace." In *Handbook of Violence*, edited by Albert Roberts, John Wodarski, and Lisa Rapp-Paglicci, 414–27. Hoboken, NJ: Wiley.

Brzozowski, Jodi-Anne, and Robyn Brazeau. 2008. "What Are the Trends in Self-Reported Spousal Violence in Canada?" Statistics Canada. http://www.statcan.gc.ca/pub/89-630-x/2008001/article/10661-eng.htm.

Buchwald, Emilie, Pamela Fletcher, and Martha Roth, eds. 1995. *Transforming a Rape Culture*. Minneapolis: Milkweed Editions.

Bull, Hedley. 1977. *The Anarchical Society*. New York: Columbia University Press.

Burgess, Ann, and Albert Roberts. 2002. "Violence within Families through the Life Span." In *Handbook of Violence*, edited by Albert Roberts, John Wodarski, and Lisa Rapp-Paglicci, 3–33. Hoboken, NJ: Wiley.

Burrowes, Robert. 1996. *The Strategy of Nonviolent Defense: A Gandhian Approach*. Albany: State University of New York Press.

Burton, John. 1990a. *Conflict: Human Needs Theory*. London: Macmillan.

———. 1990b. *Conflict: Resolution and Prevention Theory*. London: Macmillan.

———. 1997. *Violence Explained: The Sources of Conflict, Violence, and Crime and Their Prevention*. Manchester, UK: Manchester University Press.

Butts, Jeffrey, and Daniel Mears. 2001. "Reviving Juvenile Justice in a Get-Tough Era." *Youth and Society* 33(2): 169–98.

Byrne, Sean. 1995. "Conflict Regulation or Conflict Resolution: Third Party Intervention in the Northern Ireland Conflict; Prospects for Peace." *Terrorism and Political Violence* 7(2): 1–24.

———. 1997a. *Growing Up in a Divided Society: The Impact of Conflict on Belfast Schoolchildren.* Cranbury, NJ: Associated University Presses.

———. 1997b. "The Politics of a New Era in Northern Ireland: Belfast Schoolchildren's Images of Political Conflict and Social Change." *Mind and Human Interaction* 7(2): 52–71.

———. 1999. "Israel, Northern Ireland and South Africa at a Cross-Roads: Understanding Intergroup Conflict, Peacebuilding and Conflict Resolution in Ethnopolitical Conflicts." *International Journal of Intergroup Tensions* 28(3/4): 235–53.

———. 2000. "Power Politics as Usual in Cyprus and Northern Ireland: Divided Islands and the Roles of External Ethno-Guarantors." *Nationalism and Ethnic Politics* 6(1): 1–24.

———. 2001. "Transformational Conflict Resolution and the Northern Ireland Conflict." *International Journal on World Peace* 28(2): 3–22.

———. 2002. "Toward Tractability: The 1993 South African Record of Understanding and the 1998 Northern Ireland Good Friday Agreement." *Irish Studies in International Affairs* 13(1): 135–49.

———. 2003. "Linking Theory to Practice: How Cognitive Psychology Informs the Collaborative Problem-Solving Process for Third Parties." *International Journal of Peace Studies* 8(1): 29–44.

———. 2007. "Mired in Intractability: The Roles of External Ethno-Guarantors and Primary Mediators in Cyprus and Northern Ireland." *Conflict Resolution Quarterly* 24(2): 149–72.

———. 2009a. *Economic Assistance and the Northern Ireland Conflict: Building the Peace Dividend.* Cranbury, NJ: Associated University Presses.

———. 2009b. "The Politics of Peace and War in Northern Ireland." In *Regional and Ethnic Conflicts: Perspectives from the Front Lines,* edited by George Irani, Vamik Volkan, and Judy Carter, 212–26. New York: Prentice Hall.

Byrne, Sean, and Michael Ayulo. 1998. "External Economic Aid in Ethno-Political Conflict: A view from Northern Ireland." *Security Dialogue* 29(4): 219–33.

Byrne, Sean, and Neal Carter. 1996. "Social Cubism: Six Social Forces of Ethnoterritorial Politics in Northern Ireland and Quebec." *Peace and Conflict Studies* 3(2): 52–72.

Byrne, Sean, Neal Carter, and Jessica Senehi. 2003. "Social Cubism and Social Conflict: Analysis and Resolution." *Journal of International and Comparative Law* 8(3): 725–40.

Byrne, Sean, James Fergusson, Eyal Ben-Ari, and Kobi Michael. 2006. "Old Conflict, New Challenges: Peace-Building in Israeli-Palestinian Relations." Bison Paper 8, Centre for Defence and Security Studies. Winnipeg: University of Manitoba.

Byrne, Sean, and Cynthia Irvin. 2001. "Economic Aid and Policymaking: Building the Peace Dividend in Northern Ireland." *Policy and Politics* 29(1): 413–29.

———. 2002. "A Shared Common Sense: Perceptions of the Material Effects and Impacts of Economic Growth in Northern Ireland." *Civil Wars* 5(1): 55–86.

———, eds. Paul Dixon, Brian Polkinghorn, and Jessica Senehi, asso. eds. 2000. *Reconcilable Differences: Turning Points in Ethnopolitical Conflict.* West Hartford, CT: Kumarian.

Byrne, Sean, Cynthia Irvin, and Eyob Fissuh. 2009. "The Perception of Economic Assistance in Northern Ireland and Its Role in the Peace Process." In *Handbook of Conflict Analysis and Resolution,* edited by Dennis Sandole, Sean Byrne, Ingrid Sandole-Starosta, and Jessica Senehi, 475–94. London: Routledge.

Byrne, Sean, and Loraleigh Keashly. 2000. "Working with Ethno-Political Conflict: A Multi-Modal Approach to Conflict Intervention." *International Peacekeeping* 7(1): 97–120.

Byrne, Sean, Colleen McLeod, and Brian Polkinghorn. 2004. "University Students from Four Ethnopolitical Conflict Zones: An Exploratory Study of Images of Self and Country." *Peace and Conflict Studies* 11(2): 13–34.

Byrne, Sean, and Jessica Senehi. 2009. "Conflict Analysis and Resolution as a Multidiscipline: A Work in Progress." In *Handbook of Conflict Analysis and Resolution,* edited by Dennis Sandole, Sean Byrne, Ingrid Sandole-Starosta, and Jessica Senehi, 1–17. London: Routledge.

Byrne, Sean, Chuck Thiessen, and Eyob Fissuh. 2007. "Economic Assistance and Peacebuilding in Northern Ireland." *Peace Research: Canadian Journal of Peace and Conflict Studies,* 39 (1/2): 7–22.

Cairns, Ed. 1996. *Children and Political Violence.* Cambridge, UK: Blackwell.

Cameron, Carroll. 1995. *Domestic Violence.* Miami: Home Study Educators Inc.

Campbell, Kirsten. 2003. "Rape as a 'Crime against Humanity': Trauma, Law and Justice in the ICTY." *Journal of Human Rights* 2(4): 507–15.

Capra, Fritjof. 1996. *The Web of Life: A New Scientific Understanding of Living Systems*. New York: Anchor.

Caprioli, Mary, and Mark A. Boyer. 2001. "Gender, Violence, and International Crisis." *Journal of Conflict Resolution* 45(4): 503–18.

Caringella-MacDonald, Susan, and Drew Humphries. 1991. "Sexual Assault: Individual and Community Level Options in the Wake of Reform." In *Criminology as Peacemaking,* edited by Harold E. Pepinsky and Richard Quinney, 98–114. Bloomington: Indiana University Press.

Carment, David, and Patrick James. 1998. "Escalation of Ethnic Conflict." *International Politics* 35: 65–82.

Carnegie Commission on Preventing Deadly Conflict. 1997. *Preventing Deadly Conflict*. Washington, DC: Carnegie Corporation of New York.

Carsten, F. L. 1969. *The Rise of Fascism*. Berkeley: University of California Press.

Carter, Neal, and Sean Byrne. 2000. "The Dynamics of Social Cubism: A View from Northern Ireland and Quebec." In *Reconcilable Differences: Turning Points in Ethnopolitical Conflicts,* edited by Sean Byrne and Cynthia Irvin, Paul Dixon, Brian Polkingham, and Jessica Senehi, assoc. eds., 41–65. West Hartford, CT: Kumarian.

Carter, Judy, George Irani, and Vamik Volkan, eds. 2009. *Regional and Ethnic Conflicts: Perspectives from the Front Lines*. New York: Prentice Hall.

Chappell, Duncan, and Vittorio Di Martino. 2001. *Violence at Work*. International Labour Organization. http://www.ilo.org/public/libdoc /ilo/2006/106B09_110_engl.pdf.

Chasin, Barbara. 1998. *Inequality and Violence in the United States*. Amherst, NY: Humanity Books.

Cheldelin, Sandra, Daniel Druckman, and Larissa Fast, eds. 2003. *Conflict: From Analysis to Intervention*. New York: Continuum.

Chiarello, Christine, Jessica Senehi, and Sara Nuding. 1987. "Semantic Priming with Abstract and Concrete Words: Differential Asymmetry May Be Post-Lexical." *Brain and Language* 28: 136–62.

Chiarello, Christine, Jessica Senehi, and Marie Soulier. 1986. "Viewing Conditions and Hemispheric Asymmetry for the Lexical Decision." *Neuropsychologia* 24: 521–30.

Christie, Daniel J. 2001. "Peacebuilding Approaches to Social Justice." In *Peace, Conflict and Violence: Peace Psychology for the 21st Century,* edited by Daniel J. Christie, Richard V. Wagner, and Deborah DuNann Winter, 277–81. Upper Saddle River, NJ: Prentice Hall.

Christie, Daniel J., Wagner, Richard V., and Deborah DuNann Winter. 2001. "Introduction to Peace Psychology." In *Peace, Conflict and*

*Violence: Peace Psychology for the 21st Century,* edited by Daniel J. Christie, Richard V. Wagner, and Deborah DuNann Winter, 1–14. Upper Saddle River, NJ: Prentice Hall.

Clinard, Marshall, and Peter Yeager. 1980. *Corporate Crime.* New York: Free Press.

———. 1990. *Corporate Corruption: The Abuse of Power.* New York: Praeger.

Coffey, Brian, and Stephen Woolworth. 2004. "Destroy the Scum, and Then Neuter Their Families: The Web Forum as a Vehicle for Community Discourse?" *Social Science Journal* 41: 1–14.

Cohen, Raymond. 1997. *Negotiating across Cultures: International Communication in an Interdependent World.* Washington, DC: United States Institute of Peace Press.

Cohn, I., and G. Goodwin-Gill. 1994. *Child Soldiers: The Role of Children in Armed Conflicts.* New York: Oxford University Press.

Coleman, James, ed. 1994. *The Criminal Elite: The Sociology of White-Collar Crime.* 3rd ed. New York: St. Martin's.

Coleman, Valerie. 1994. "Lesbian Battering: The Relationship between Personality and the Perpetration of Violence." *Violence and Victims* 2: 139–52.

Coles, Robert. 1986. *The Political Life of Children.* Boston: Houghton Mifflin.

Conly, Catherine, Patricia Kelly, Paul Mahanna, and Lynn Warner. 1993. *Street Gangs: Current Knowledge and Strategies.* Washington, DC: National Institute of Justice.

Conroy, John. 2001. *Unspeakable Acts, Ordinary People: The Dynamics of Torture.* Berkeley: University of California Press.

Cooper, Rabbi Abraham. 1998. *The New Lexicon of Hate: The Changing Tactics, Language and Symbols of America's Extremists.* Los Angeles: Simon Wiesenthal Centre.

Cortright, David. 2006. *Beyond Gandhi: Nonviolence for an Age of Terrorism.* Boulder, CO: Paradigm.

Cortright, David, and George Lopez, eds. 2000. *The Sanctions Decade: Assessing UN Strategies in the 1990s.* Boulder, CO: Lynne Rienner.

Coser, Lewis. 1965. *The Function of Social Conflict.* Glencoe, IL: Free Press.

Covey, Jack, Michael Oziedzic, and Leonard Hawley. 2005. *The Quest for Viable Peace: International Intervention and Strategies for Conflict Transformation.* Washington, DC: United States Institute of Peace Press.

Curle, Adam. 1971. *Making Peace.* London: Tavistock.

Daiute, Colette. 2003. "Negotiating Violence Prevention." *Journal of Social Issues* 59(1): 83–101.

Darby, John. 2001. *The Effects of Violence on Peace Processes.* Washington, DC: United States Institute of Peace Press.

Davis, James. 1991. *Who Is Black? One Nation's Definition.* Pittsburgh: Pennsylvania State University.

DeKeseredy, Walter, and Martin Schwartz. 1991. "British Left Realism on the Abuse of Women." In *Criminology as Peacemaking,* edited by Harold E. Pepinsky and Richard Quinney, 154–72. Bloomington: Indiana University Press.

de Lauretis, Teresa. 1987. *Technologies of Gender.* Bloomington: Indiana University Press.

de Mesquita, Bueno Bruce. 1981. *The War Trap.* New Haven, CT: Yale University Press.

Denenberg, Richard, and Mark Braverman. 2001. *The Violence-Prone Workplace: A New Approach to Dealing with Hostile, Threatening, and Uncivil Behavior.* Ithaca, NY: Cornell University Press.

de Silva, K. M. 1997. "Sri Lanka: Surviving Ethnic Strife." *Journal of Democracy* 8(1): 97–111.

Deutsch, Karl. 1957. *Political Community and the North Atlantic Area: International Organization in the Light of Historical Experience.* Princeton, NJ: Princeton University Press.

Deutsch, Morton, Patrick Coleman, and Eric Marcus, eds. 2006. *The Handbook of Conflict Resolution: Theory and Practice.* San Francisco: Jossey-Bass.

Diamond, Louise, and John McDonald. 1996. *Multi-Track Diplomacy: A Systems Approach to Peace.* West Hartford, CT: Kumarian.

Diehl, Paul, and Joseph Lepgold, eds. 2003. *Regional Conflict Management.* Boulder, CO: Rowman and Littlefield.

Dixon, Paul. 2000. *Northern Ireland: Power, Ideology and Reality.* London: Macmillan.

———. 2007. *The Northern Ireland Peace Process: Choregraphy and Theatrical Politics.* London: Routledge.

Dodge, C. P., and M. Raundalen. 1987. *War, Violence, and Children in Uganda.* Oslo: Norwegian University Press.

Doi, Karyn. 2001. "America's Anti-Violence Campaign: The Use of Mediation to Reduce the Incidence of Workplace Violence." *Risk: Health, Safety & Environment* 12(1/2): 133–41.

Doyle, Michael. 2001. "War Making and Peace Making? The United Nations' Post–Cold War Record." In *Turbulent Peace: The Challenges of Managing International Conflict,* edited by Chester Crocker, Fen

Osler Hampson, and Pamela Aall, 529–60. Washington, DC: United States Institute of Peace Press.

Duhart, Detis. 2001. "Violence in the Workplace, 1993–1999." U.S. Department of Justice, National Crime Victimization Survey: Office of Justice Programs, Bureau of Justice Statistics. http://bjs.ojp.usdoj.gov/content/pub/pdf/vw99.pdf.

DuNann Winter, Deborah, and Dana C. Leighton. 2001. "Structural Violence." In *Peace, Conflict and Violence: Peace Psychology for the 21st Century,* edited by Richard V. Wagner, Deborah DuNann Winter, and Daniel J. Christie, 99–101. Upper Saddle River, NJ: Prentice Hall.

Dunn, David. 2004. *From Power Politics to Conflict Resolution: Assessing the Work of John Burton.* London: Palgrave Macmillan.

Dutton, Donald. 2007. *The Abusive Personality: Violence and Control in Intimate Relationships.* 2nd ed. New York: Guilford.

Eckhardt, Christopher, Julia Babcock, and Susan Homack. 2004. "Partner Assaultive Men and the Stages and Processes of Change." *Journal of Family Violence* 19(2): 81–93.

Edelman, Marian Wright. 1992. *The Measure of Our Success: A Letter to My Children.* New York: Harper.

Edelstein, Jillian. 2002. *Truth and Lies: Stories from the Truth and Reconciliation Commission in South Africa.* New York: New Press.

Elders, Glenn. 1974. *Children of the Great Depression.* Chicago: University of Chicago Press.

Elias, Robert. 1997. "A Culture of Violent Solutions." In *The Web of Violence: From Interpersonal to Global,* edited by Lester Jennifer Turpin and Lester R. Kurtz, 117–48. Chicago: University of Illinois Press.

Ellison, Christopher, and John Bartwoski. 1997. "Religion and the Legitimation of Violence: Conservative Protestantism and Corporal Punishment." In *The Web of Violence: From Interpersonal to Global,* edited by Lester Jennifer Turpin and Lester R. Kurtz, 45–68. Chicago: University of Illinois Press.

Elsass, Peter. 1997. *Treating Victims of Torture and Violence: Theoretical, Cross-Cultural, and Clinical Implications.* New York: New York University Press.

Englander, Elizabeth. 2007. *Understanding Violence.* 3rd ed. Mahwah, NJ: Lawrence Erlbaum.

Enloe, Cynthia. 1993. *The Morning After: Sexual Politcs at the End of the Cold War.* Berkley: University of California Press.

———. 2000. *Manoeuvres: The International Politics of Militarizing Women's Lives*. Berkeley: University of California Press.

———. 2001. *Bananas, Beaches, and Bases: Making Feminist Sense of International Politics*. 2nd ed. Berkeley: University of California Press.

Erikson, Erik. 1950. *Childhood and Society*. New York: Norton.

Escobar, Arturo. 1995. *Encountering Development: The Making and Unmaking of the Third World*. Princeton, NJ: Princeton University Press.

Espiritu, Antonia. 2004. "Racial Diversity and Hate Crime Incidents." *Social Science Journal* 41: 197–208.

Fanning, Bryan. 2002. *Racism and Social Change in the Republic of Ireland*. Manchester, UK: Manchester University Press.

Fanon, Frantz. 1965. *The Wretched of the Earth*. Boston: Beacon.

Federal Bureau of Investigation. 1997. "Trends in Anti-Gay Violence: Number of Incidents, Offenses, Victims, and Offenders by Bias Motivation." http://www.fbi.gov/about-us/cjis/ucr/hate-crime/1997.

Ferguson, Niall. 2006. *War of the World: Twentieth-Century Conflict and the Descent of the West*. New York: Penguin.

Finlayson, Alan. 1988. "Psychology, Psychoanalysis and Theories of Nationalism." *Nations and Nationalism* 4(2): 145–62.

Fisher, Bonnie, and Elaine Gunnison. 2001. "Violence in the Workplace: Gender Similarities and Differences." *Journal of Criminal Justice* 9(2): 145–55.

Fisher, Roger, and William Ury. 1981. *Getting to Yes: Negotiating Agreement without Giving In*. New York: Penguin.

Fisher, Ronald J. 1997. *Interactive Conflict Resolution: Pioneers, Potential, and Prospects*. Syracuse, NY: Syracuse University Press.

Fisk, Robert. 2005. *The Great War for Civilization: The Conquest of the Middle East*. London: UK General Books.

Fitzduff, Mari. 1996. *Beyond Violence: Conflict Resolution Processes in Northern Ireland*. Tokyo: United Nations University.

Fitzgerald, Louise, and Sandra Shullman. 1993. "Sexual Harassment: A Research Analysis and Agenda for the 1990s." *Journal of Vocational Behavior* 42(1): 5–27.

Fitzgerald, Louise, Fritz Drasgow, Charles Hulin, Michele Gelfand, and Vicki Magley. 1997. "Antecedents and Consequences of Sexual Harassment in Organizations: A Test of an Integrated Model." *Journal of Applied Psychology* 82(4): 578–89.

Foer, Franklin. 2004. *How Soccer Explains the World: An Unlikely Theory of Globalization*. New York: Harper Perennial.

Ford, Nicholas. 1990. "The Social Context of the Emergence of HIV in Thailand." *Journal of Population and Social Studies* 2(2): 223–37.

Foucault, Michel. 1979. *Discipline and Punish: The Birth of the Prison.* New York: Vintage.

———. 1993. *The Archaeology of Knowledge and the Discourse on Language.* New York: Barnes and Noble. First published 1972.

Frankl, Viktor. 1984. *Man's Search for Meaning.* New York: Simon and Schuster.

Fredrickson, George. 1995. *Black Liberation: A Comparative History of Black Ideologies in the United States and South Africa.* Oxford: Oxford University Press.

Freire, Paulo. 1999. *Pedagogy of the Oppressed.* New York: Continuum. First published 1970.

Freud, Sigmund. 1949. *An Outline of Psycho-Analysis.* New York: Norton.

Fry, Douglas. 2006. *The Human Potential for Peace: An Anthropological Challenge to Assumptions about War and Violence.* Oxford: Oxford University Press.

Funk, Nathan, and Abdul Aziz Said. 2008. *Islam and Peacemaking in the Middle East.* Boulder, CO: Lynne Rienner.

Gallant, Michelle. 2009. "Law and Legal Processes in Resolving International Conflicts." In *Handbook of Conflict Analysis and Resolution,* edited by Dennis Sandole, Sean Byrne, Ingrid Sandole-Starosta, and Jessica Senehi, 394–404. London: Routledge.

Galtung, Johan. 1985. "Twenty-Five Years of Peace Research: Ten Challenges and Some Responses." *Journal of Peace Research* 22(2): 141–58.

———. 1990. "Cultural Violence." *Journal of Peace Research* 27(3): 291–305.

———. 1996. *Peace by Peaceful Means: Peace and Conflict, Development and Civilization.* Thousand Oaks, CA: Sage.

———. 2006. "Theoretical Challenges of Peace Building with and for Youth." In *Troublemakers or Peacemakers? Youth and Post-Accord Peace Building,* edited by Siobhán McEvoy-Levy, 259–80. Notre Dame, IN: Notre Dame University Press.

———. 2009. "Toward a Conflictology: The Quest for Transdisciplinarity." In *Handbook of Conflict Analysis and Resolution,* edited by Dennis Sandole, Sean Byrne, Ingrid Sandole-Starosta, and Jessica Senehi, 509–22. London: Routledge.

Galtung, Johan, Carl G. Jacobsen, and Kai Frithjof Brand-Jacobsen. 2002. *Searching for Peace: The Road to TRANSCEND.* London: Pluto.

Gandhi, Mohandas. 1992. "Ahimsa, or the Way of Nonviolence." In *A Peace Reader: Essential Readings on War, Justice, Nonviolence and World Order,* edited by Joseph Fahey and Richard Armstrong, 171–76. Mahwah, NJ: Paulist Press.

Garbarino, James. 1999. *Lost Boys: Why Our Sons Turn Violent and How We Can Save Them.* New York: Anchor Books.

———. 2003. *And Words Can Hurt Forever: How to Protect Adolescents from Bullying, Harassment, and Emotional Violence.* New York: Simon and Schuster.

Garbarino, James, and Kathleen Kostelny. 1997. "What Children Can Tell Us about Living in a War Zone." In *Children in a Violent Society,* edited by J. D. Osofsky, 32–41. New York: Guilford.

Gates, Henry Louis, ed. 1986. *"Race," Writing, and Difference.* Chicago: University of Chicago Press.

Gaudiosi, John. 2009. *Child Maltreatment.* Washington, DC: U.S. Department of Health and Human Services, Administration on Children, Youth and Families. http://www.acf.hhs.gov/programs/cb/pubs/cm09/cm09.pdf.

Geller, Daniel, and J. David Singer. 1998. *Nations at War: A Scientific Study of International Conflict.* Cambridge: Cambridge University Press.

Gelles, Richard J. 1997. *Intimate Violence in Families.* Thousand Oaks, CA: Sage.

Gelles, Richard J., and Donileen Loeske, eds. 1993. *Current Controversies on Family Violence.* Newbury Park, CA: Sage.

Gelles, Richard J., and Murray A. Strauss. 1989. *Intimate Violence: The Causes and Consequences of Abuse in the American Family.* New York: Touchstone Books.

Gerstenfeld, Phyllis Behrens. 2003. *Hate Crimes: Causes, Controls, and Controversies.* London: Sage.

Gerstenfeld, Phyllis Behrens, and Diana R. Grant. 2003. *Crimes of Hate: Selected Readings.* London: Sage.

Gill, Martin, Bonnie Fisher, and Vaughan Bowie. 2002. *Violence at Work: Causes, Patterns, and Prevention.* Devon, UK: Willan.

Gilligan, Carol. 1993. *In a Different Voice: Psychological Theory and Women's Development.* Boston: Harvard University Press.

Gilpin, Robert. 1983. *War and Change in World Politics.* Cambridge: Cambridge University Press.

Girard, Renée. 1979. *Violence and the Sacred.* Baltimore: Johns Hopkins University Press.

Giulianotti, Richard, Norman Bonney, and Mike Hepworth. 1994. *Football, Violence and Social Identity.* New York: Routledge.

Glenn, John. 1997. "Nations and Nationalism: Marxist Approaches to the Subject." *Nationalism and Ethnic Politics* 3(2): 79–100.

Golden, John, Craig Johnson, and Rebecca Lopez. 2002. "Sexual Harassment in the Workplace: Exploring the Effects of Attractiveness on Perception of Harassment." *Sex Roles* 45 (11/12): 767–84.

Goldstein, Joshua. 2003. *War and Gender: How Gender Shapes the War System and Vice Versa.* Cambridge: Cambridge University Press.

Goldstone, Jack, Ted Robert Gurr, and Farrokh Moshiri. 1992. *Revolutions of the Late Twentieth Century.* London: HarperCollins.

Goleman, Daniel. 1995. *Emotional Intelligence.* New York: Bantam.

———. 1997. *Emotional Intelligence: Why It Can Matter More Than IQ.* New York: Bantam.

Green, Donald, Dara Strolovitch, Janelle Wong, and Robert Bailey. 2001. "Measuring Gay Populations and Antigay Hate Crime." *Social Science Quarterly* 82(2): 281–96.

Griffin, Ricky, and Anne O'Leary-Kelly, eds. 2004. *The Dark Side of Organizational Behavior.* San Francisco: Jossey-Bass.

Griffin, Susan. 1992. *A Chorus of Stones: The Private Life of War.* New York: Anchor.

Grossman, Dave, and Gloria DeGaetano. 1999. *Stop Teaching Our Kids to Kill: A Call to Action against TV, Movie, and Video Game Violence.* New York: Crown.

Guelke, Adrian. 1988. *Northern Ireland: The International Perspective.* Dublin: Macmillan.

Gugelberger, G., and M. Kearney. 1991. "Voices for the Voiceless: Testimonial Literature in Latin America." *Latin American Perspectives* 18(3): 3–14.

Gunder Frank, Andre. 1971. *Capitalism and Underdevelopment in Latin America.* London: Penguin.

Gurr, Ted Robert. 1970. *Why Men Rebel.* Princeton, NJ: Princeton University Press.

———. 1993. *Minorities at Risk: A Global View of Ethnopolitical Conflicts.* Washington, DC: United States Institute of Peace.

Haas, Ernest. 1976. *The Uniting of Europe: Political, Social and Economic Forces, 1950–1957.* Stanford, CA: Stanford University Press.

Hacker, Andrew. 1995. *Two Nations: Black and White, Separate, Hostile, Unequal.* New York: Ballantine.

Hagan, John, and Holly Foster. 2001. "Youth Violence and the End of Adolescence." *American Sociological Review* 66(6): 874–99.

Hanh, Thich Nhat, and Daniel Berrigan. 1993. *Love in Action: Writings on Nonviolent Change.* Berkeley: Parallax.

Harding, Sandra, ed. 1987. *Feminism and Methodology.* Bloomington: Indiana University Press.

Harper, Gary. 2004. *The Joy of Conflict Resolution: Transforming Victims, Villains, and Heroes in the Workplace and at Home.* Gabriola Island, British Columbia: New Society Publishers.

Harris, Ian, and Mary Lee Morrison Harris. 2003. *Peace Education.* Jefferson, NC: McFarland.

Harris, M. Kay. 1991. *Moving into the New Millennium.* Bloomington: Indiana University Press.

Harris, Rosemary. 1972. *Prejudice and Tolerance in Ulster: A Study of Neighbors and 'Strangers' in a Border Community.* Manchester, UK: Manchester University Press.

Haufler, Virginia. 2001. "Is There a Role for Business in Conflict Management?" In *Turbulent Peace: The Challenges of Managing International Conflict,* edited by Chester Crocker, Fen Osler Hampson, and Pamela Aall, 659–76. Washington, DC: United States Institute of Peace Press.

Hechter, M. 1975. *Internal Colonialism: The Celtic Fringe in British National Development, 1536–1966.* London: Routledge.

Herek, Gregory, and Kevin Berrill. 1992. *Hate Crimes: Confronting Violence against Lesbians and Gay Men.* Thousand Oaks, CA: Sage.

Herman, Judith. 2001. *Trauma and Recovery: The Aftermath of Violence—From Domestic Abuse to Political Terror.* New York: Basic Books.

Hermann, Margaret. 1986. *Political Psychology: Contemporary Problems and Issues.* San Francisco: Jossey-Bass.

———. 1999. "Exploring Deeper Wisdoms of Mediation: Notes from the Edge." *Peace and Conflict Studies* 6(1): 7–19.

———. 2008. *Advances in Political Psychology: Managing Crises in an Uncertain World.* Amsterdam: Elseiver Science.

Hirschsohn, P. 1996. "Negotiating a Democratic Order in South Africa: Learning from Mediation and Industrial Relations." *Negotiation Journal* 12(2): 138–49.

Hobbes, Thomas. 1904. *Leviathan: Or the Matter, Forme, and Power of a Commonwealth, Ecclesiasticall and Civill.* Cambridge: Cambridge University Press.

Hocker, Joyce, and William Wilmot. 1995. *Interpersonal Conflict.* Madison, WI: Brown and Benchmark.

Hoffman, Kristi L., and John Edwards. 2004. "An Integrated Theoretical Model of Sibling Violence and Abuse." *Journal of Family Violence* 19(3): 185–200.

Homer-Dixon, Thomas. 2001. *The Ingenuity Gap: Can We Solve the Problems of the Future?* New York: Vintage.

———. 2007. *The Upside of Down: Catastrophe, Creativity and the Renewal of Civilization.* New York: Vintage.

Honey-Knopp, Fay. 1991. "Community Solutions to Sexual Violence: Feminist/Abolitionist Perspectives." In *Criminology as Peacemaking,* edited by Harold E. Pepinsky and Richard Quinney, 181–93. Bloomington: Indiana University Press.

Honneth, Axel. 1995. *The Struggle for Recognition: The Moral Grammar of Social Conflict.* Cambridge, MA: MIT Press.

Honneth, Axel, and John Farrell. 1997. "Recognition and Moral Obligation." *Social Research* 64(1): 16–35.

hooks, bell. 1990. *Yearning: Race, Gender, and Cultural Politics.* Boston: South End.

Horowitz, Donald. 2000. *Ethnic Groups in Conflict.* Berkeley: University of California Press.

Howard, Donna, and Min Qi Wang. 2003. "Psychosocial Factors Associated with Adolescent Boys' Reports of Dating Violence." *Adolescence* 38 (5): 519–33.

Howard, Jack. 2002. "Workplace Violence in Organizations: An Exploratory Study of Organizational Prevention Techniques." *Employee Responsibility and Rights Journal* 13(2): 57–75.

Howell, James. 2003. *Preventing and Reducing Juvenile Delinquency: A Comprehensive Framework.* Thousand Oaks, CA: Sage.

Hoy, Paula. 1998. *Players and Issues in International Aid.* West Hartford, CT: Kumarian.

Huggins, Martha, and Myriam Mesquita. 2000. "Civic Invisibility, Marginality, and Moral Exclusion: The Murders of Street Youth in Brazil." In *Children of the Streets of the Americas: Globalization, Homelessness and Education in the United States, Brazil and Cuba,* edited by Roslyn Arlin Mickelson, 157–270. New York: Routledge.

Irvin, Cynthia. 1999. *Militant Nationalism: Between Movement and Party in Northern Ireland and the Basque Country.* Duluth: University of Minnesota Press.

Janis, Irving. 1972. *Victims of Groupthink.* Boston: Houghton Mifflin.

Jenness, Valerie. 2007. "The Emergence, Content and Institutionalization of Hate Crime Law: How a Diverse Policy Community Produced a Modern Legal Fact." *Annual Review of Law and Social Science* 3(1): 141–60.

Jenson, Jeffrey, and Matthew Howard, eds. 1999. *Youth Violence: Current Research and Recent Practice Innovations*. Washington, DC: National Association of Social Workers Press.

Jeong, Ho-Won. 2000a. *Peace and Conflict Studies: An Introduction*. London: Ashgate.

———, ed. 2000b. *The New Agenda for Peace Research*. Aldershot, UK: Ashgate.

———. 2005. *Peacebuilding in Post-Conflict Societies: Strategy and Process*. Boulder, CO: Lynne Reinner.

———. 2008. *Understanding Conflict and Conflict Analysis*. Thousand Oaks, CA: Sage.

———. 2009. *Conflict Management and Resolution: An Introduction*. London: Routledge.

Jervis, Robert. 1976. *Perception and Misperception in International Politics*. Princeton, NJ: Princeton University Press.

Johnson, D., and R. Johnson. 1996. "Conflict Resolution and Peer Mediation Programs in Elementary and Secondary Schools: A Review of the Research." *Review of Educational Research* 66(4): 459–506.

Jones, William. 1997. *Is God a White Racist? A Preamble to Black Theology*. Boston: Beacon.

Junhong, Chu. 2001. "Prenatal Sex Determination and Sex-Selective Abortion in Rural Central China." *Population and Development Review* 2(27): 259–81.

Kagan, Donald. 1995. *On the Origins of War*. New York: Doubleday.

Kaldor, Mary. 2007. *New and Old Wars: Organized Violence in a Global Era*. Palo Alto, CA: Stanford University Press.

Karp, David, and Beau Breslin. 2001. "Restorative Justice in School Communities." *Youth and Society* 33(2): 249–72.

Katz, Neil, and John Lawyer. 1985. *Communication and Conflict Resolution Skills*. Dubuque, IA: Kendall/Hunt.

Kaufman, Edy, and Manuel Hassassian. 2009. "Understanding Our Israeli-Palestinian Conflict and Searching for Its Resolution." In *Regional and Ethnic Conflicts: Perspectives from the Front Lines,* edited by George Irani, Vamik Volkan, and Judy Carter, 87–129. New York: Prentice Hall.

Kaufman, Stuart. 2001. *Modern Hatreds: The Symbolic Politics of Ethnic War*. Ithaca, NY: Cornell University Press.

Keashly, Loraleigh, and Ron Fisher. 1996. "A Contingency Perspective on Conflict Interventions: Theoretical and Practical Considerations." In *Resolving International Conflicts: The Theory and Practice of Mediation,* edited by Jacob Bercovitch, 235–63. Boulder, CO: Lynne Rienner.

Keashly, Loraleigh, and Steve Harvey. 2006. "Workplace Emotional Abuse." In *Handbook of Workplace Violence,* edited by Kevin Kelloway, Julian Barling, and Joseph Hurrell, 95–120. Thousand Oaks, CA: Sage.

Keashly, Loraleigh, Virginia Trott, and Lynne MacLean. 1994. "Abusive Behavior in the Workplace: A Preliminary Investigation." *Violence and Victims* 9(4): 341–57.

Keethaponcalon, Soospaili. 2001. "Underage Soldiers and Intervention: The Global Challenge of Violence Reduction and Conflict Resolution." PhD dissertation, Department of Conflict Analysis and Resolution, Nova Southeastern University.

Kegley, Charles, and Eugene Wittkopf. 2006. *World Politics: Trend and Transformation.* Florence, KY: Wadsworth.

Kelman, Herbert. 1991. "Interactive Problem-Solving: The Uses and Limits of a Therapeutic Model for the Resolution of International Conflicts." In *The Psychodynamics of International Relationships,* edited by Joseph Montville, Vamik Volkan, and Demetrios Julius, 145–60. Boston: Lexington Books.

———. 1997. "Negotiating National Identity and Self-Determination in Ethnic Conflicts: The Choice between Pluralism and Ethnic Cleansing." *Negotiation Journal* 13(4): 327–40.

Kelman, Herbert, and Stephen Cohen. 1976. "The Problem-Solving Workshop: A Social Psychological Contribution to the Resolution of International Conflict." *Journal of Peace Research* 13(2): 79–90.

Kennedy, Daniel, Robert Homant, and Michael Homant. 2004. "Perception of Injustice as a Predictor of Support for Workplace Aggression." *Journal of Business and Psychology* 18(3): 323–36.

Kenny, James. 2002. "The Process of Employee Violence: The Building of a Workplace Explosion." In *Violence at Work: Causes, Patterns and Prevention,* edited by Bonnie Fisher, Martin Gill, and Vaughan Bowie, 76–89. Devon, UK: Willan.

Keohane, Robert Owen, and Joseph Nye. 1989. *Power and Interdependence.* New York: Foresman.

Kerr, John. 1994. *Understanding Soccer Hooliganism.* Buckingham, UK: Open University Press.

Kilbourne, Jean. 1995. *Pack of Lies.* Cambridge, MA: Media Education Foundation.

King, Martin Luther, Jr. 1958. *Stride toward Freedom: The Montgomery Story.* San Francisco: Harper.

———. 1992. *I Have a Dream: Writings and Speeches That Changed the World.* San Francisco: Harper.

Kinney, Joseph. 1992. *Breaking Point: The Workplace Violence Epidemic and What to Do about It*. Chicago: National Safe Workplace Institute.

Kira, Ibrahim, Adnan Hammad, Linda Lewandowski, Thomas Templin, Vidya Ramaswamy, Bulent Ozkan, and Jamal Mohanesh. 2007. "Health Issues in the Arab American Community: The Physical and Mental Status of Iraqi Refugees and Its Etiology." *Ethnicity and Disease* 17(2): 3–79.

Kivel, Paul. 1997. *Uprooting Racism: How White People Can Work for Racial Justice*. Gabriola Island, British Columbia: New Society Publishers.

Klare, Michael. 2002. *Resource Wars: The New Landscape of Global Conflict*. New York: Owl Books.

———. 2008. *Rising Powers, Shrinking Planet: The New Geopolitics of Energy*. New York: Henry Holt Metropolitan.

Klein, Ruth, and Anita Bromberg. 2003. *Audit of Anti-SemiticIncidents: Patterns of Prejudice in Canada*. Toronto: League for Human Rights of B'Nai Brith Canada.

Knight, Nick. 1983. *Skinhead*. New York: Omnibus.

Koo, Katrina Lee. 2002. "Confronting a Disciplinary Blindness: Women, War and Rape in the International Politics of Security." *Australian Journal of Political Science* 3(37): 525–36.

Kozol, Jonathan. 1991. *Savage Inequalities: Children in America's Schools*. New York: Crown.

Kriesberg, Louis. 1998. *Constructive Conflicts: From Escalation to Resolution*. Lanham, MD: Rowman and Littlefield.

Kulchyski, Peter. 2005. *Like the Sound of a Drum: Aboriginal Cultural Politics in Denendeh and Nunavut*. Winnipeg: University of Manitoba Press.

Kuypers, Joseph. 1992. *Man's Will to Hurt: Investigating the Causes, Supports and Varieties of His Violence*. Halifax, Nova Scotia: Fernwood Books.

Kwan Koon, Young. 2003. "Introduction: Power Cycle Theory and the Practice of International Relations." *International Political Science Review* 24(1): 5–12.

Landau, Sy, Barbara Landau, and Daryl Landau. 2001. *From Conflict to Creativity: How Resolving Workplace Disagreements Can Inspire Innovation and Productivity*. San Francisco: Jossey-Bass.

Langhinrichsen-Rohling, Jennifer, Mark Hankla, and Colleen Dostal Stormberg. 2004. "The Relationship Behavior Networks of Young

Adults: A Test of the Intergenerational Transmission of Violence Hypothesis." *Journal of Family Violence* 19(3): 139–51.

Laue, Jim, and Gerald Cormick. 1978. "The Ethics of Intervention in Community Disputes." In *The Ethics of Social Intervention,* edited by Herbert Kelman, Gordon Bermant, and Donal Warwick, 205–32. Washington, DC: Halsted.

Laurer, Teresa M. 2002. *The Truth about Rape.* Gold River, CA: RapeRecovery.com. http://www.raperecovery.com/pdf_files/truth_about_rape_preview.pdf.

Leather, Phil, Tom Cox, and Bill Farnsworth. 1990. "Violence at Work: An Issue for the 1990s." *Work and Stress* 4(1): 3–5.

Leatherman, Janie, and Nadezhda Griffin. 2009. "Ethnical and Gendered Dilemmas of Moving from Emergency Response to Development in 'Failed' States." In *Handbook of Conflict Analysis and Resolution,* edited by Dennis Sandole, Sean Byrne, Ingrid Sandole-Starosta, and Jessica Senehi, 352–66. London: Routledge.

Lederach, John Paul. 1995. *Peace by Peaceful Means: Conflict Transformation across Societies.* Syracuse, NY: Syracuse University Press.

———. 1997. *Building Peace: Sustainable Reconciliation in Divided Societies.* Washington, DC: United States Institute of Peace Press.

———. 1999. *The Journey toward Reconciliation.* Scottsdale, Windsor, Ontario: Herald.

———. 2005. *The Moral Imagination: The Art and Soul of Building Peace.* Oxford: Oxford University Press.

Ledray, Linda. 1994. *Recovering from Rape.* New York: Owl Books.

Lenin, Vladamir. 1969. *Imperialism and the Highest Stage of Capitalism.* New York: International Publishers.

Lentz, Theodore, ed. 1976. *Humanatroitism: Human Interests in Peace and Survival.* St. Louis: Future Press.

Levitt, Steven, and Stephen Dubner. 2009. *Freakonomics: A Rogue Economist Explores the Hidden Side of Everything.* New York: Harper Perennial.

Lieberfeld, Daniel. 1999. "Conflict Ripeness Revisited: The South African and Israeli/Palestinian Cases." *Negotiation Journal* 15(1): 63–82.

Liebow, Elliot. 1967. *Tally's Corner: A Study of Negro Streetcorner Men.* Boston: Little, Brown.

Lifton, Robert Jay. 1997. "Doubling: The Faustian Bargain." In *The Web of Violence: From Interpersonal to Global,* edited by Jennifer Turpin and Lester Kurtz, 29–44. Chicago: University of Illinois Press.

Little, David. 1994. *Sri Lanka: The Invention of Enmity.* Washington, DC: United States Institute of Peace Press.

Loewenberg, Peter. 1971. "The Psychohistorical Origins of the Nazi Youth Cohort." *American Historical Review* 76(5): 1457–502.

Loffreda, Beth. 2001. *Losing Matt Sheppard: Life and Politics in the Aftermath of Anti-Gay Murder.* New York: Columbia University Press.

Lorenz, Konrad. 1937. "Imprinting." *Auk* 54(1): 245–73.

Lundy, Sandra. 1993. "Abuse That Dare Not Speak Its Name: Assisting Victims of Lesbian and Gay Domestic Violence in Massachusetts." *New England Law Review* 28(1): 273–311.

Macbeth, Fiona, and Nic Fine. 1995. *Playing with Fire: Creative Conflict Resolution for Young Adults.* Philadelphia: New Society Publishers.

MacGinty, Roger. 2001. "Ethno-National Conflict and Hate Crime." *American Behavioral Scientist* 45(4): 639–53.

———. 2006. *No War, No Peace: The Rejuvenation of Stalled Peace Processes and Peace Accords.* Basingstoke, UK: Palgrave Macmillan.

MacGinty, Roger, and Andrew Williams. 2009. *Conflict and Development.* London: Routledge.

Machiavelli, Niccolo. 1977. *The Prince.* New York: Norton.

MacLeod, Jay. 1995. *Ain't No Makin' It: Aspirations and Attainment in a Low-Income Neighborhood.* Boulder, CO: Westview.

Mader, Gerald, ed. 1995. *Declaration of Schlaining against Racism, Violence and Discrimination.* Stadtschlaining, Austria: A-7461 Commission for UNESCO and European University Centre for Peace Studies.

Marable, Manning. 1997. *Black Liberation in Conservative America.* Boston: South End.

Margalit, Avishai. 1996. *The Decent Society.* Cambridge: Harvard University Press.

Marten, G. G. 2004. *Human Ecology: Basic Concepts for Sustainable Development.* London: Earthscan.

Maslow, Abraham. 1967. "Self-Actualization and Beyond." In *Challenges of Humanistic Psychology,* edited by James Bugental, 278–81. New York: McGraw-Hill.

———. 1968. *Toward a Psychology of Science.* New York: Van Nostrand.

Mason, Alex. 2004. "Predicting Depression, Social Phobia, and Violence in Early Adulthood from Childhood Behavior Problems." *Journal of American Academy of Childhood Adolescent Psychiatry* 43(3): 307–15.

Masson, Sophie. 2002. "Jean-Marie Le Pen and the French Paradox." *European Business Review* 14(5): 383–89.

Mathers, Colin. 2005. "Uncertainty and Data Availability for the Global Burden of Disease Estimates, 2000–2002." http://www.who.int/healthinfo/publications/boduncertaintypaper2002.pdf.

Matic, Mislav, Sean Byrne, and Eyob Fissuh Ghebretsadik. 2007. "Awareness and Process: The Role of European Union Peace II Fund and the International Fund for Ireland in Building the Peace Dividend in Northern Ireland." *Journal of Conflict Studies* 27(1): 105–25.

Matinuddin, Kamal. 1999. *The Taliban Phenomenon: Afghanistan, 1994–1997.* Oxford: Oxford University Press.

McEvoy-Levy, Siobhán, ed. 2006. *Troublemakers or Peacemakers? Youth and Post-Accord Peace Building.* Notre Dame, IN: Notre Dame University Press.

McFarlin, Susan, William Fals-Stewart, Debra Major, and Elaine Justice. 2001. "Alcohol Use and Workplace Aggression: An Examination of Perpetration and Victimization." *Journal of Substance Abuse* 13(3): 303–21.

McGarry, John. 1998. "Political Settlements in Northern Ireland and South Africa." *Political Studies* 46(5): 1–17.

McGarry, John, and Brendan O'Leary. 1995. *Explaining Northern Ireland: Broken Images.* Cambridge, UK: Blackwell.

McLaughlin, Daniel. 1993. "Personal Narratives for School Change in Navajo Settings." In *Naming Silenced Lives: Personal Narratives and Processes of Educational Change,* edited by Daniel McLaughlin and William G. Tierney, 95–118. New York: Routledge.

Melucci, Alberto, John Keane, and Paul Mier, eds. 1989. *Nomads of the Present: Social Movements and Individual Needs in Contemporary Society.* Philadelphia: Temple University Press.

Memmi, Albert. 1967. *The Colonizer and the Colonized.* Boston: Beacon.

Merkl, Peter, and Leonard Weinberg. 1997. *The Revival of Right Wing Extremism in the 90's.* London: Frank Cass.

Merry, Sally Engle. 2006. *Human Rights and Gender Violence: Translating International Law into Social Justice.* Chicago: University of Chicago Press.

Mertus, Julie. 2008. *Bait and Switch: Human Rights and U.S. Foreign Policy.* London: Routledge.

Miall, Hugh, Tom Woodhouse, and Oliver Ramsbotham. 1999. *Contemporary Conflict Resolution: The Prevention, Management and Transformation of Deadly Conflicts.* Cambridge, UK: Polity.

Miczek, Klaus, Allan Mirsky, Gregory Carey, Joseph DeBold, and Adrian Raine. 1994. "An Overview of Biological Influence on Violent

Behavior." In *Understanding and Preventing Violence: Biobehavioral Influences,* Vol. 2, edited by Albert Reiss, Klaus Miczek, and Jeffrey Roth, 1–20. Washington, DC: National Academy Press.

Milgram, Stanley. 1974. *Obedience to Authority: An Experimental View.* New York: Harper and Row.

Miller, David. 1978. *The Queen's Rebels: Ulster Loyalism in Historical Perspective.* Dublin: University College Dublin.

Mills, Charles. 1997. *The Racial Contract.* Ithaca, NY: Cornell University Press.

Minow, Martha. 1998. "Between Vengeance and Forgiveness: South Africa's Truth and Reconciliation Commission." *Negotiation Journal* 14: 319–57.

Miranda, Dave, and Michel Claes. 2004. "Rap Music Genres and Deviant Behaviors in French-Canadian Adolescents." *Journal of Youth and Adolescents* 33(2): 113–22.

Mitchell, Kimberly, and David Finkelhor. 2001. "Risk of Crime Victimization among Youth Exposed to Domestic Violence." *Journal of Interpersonal Violence* 16(9): 944–64.

Mitrany, David. 1966. *A Working Peace System.* New York: Quadrangle Books.

Mokhiber, Russel. 1989. *Corporate Crime and Violence: Big Business Power and the Abuse of Public Trust.* San Francisco: Sierra Club Books.

Montgomery County Government. 1995. *STOP Hate/Violence Juvenile Offender Program.* Rockville, MD: Montgomery County Government.

Monti, Daniel. 1994. *Wannabe: Gangs in Suburbs and Schools.* New York: Wiley Blackwell.

Montville, Joseph. 1981. *Conflict and Peacemaking in Multiethnic Societies.* New York: Lexington Books.

Moran, Emilio. 2006. *People and Nature: An Introduction to Human Ecological Relations.* Cambridge, UK: Blackwell.

Morgenthau, Hans. 1948. *Politics Among Nations: The Struggle for Power and Peace.* New York: Knopf.

National Victim Center. 1992. *National Woman's Survey.* Washington, DC: National Victim Center and Crime Victims Research and Treatment Center, U.S. Department of Justice.

Nayak, Madhabika, Christina Byrne, Mutsumi Martin, and Anna George Abraham. 2003. "Attitudes toward Violence against Women: A Cross-Nation Study." *Sex Roles* 49(7/8): 333–42.

Nighswander, Maggie, and Jocelyn Proulx. 2007. "Children First: A Guide for Service Providers Working with Children Exposed to Family Violence." Unpublished Report for RESOLVE, University of Manitoba, Winnipeg, Manitoba.

Nordstrom, Carolyn. 2006. "The Jagged Edge of Peace: The Creation of Culture and War Orphans in Angola." In *Troublemakers or Peacemakers? Youth and Post-Accord Peace Building,* edited by Siobhán McEvoy-Levy, 117–38. Notre Dame, IN: Notre Dame University Press.

Oberschall, Anthony. 2008. *Conflict and Peace in Divided Societies: Responses to Ethnic Violence.* London: Routledge.

O'Donnell, Christopher, Angie Smith, and Jeanne Madison. 2002. Using Demographic Risk Factors to Explain Variations in the Incidence of Violence against Women. *Journal of Interpersonal Violence* 12(17): 1239–62.

Office of Democratic Institutions and Human Rights. 2006. *Hate Crimes in the OSCE Region: Incidents and Responses.* Warsaw: Organization for Security and Cooperation in Europe.

O'Leary, Brendan, and John McGarry. 1993. *The Politics of Antagonism: Understanding Northern Ireland.* Atlantic Highlands, NJ: Athlone.

———. 1997. "The Conservative Stewardship of Northern Ireland, 1979–97: Sound-Bottomed Contradictions or Slow Learning." *Political Studies* 45(3): 663–76.

Olson-Lounsberry, Marie, and Fred Pearson. 2009. *Civil Wars: Internal Struggles, Global Consequences.* Toronto: University of Toronto Press.

O'Malley, Padraig. 1992. *Biting at the Grave: The Irish Hunger Strikes and the Politics of Despair.* Boston: Houghton Mifflin.

Organski, A. F. K. 1958. *World Politics.* New York: Knopf.

Paludi, Michele, Rudy Nydegger, and Carmen Paludi. 2006. *Understanding Workplace Violence: A Guide for Managers and Employees.* Westport, CT: Praeger.

Paris, Roland. 2004. *At War's End: Building Peace after Civil Conflict.* Cambridge: Cambridge University Press.

Pearson, Fred. 2001. "Dimensions of Conflict Resolution in Ethnopolitical Disputes." *Journal of Peace Research* 38(3): 275–88.

Pearson, Fred, and Marie Olson-Lounsberry. 2009. "The Challenge of Operationalizing Key Concepts in Conflict Resolution Theory in International and Subnational Conflicts." In *Handbook of Conflict Analysis and Resolution,* edited by Dennis Sandole, Sean Byrne, Ingrid Sandole-Starosta, and Jessica Senehi, 69–82. London: Routledge.

Pearson, Fred, and Marty Rochester. 1992. *International Relations: The Global Condition in the Late Twentieth Century.* New York: McGraw-Hill.

Pence, Ellen, and Michael Paymar. 1993. *Education Groups for Men Who Batter: The Duluth Model.* New York: Springer Publishing.

Perkins, John. 2007. *Secret History of the American Empire*. London: Dutton.

Perry, Barbara. 2001. *In the Name of Hate: Understanding Hate Crimes*. New York: Routledge.

Perry, John. 2008. *Catholics and Slavery: A Compromising History*. Ottawa: Novalis.

Perryman, Mark. 2002. *Hooligan Wars: Causes and Effects of Football Violence*. Trafalgar Square: Mainstream Publishing.

Peters, W. A. 1971. *A Class Divided*. New York: Doubleday.

Philbrick, Jane Hass, Marcia Sparks, Marsha Hass, and Steven Arsenault. 2003. "Workplace Violence: The Legal Costs Can Kill You." *American Business Review* 21(1): 84–90.

Pieterse, Jan Nederveen. 1997. "Deconstructing/Reconstructing Ethnicity." *Nations and Nationalism* 3(3): 365–95.

Pilisuk, Marc. 2008. *Who Benefits from Global Violence and War: Uncovering A Destructive System*. Westport, CT: Praeger.

Pinheiro, Paulo Sergio. 2007. *UN Secretary General's Study on Violence against Children*. http://www.unviolencestudy.org/.

Polkinghorn, Brian, and Sean Byrne. 2001. "Between War and Peace: An Examination of Conflict Management Styles in Four Conflict Zones." *International Journal of Conflict Management* 12(1): 23–46.

Porritt, Jonathon, and David Winner. 1988. *The Coming of the Greens*. London: Fontana/Collins.

Power, Samantha. 2007. *A Problem from Hell: America and the Age of Genocide*. New York: Harper Perennial.

Price, Joshua M. 2002. "The Apotheosis of Home and the Maintenance of Spaces of Violence." *Hypatia* 17(4): 39–70.

Princen, Thomas. 1991. *Intermediaries in International Conflicts*. Princeton, NJ: Princeton University Press.

Prothrow-Stith, Deborah. 1991. *Deadly Consequences: How Violence Is Destroying Our Teenage Population and a Plan to Begin Solving the Problem*. New York: Harper Perrenial.

Prothrow-Stith, Deborah, and Howard Spivak. 2004. *Murder Is No Accident: Understanding and Preventing Youth Violence in America*. San Francisco: Jossey-Bass.

Raine, Adrian. 2002. "Biosocial Studies of Antisocial and Violent Behavior in Children and Adults: A Review." *Journal of Abnormal Child Psychology* 30(4): 311–26.

Ramdial, Sandra. 2002. "Conflict, Complexity and Women: Wife Battering on the Island Paradise of Trinidad." PhD dissertation,

Department of Conflict Analysis and Resolution, Nova Southeastern University.

Randall, Margaret. 1991. "Reclaiming Voices: Notes on New Female Practices in Journalism." *Latin American Perspectives* 18: 103–13.

Randall, Peter. 1997. *Adult Bullying: Perpetrators and Victims.* New York: Routledge.

Rapoport, Anatol. 1992. *Peace: An Idea Whose Time Has Come.* Ann Arbor: University of Michigan Press.

———. 1997. *The Origins of Violence: Approaches to the Study of Conflict.* New Brunswick, NJ: Transactions Publishers.

———. 1999. *Rituals and Religion in the Making of Humanity.* Cambridge: Cambridge University Press.

Raviv, Amiram, Louis Oppenheimer, and Daniel Bar-Tal, eds. 1999. *How Children Understand War and Peace: A Call for International Peace Education.* San Francisco: Jossey-Bass.

Rayburn, Nadine, Margaret Mendoza, and Gerald Davison. 2003. "Bystanders' Perceptions of Perpetrators and Victims of Hate Crime." *Journal of Interpersonal Violence* 18(9): 1055–74.

Reeves, Carol Anne. 2004. "When the Dark Side of Families Enters the Workplace." In *The Dark Side of Organizational Behavior,* edited by Rickey Griffin and Anne O'Leary-Kelly, 103–28. San Francisco: Wiley.

Reiss, Albert, and Jeffrey Roth. 1993. *Understanding and Preventing Violence,* Vol. 1. Washington, DC: National Academy Press.

Renzetti, Claire. 1992. *Violent Betrayal: Partner Abuse in Lesbian Relationships.* Newbury Park, CA: Sage.

Reza, W. K., and Ernesto Barger. 1994. *The Farm Labor Movement in the Midwest.* Austin: University of Texas.

Rice, Brian. 2011 "Relationships with Human and Non-Human Species and How They Apply toward Peace-Building and Leadership in Indigenous Societies." In *Critical Issues in Peace and Conflict Studies: Theory, Practice, and Pedagogoy,* edited by Thomas Matyok, Jessica Senehi, and Sean Byrne, 199–277. Lanham, MD: Lexington Books.

Richey, Lisa Ann. 2008. *Population Politics and Development: From the Policies to the Clinics.* London: Palgrave Macmillan.

Ridgeway, James. 1995. *Blood in the Face: The Ku Klux Klan, Aryan Nations, Nazi Skinheads, and the Rise of a New White Culture.* New York: Thunder's Mouth.

Riger, Stephanie. 2002. "The Radiating Impact of Intimate Partner Violence." *Journal of Interpersonal Violence* 17(2): 184–205.

Rogers, Carl. 1942. *Counseling and Psychotherapy.* Boston: Houghton Mifflin.

———. 1951. *Client Centered Therapy.* Boston: Houghton Mifflin.

Rogers, Kimberly Ann, and Duncan Chappell. 2003. *Preventing and Responding to Violence at Work.* Geneva: International Labor Office.

Rogers, Paul. 2007. *Towards Sustainable Security: Alternatives to the War on Terror.* London: Oxford Research Group.

———. 2008. *Why We're Losing the War on Terror.* Cambridge, UK: Polity.

Ross, Florence. 2002. "A New Age for Old Age: The Changing Paradigm of the Older Person Worldwide; Elders as Citizen Diplomats, Leaders for Social Change." PhD dissertation, Department of Conflict Analysis and Resolution, Nova Southeastern University.

———. 2003. "Call to Action to Elders Worldwide: The Need to Highlight Their Abilities, Wisdom and Compassion as Citizen Diplomats and Leaders for Social Change." *Peace and Conflict Studies* 10(1): 116–23.

Ross, Marc Howard. 1993. *The Management of Conflict: Interpretations and Interests in Comparative Perspective.* New Haven, CT: Yale University Press.

———. 1998. "Democracy as Joint Problem-Solving: Addressing Interests and Identities in Divided Societies." *Nationalism and Ethnic Politics* 4(4): 19–46.

———. 2007. *Cultural Contestation in Ethnic Conflict.* Princeton, NJ: Princeton University Press.

Rothman, Jay. 1992. *From Confrontation to Cooperation: Resolving Ethnic and Regional Conflict.* Newbury Park, CA: Sage.

———. 1997. *Resolving Identity Based Conflicts in Nations, Organizations, and Communities.* San Francisco: Jossey- Bass.

Rouhana, Nadim, and Susan Korper. 1996. "Dealing with the Dilemmas Posed by Power Asymmetry in Intergroup Conflict." *Negotiation Journal* 13(2): 353–66.

Rude, George. 1959. *The Crowd and the French Revolution.* Oxford: Oxford University Press.

Rutstein, Nathan. 1997. *Coming of Age at the Millennium: Embracing the Oneness of Human Kind.* Washington, DC: Global Classroom.

Ryan, Stephen. 2007. *The Transformation of Violent Intercommunal Conflict.* Aldershot, UK: Ashgate.

Sachs, Jeffrey. 2006. *The End of Poverty: Economic Possibilities for Our Time.* New York: Penguin.

Sahadevan, P. 1997. "Resistance to Resolution: Explaining the Intractability of Ethnic Conflict in Sri Lanka." *International Journal of Group Tensions* 27(1): 19–41.

Salter, Malcolm. 2008. *Innovation Corrupted: The Origins and Legacy of Enron's Collapse*. Boston: Harvard University Press.

Sampson, Cynthia, and John Paul Lederach, eds. 2000. *From the Ground Up: Mennonite Contributions to International Peacebuilding*. Oxford: Oxford University Press.

Sandole, Dennis. 1998. "A Comprehensive Mapping of Conflict Resolution: A Three-Pillar Approach." *Peace and Conflict Studies* 5(2): 1–25.

———. 2003. "Typology." In *Conflict: From Analysis to Intervention*, edited by Sandra Cheldelin, Daniel Druckman, and Larissa Fast, 39–55. New York: Continuum International.

Sandole, Dennis, Sean Byrne, Ingrid Sandole-Starosta, and Jessica Senehi, eds. 2009. *Handbook of Conflict Analysis and Resolution*. London: Routledge.

Saunders, Harold. 2001. *Public Peace Process: Sustained Dialogue to Transform Racial and Ethnic Conflicts*. London: Palgrave.

Schabas, William. 2001. "International Law and Response to Conflict." In *Turbulent Peace: The Challenges of Managing International Conflict*, edited by Chester Crocker, Fen Osler Hampson, and Pamela Aall, 603–18. Washington, DC: United States Institute of Peace Press.

Schell, Bernadette. 2003. "The Prevalence of Sexual Harassment, Stalking, and False Victimization Syndrome (FVS) Cases and Related Human Resource Management Policies in a Cross-Section of Canadian Companies from January 1995 through January 2000." *Journal of Family Violence* 18(6): 351–60.

Schellenberg, James. 1996. *Conflict Resolution: Theory, Research, and Practice*. Albany: State University of New York Press.

Schelling, Thomas. C. 1981. *The Strategy of Conflict*. Boston: Harvard University Press.

Schirch, Lisa. 2004. *Ritual and Symbol in Peacebuilding*. West Hartford, CT: Kumarian.

Schlosser, Eric. 2001a. *Fast Food Nation: The Dark Side of the All-American Meal*. New York: Houghton Mifflin.

———. 2001b. "The Chain Never Stops." *Mother Jones*, July–August, 1–9.

Schoenfelder, Christel. 2001. "Comment: Timeout! Prosecuting Juveniles for Sports-Related Violence and the Effect on Contact Sports." *Journal of Juvenile Law* 22(1): 139–58.

Schwartz, Michael. 2008. *War without End: The Iraq War in Context*. Chicago: Haymarket Books.

Schwerin, Edward. 1995. *Mediation, Citizen Empowerment, and Transformational Politics*. Westport, CT: Praeger.

Scimecca, Joseph A. 1991. "Conflict Resolution in the United States: The Emergence of a Profession." In *Conflict Resolution: Cross-Cultural Perspectives*, edited by Peter Black, Kevin Avruch, and Joseph Scimecca, 19–40. Westport, CT: Greenwood.

Sedlak, Andrea, Jane Mettenberg, Monica Basena, Ian Petta, Karla McPherson, Angela Greene, and Spencer Li. 2010. Fourth National Incidence Study of Child Abuse and Neglect (NIS-4): Report to Congress. Washington, DC: U.S. Department of Health and Human Services. http://www.acf.hhs.gov/programs/opre/abuse_neglect/natl_incid/index.html.

Sekulic, Dusko. 1997. "The Creation and Dissolution of the Multinational State: The Case of Yugoslavia." *Nations and Nationalism* 3(2): 165–79.

Seligman, Martin, Steven Maier, and Richard Solomon. 1971. "Unpredictable and Uncontrollable Aversive Events." In *Aversive Conditioning and Learning*, edited by F. R. Brush, 347–400. New York: Academic Press.

Senehi, Jessica. 1996. "Language, Culture and Conflict: Storytelling as a Matter of Life and Death." *Mind and Human Interaction* 7(3): 150–64.

———. 2000. "Constructive Storytelling in Inter-Communal Conflicts: Building Community, Building Peace." In *Reconcilable Differences: Turning Points in Ethnopolitical Conflict*, edited by Sean Byrne and Cynthia Irvin, Paul Dixon, Brian Polkingham, and Jessica Senehi, assoc. eds., 96–114. West Hartford, CT: Kumarian.

———. 2002. "Constructive Storytelling: A Peace Process." *Peace and Conflict Studies* 9(2): 41–63.

———. 2009a. "Building Peace: Storytelling to Transform Conflicts Constructively." In *Handbook of Conflict Analysis and Resolution*, edited by Dennis Sandole, Sean Byrne, Ingrid Sandole-Starosta, and Jessica Senehi, 199–212. London: Routledge.

———. 2009b. "The Role of Constructive, Transcultural Storytelling in Ethnopolitical Conflict Transformation in Northern Ireland." In *Regional and Ethnic Conflicts: Perspectives from the Front Lines*, edited by George Irani, Vamik Volkan, and Judy Carter, 227–37. New York: Prentice Hall.

Senehi, Jessica, and Sean Byrne. 2006. "From Violence toward Peace: The Role of Storytelling for Youth Healing and Political Empowerment after Conflict." In *Troublemakers or Peacemakers? Youth and Post-Accord Peace Building,* edited by Siobhán McEvoy-Levy, 235–58. Notre Dame, IN: University of Notre Dame Press.

Senehi, Jessica, and Marcie Hawranik. 2009. "Politics." In *Encyclopedia of Women's Folklore and Folklife,* edited by Liz Locke, Theresa Vaughan, and Pauline Greenhill, 463–69. Santa Barbara, CA: Greenwood.

Senehi, Jessica, Stephen Ryan, and Sean Byrne. 2010. "Introduction: Peacebuilding, Reconciliation and Transformation." *Peace and Conflict Studies* 17(1): 1–43.

Senese, Paul, and John Vasquez. 2008. *The Steps to War: An Empirical Study.* Princeton, NJ: Princeton University Press.

Sharp, Gene. 2005. *Waging Nonviolent Struggle: 20th Century Practice and 21st Century Potential.* Boston: Extending Horizons Books.

Sherif, Muzafer, O. J. Harvey, B. Jack White, William R. Hood, and Carolyn W. Sherif. 1961. *Intergroup Conflict and Cooperation: The Robbers Cave Experiment.* Tulsa: University of Oklahoma.

Silver, Dan. 1997. *The New Civil War: The Lesbian and Gay Struggle for Civil Rights.* Laval: Grolier.

Simon, David. 1996. *Elite Deviance.* Boston: Allyn and Bacon.

Singer, J. David. 1962. *Deterence, Arms Control, and Disarmament.* Columbus: Ohio Strategy Press.

Sislin, John, and Frederic Pearson. 2001. *Arms and Ethnic Conflict.* Boulder, CO: Rowman and Littlefield.

Skinner, B. F. 1938. *The Behavior of Organicisms.* Englewood Cliffs, NJ: Prentice Hall.

Skocpol, Theda. 1979. *States and Social Revolutions.* Cambridge: Cambridge University Press.

Smith, Anthony. 1996. "Culture, Community and Territory: The Politics of Ethnicity and Nationalism." *International Affairs* 72(3): 445–58.

Smith, Philip. 1997. "Civil Society and Violence: Narrative Forms and the Regulation of Social Conflict." In *The Web of Violence: From Interpersonal to Global,* edited by Jennifer Turpin and Lester Kurtz, 91–116. Chicago: University of Illinois Press.

Smith, Paige Hall. 2003. "A Longitudinal Perspective on Dating Violence among Adolescent and College-Age Women." *American Journal of Public Health* 93(7): 1104–9.

Smock, David, ed. 2002. *Interfaith Dialogue and Peacebuilding.* Washington, DC: United States Institute of Peace Press.

Snyder, Anna. 2003. *Setting the Agenda for Global Peace: Conflict and Consensus Building.* Aldershot, UK: Ashgate.

Sommers, Jennifer, Terry Schell, and Stephen Vodanovich. 2002. "Developing a Measure of Individual Differences in Organizational Revenge." *Journal of Business and Psychology* 17(2): 207–22.

Southern Poverty Law Center. 1999. *Ten Ways to Fight Hate: A Community Response Guide*. Montgomery, AL: Southern Poverty Law Center.

Spender, Dale. 1982. *Women of Ideas: And What Men Have Done to Them*. New York: HarperCollins.

Staub, Ervin. 1992. *The Roots of Evil: The Origins of Genocide and Other Group Violence*. Cambridge: Cambridge University Press.

Stein, Janice, David Robertson Cameron, John Ibbitson, Will Kymlicka, John Meisel, Haroon Siddiqui, and Michael Valpy. 2007. *Uneasy Partners: Multiculturalism and Rights in Canada*. Waterloo: Wilfred Laurier.

Steinberg, Stephen. 2002. *The Ethnic Myth: Race, Ethnicity, and Class in America*. Boston: Beacon.

Steinmetz, Suzanne, and Murray Straus. 1973. "The Family as Cradle of Violence." *Society* 10(6): 50–56.

Stephens, John. 1994. "Gender Conflict: Connecting Feminist Theory and Conflict Resolution Theory and Practice." In *Conflict and Gender*, edited by Judy Beinstein Miller and Anita Taylor. New York: Hampton.

Stewart, Angela J. 2004. "Victimization and Posttraumatic Stress Disorder among Homeless Adolescents." *Journal of American Academy of Child Adolescent Psychiatry* 43(3): 325–31.

Stoessinger, John. 1990. *Why Nations Go to War*. New York: St. Martin's.

Strahl, Barbara Simons. 2004. "Implementing the FORUM Program." PhD dissertation, Department of Conflict Analysis and Resolution, Nova Southeastern University.

Straker, Gill. 1992. *Faces in the Revolution: The Psychological Effects of Violence on Township Youth in South Africa*. Athens: Ohio University Press.

Strauss, Murray, and Denise Donnelly. 2000. *Beating the Devil Out of Them: Corporal Punishment in American Families*. Lanham, MD: Lexington Books.

Strobel, Warren. 2001. "Information and Conflict." In *Turbulent Peace: The Challenges of Managing International Conflict*, edited by Chester Crocker, Fen Osler Hampson, and Pamela Aall, 677–95. Washington, DC: United States Institute of Peace Press.

Stromquist, Shelton, and Marvin Bergman, eds. 1997. *Unionizing the Jungles: Labor and Community in the Twentieth-Century Meatpacking Industry*. Dubuque: University of Iowa Press.

Suall, Erwin. 1995. *Skinhead International: A Worldwide Survey of Neo-Nazi Skinheads*. New York: Anti-Defamation League of B'Nai B'Rith.

Suresh, Kanekar, and Veenapani Seksaria. 1993. "Acquaintance versus Stranger Rape: Testing the Ambiguity Reduction Hypotheses." *European Journal of Social Psychology* 23(5): 485–94.

Sylvester, Christine. 2002. *Feminist International Relations: An Unfinished Journey*. Cambridge: Cambridge University Press.

Talentino, Andrea. 2005. *Intervention After the Cold War: The Evolution of Theory and Practice*. Athens, OH: Ohio University Press.

Tangri, Sandra, Martha Burt, and Leanor Johnson. 1982. "Sexual Harassment at Work: Three Explanatory Models." *Journal of Social Issues* 38(4): 35–54.

Tickner, Ann. 1992. *Gender in International Relations: The Feminist Perspectives on Achieving Global Security*. New York: Columbia University Press.

———. 2001. *Gendering World Politics: Issues and Approaches in the Post-Cold War Era*. New York: Columbia University Press.

Tifft, Larry, and Lyn Markham. 1991. "Battering Women and Battering Central Americans: A Peacemaking Synthesis." In *Criminology as Peacemaking*, edited by Harold E. Pepinsky and Richard Quinney, 114–53. Bloomington: Indiana University Press.

Tobin, Timothy. 2001. "Organizational Determinants of Violence in the Workplace." *Aggression and Violent Behavior* 6: 91–102.

Tsing, Anna Lowenhaupt. 2005. *Friction: An Ethnography of Global Connection*. Princeton, NJ: Princeton University Press.

Tucker, Robert. 1972. *The Marx-Engels Reader*. New York: Norton.

Turner, James, and Michael Gelles. 2003. *Threat Assessment: A Risk Management Approach*. London: Routledge.

Turpin, Jennifer, and Lester Kurtz, eds. 1997. *The Web of Violence: From Interpersonal to Global*. Champaign: University of Illinois Press.

Tuso, Hamdesa. 1997. "Ethiopia: The New Political Order and Ethnic Conflict during the Post Cold War Era." *Africa Journal* 52: 343–64.

———. 1999. "Indigenous Processes of Conflict Resolution in Oromo Society." In *Traditional Cures for Modern Conflicts: African Conflict "Medicine,"* edited by William Zartman, 79–93. Boulder, CO: Lynne Rienner.

———. 2000. "Constructed on a Sand Foundation: The Crisis of U.S. Foreign Policy toward the Horn of Africa during the Post Cold War Era." *Horn of Africa Journal* 27: 19–31.

————. 2011. "Indigenous Processes of Conflict Resolution: Neglected Methods of Peacemaking by the New Field of Conflict Resolution." In *Critical Issues in Peace and Conflict Studies: Thoery, Practice, and Pedagogy*, edited by Thomas Matyok, Jessica Senehi, and Sean Byrne, 245–70. Lanmam, MD: Lexington Books.

Umbreit, M. 1995. *Mediating Interpersonal Conflicts: A Pathway to Peace.* West Concord, MN: CPI Publishing.

United Nations Children's Fund. 2008. *The State of the World's Children, 2009: Maternal and Newborn Health.* New York: United Nations Children's Fund. http://www.unicef.org/publications/files/SOWC_2009_Main__Report__03112009.pdf.

United Nations Development Fund for Women. 2007. Say No: UNiTE to Violence against Women. http://www.saynotoviolence.org/.

Ury, William. 2000. *The Third Side: Why We Fight and How We Can Stop.* New York: Penguin.

————. 2002. *Must We Fight: From the Battlefield to the Schoolyard, a New Perspective on Violent Conflict and Its Prevention.* San Francisco: Jossey-Bass.

Ury, William, Jeanne Brett, and Stephen Goldberg. 1993. *Getting Disputes Resolved: Designing Systems to Cut the Costs of Conflict.* Cambridge, MA: PON Books.

Uvin, Peter. 2004. *Human Rights and Development.* West Hartford, CT: Kumarian.

Vallee, Brian. 2007. *The War on Women: Elly Armour, Jane Hurshman, and Criminal Domestic Violence in Canadian Homes.* Toronto: Key Porter Books.

Vasquez, John. 1993. *The War Puzzle.* Cambridge: Cambridge University Press.

Vestal, Anita. 2001. "How Teacher Training in Conflict Resolution and Peace Education Influences Attitudes, Interactions and Relationships in Head Start Centres." PhD dissertation, Department of Conflict Analysis and Resolution, Nova Southeastern University.

Vickers, Margaret. 2001. "Bullying as Unacknowledged Organizational Evil: A Researcher's Story." *Employee Responsibility and Rights Journal* 13(4): 205–17.

Vogler, Richard. 1991. *Reading the Riot Act: The Magistracy, the Police, and the Army in Civil Disobedience.* New York: McGraw-Hill.

Volkan, Vamik. 1992. "Psychological Dimensions of Conflict: Redefining Our Approach to Ethnic Conflicts by Taking a Psychological Point of View." Working Paper Series. Atlanta: Carter Center of Emory University.

———. 1998. *Blood Lines: From Ethnic Pride to Ethnic Terrorism.* Boulder, CO: Westview.

Vygotsky, Lev S. 1978. "Thinking and Speech." In *The Collected Works of Lev S. Vygotsky,* edited by Robert W. Rieber and Aaron S. Cartin, 1–150. New York: Plenum.

Wadley, Susan Snow. 1994. *Struggling with Destiny in Karimpur, 1925–1984.* Berkeley: University of California Press.

Walker, Lenore. 2000. *The Battered Woman Syndrome.* New York: Springer.

Wall, Edmund. 2000. *Sexual Harassment: Confrontations and Decisions.* Amherst, NY: Prometheus Books.

Wallach, John. 2000. *The Enemy Has a Face: The Seeds of Peace Experience.* Washington, DC: United States Institute of Peace.

Wallensteen, Peter, ed. 2002. *Understanding Conflict Resolution: War, Peace and the Global System.* Thousand Oaks, CA: Sage.

Wallerstein, Immanuel. 2004. *World Systems Analysis: An Introduction.* Raleigh, NC: Duke University Press.

Waltz, Kenneth. 1957. *Man, the State and War.* New York: Colombia University Press.

Walzer, Michael, ed. 1995. *Toward a Global Civil Society.* Oxford: Berghahn Books.

Wartenberg, Thomas. 1990. *The Forms of Power: From Domination to Transformation.* Philadelphia: Temple University Press.

Warters, William. 1986. "Treatment of the Male Batterer: An Overview of the Field." Unpublished paper.

Watson, Gavin. 2001. *Skins.* Kingston, Ontario: Olmstead.

Watts, Meredith. 2001. "Aggressive Youth Cultures and Hate Crime." *American Behavioral Scientist* 45(4): 600–615.

Webel, Charles, and Johan Galtung, eds. 2007. *Handbook of Peace and Conflict Studies.* Thousand Oaks, CA: Sage.

Welch, Michael. 2003. "Moral Panic over Youth Violence: Wilding and the Manufacture of Menace in the Media." *Youth and Society* 34(1): 3–30.

Wessells, Michael. 2006. *Child Soldiers: From Violence to Protection.* Cambridge: Harvard University Press.

Wessells, Michael, and Davidson Jonah. 2006. "Recruitment and Reintegration of Former Youth Soldiers in Sierra Leone: Challenges of Reconciliation and Post-Accord Peace Building." In *Troublemakers or Peacemakers? Youth and Post-Accord Peace Building,* edited by Siobhán McEvoy-Levy, 27–48. Notre Dame, IN: Notre Dame University Press.

West, Cornel. 1990. "The New Cultural Politics of Difference." In *Out There: Marginalization and Contemporary Cultures*, edited by Russell Furguson. New York: New Museum of Contemporary Art.

———. 1994. *Keeping Faith: Philosophy and Race in America*. New York: Routledge.

———. 2001. *Race Matters*. New York: Vintage Books.

White, Ralph. 1996. "Why the Serbs Fought: Motives and Misperceptions." *Peace and Conflict: Journal of Peace Psychology* 2(2): 109–28.

Whyte, John. 1990. *Interpreting Northern Ireland*. Oxford: Clarendon.

Williams, Mary, ed. 1999. *Child Labor and Sweatshops*. San Diego: Greenhaven.

Wilmer, Franke. 2002. *The Social Construction of Man, the State, and War: Identity, Conflict, and Violence in Former Yugoslavia*. London: Routledge.

Wilson, Warren. 2006. *Tied to the Great Packing Machine: The Midwest and Meatpacking*. Des Moines: University of Iowa Press.

Wiseman, Jacqueline. 1979. *Stations of the Lost: The Treatment of Skid Row Alcoholics*. Chicago: University of Chicago Press.

Wittkopf, Eugene. 1994. *The Future of American Foreign Policy*. New York: Palgrave.

Wodarski, John, and Catherine Dulmus. 2002. "Preventing Workplace Violence." In *Handbook of Violence*, edited by Lisa Rapp-Paglicci, Albert Roberts, and John Wodarski, 349–77. Hoboken, NJ: Wiley.

Wolff, Stefan. 2006. *Ethnic Conflict: A Global Perspective*. Oxford: Oxford University Press.

Woolpert, Stephen, Christa Daryl Slaton, and Edward Schwerin, eds. 1998. *Transforational Politics: Theory, Study, and Practice*. Albany: State University of New York Press.

World Health Organization. 2004. *The Economic Dimensions of Interpersonal Violence*. Geneva: World Health Organization. whqlibdoc.who.int/publications/2004/9241591609.pdf.

———. 2005. *WHO Multi-Country Study on Women's Health and Domestic Violence against Women*. Geneva: World Health Organization.

Wrong, Dennis. 1995. *Power: Its Forms, Bases and Uses*. New Brunswick, NJ: Transaction Publishers.

Yoder, Kevin. 2003. "Gang Involvement and Membership among Homeless and Runaway Youth." *Youth and Society* 344(4): 411–67.

Youngs, Gillian. 2003. "Private Pain/Public Peace: Women's Rights as Human Rights and Amnesty International's Report on Violence against Women." *Journal of Women in Culture and Society* 4(28): 1209–29.

Zagar, Mitja. 2000. "Yugoslavia: What Went Wrong? Constitutional Development and Collapse of a Multiethnic State." In *Reconcilable Differences: Turning Points in Ethnopolitical Conflict,* edited by Sean Byrne and Cynthia Irvin, Paul Dixon, Brian Polkingham, and Jessica Senehi, assoc. eds., 127–53. West Hartford, CT: Kumarian.

Zariski, Raphael. 1989. "Ethnic Extremism among Ethnoterritorial Minorities in Western Europe: Dimensions, Causes, and Institutional Responses." *Comparative Politics* 21(3): 1–25.

Zartman, William. 1995. *Elusive Peace: Negotiating an End to Civil Wars.* Washington, DC: Brookings Institute.

Ziegler, David. 2001. *War, Peace and International Politics.* New York: Addison Wesley Longman.

Ziegler, Warren. 1995. *Ways of Enspiriting: Transformative Practices for the Twenty-First Century.* Denver, CO: FIA International.

Zimbardo, P. G. 1974. "On the Ethics of Intervention in Human Psychological Research: With Special Reference to the Stanford Prison Experiment." *Cognition* 2(1): 243–56.

Zimring, Franklin. 1998. *American Youth Violence.* New York: Oxford University Press.

# Index

children (*cont'd*)
  role models for, 9, 116, 222
  sexualization of, 79
  soldiers, 55, 63, 213
  *See also* domestic violence; youth
    violence
colonialism:
  and economic development, 151, 174
  and ethnopolitical conflicts, 146–47
  and Eurocentrism, 168
  and former colonies, 109
  and indigenous culture, 210
  participation of colonized in, 202
  and privilege, 145
community-based intervention
    programs, 63–65
conflict. *See* ethnopolitical conflicts;
    war culture
conflict resolution:
  by adolescents, 46, 47, 56
  and aggression, 38–39
  by citizens, 155
  and corporate violence, 131
  culture of, 40
  by elders, 39
  and indigenous businesses, 212
  international, images of, 181
  nonviolent, 3, 6
  in PACS theory, 207, 220
  and peace building, 140, 163, 220
  in political psychology, 28
  in science of peace, 41
  training in, 63, 66, 69, 96, 132,
    157–58, 159, 162, 205, 213
  violence as, 92
  for youth violence, 68–71
consciousness-raising, 202, 206, 208
Convention on the Elimination of All
    Forms of Discrimination against
    Women (CEDAW), 95
corporate violence, 122–31
  and citizens, 132

and conflict resolution, 131
interventions, 131–35
organizational culture, 134–35
*See also* workplace violence
Cyprus conflict, 141–45

Daiute, Colette, 70
Declaration of Schlaining, 118
Deraps, Bud, 210
development, responsible, 187
diplomacy:
  citizen, 155–57
  and educators, 157–58
  and external actors, 161–62
  and media, 160
  and military peacekeepers, 162
  multitrack, 154–55
  and NGOs, 158–59
  and public/private sector, 159–60
  and religious leaders, 160–61
domestic violence:
  and culture, 94–95
  cycle of battering, 88
  effect on children, 47, 53–54, 78,
    83–86, 88–90
  elder abuse, 91, 96
  factors in, 78
  intervention, 85, 86, 91–97
  and isolation, 87–88
  resources for, 85
  in same-sex relationships, 77
  sibling violence, 90–91
  state laws, 95
  statistics, 81–82, 85, 86, 87, 89–90
  as structural violence, 76, 83, 97
  types of, 86
  *See also* sexual violence
Duluth Model of intervention, 93
Duvalier, Jean-Claude "Baby Doc," 194

ecological framework, 17–18
environmental influences, 17

ECSC. *See* European Coal and Steel
Community
Edelman, Marian Wright, 39
EEC. *See* European Economic
Community
ego, 19
elder abuse, 91, 96
elders and social change, 39
Elliot, Jane, 25
emotional relearning, 32–34
employment and training intervention
programs, 67–68
Enron, 121
environmental pollution, 122, 129, 188,
208
eros, 20
ethnic hate crimes. *See* racial/ethnic
hate crimes
ethnopolitical conflicts, 139–40
and citizen diplomats, 155–57
demographic factors, 152–53
early warning contingency, 144
economic factors, 150–52, 159
and educators, 157–58
and elites, 146–47
evolution of, 142–43
example of, 138
and external actors, 161–62, 169
historical factors, 145–47
and identity, 147, 148–49, 150, 151,
152
internal, 149
interventions, 153–62
and media, 160
and military peacekeepers, 162
multitrack diplomacy, 153–54
and NGOs, 158–59
over common territory, 152–53
and political elites, 154–55
political factors, 149–50
psychocultural factors, 147–48
public/private investment and,

159–60
religious factors, 148–49
and religious leaders, 160–61
and sanctions, 151–52
social forces of, 141
ethnoviolence. *See* hate crimes
EthnoWatch, 163
EU. *See* European Union
Eurocentrism, 168
European Coal and Steel Community
(ECSC), 183–84
European Economic Community
(EEC), 184–84
European Union (EU), 18, 145, 183–84,
189
Exxon *Valdez* oil spill, 129

family intervention programs, 67
Fanon, Frantz, 20
feminism:
criticism of Freud, 19
criticism of patriarchy, 19, 39, 87
criticism of realism, 167
on demilitarism of masculinity, 168
on disempowered groups, 196
theory of violence, 39–40
Fisher, Ron, 28
Foucault, Michel, 195
Frankl, Victor, 26
Freire, Paulo, 195, 202, 208
Freud, Sigmund, 19–21
frustration aggression theory, 22

Galtung, Johan, 4, 6–7, 34, 35–36, 160,
206, 223
Gandhi, Mohandas K. (Mahatma),
41–42, 204, 206, 207, 208, 222
gangs and youth violence, 48, 56–60
GATT. *See* General Agreement on
Tariffs and Trade
General Agreement on Tariffs and
Trade (GATT), 187

media:
    on corporate violence, 124
    and ethnopolitical conflicts, 160
    and youth violence, 53, 54
migrant workers, 125
Milgram, Stanley, 24
militarism, 87, 167, 168, 176, 215. *See also*
    war culture
military peacekeepers, 162
minority males and violence, 60–62
MNCs. *See* multinational corporations
Mooney, Cyril (Sister), 211
multinational corporations (MNCs),
    159, 169, 187
multitrack diplomacy, 153–54
mutual respect, 96, 134, 199–201

NAFTA. *See* North American Free
    Trade Agreement
nationalism:
    ethnic, 139, 151, 152
    and European Union, 184
    and exclusion, 108, 139, 145, 152
    and globalization, 170
    liberation/repression via, 176
    and power, 28, 167
    and world government, 189
    and xenophobia, 177
National Incidence Study of Child
    Abuse and Neglect, Fourth
    (NIS-4), 89
negative peace, 12, 36, 186, 219
neo-Fascist hate crimes, 113–14, 117
new international economic order
    (NIEO), 174, 187, 211
New World Order, 191
NFZs. *See* Nuclear-free zones
NGOs. *See* nongovernmental
    organizations
NIEO. *See* new international economic
    order
NIS-4. *See* National Incidence Study

of Child Abuse and Neglect,
    Fourth
nongovernmental organizations
    (NGOs):
    on disease, 188
    and ethnopolitical conflicts,
        158–59
    on human rights, 214
    on international law, 188
    intervention by, 161, 163
    on nuclear weapons, 185–86
    and peace process, 161, 222
    principles of, 213
    and public support, 95
    and sanctions, 152
    and socioeconomic development,
        212
    *See also* specific organizations
nonviolence:
    as active process, 202–5
    approaches, 2
    civilian-based, 185
    and human rights, 199
    and mutual respect, 199–200
    PACS on, 6, 17
    personal responsibility, 205–8
    as prevention goal, 196
    vs. proviolent attitudes, 222
    *See also* peace
North American Free Trade Agreement
    (NAFTA), 189, 211
Nuclear-free zones (NFZs), 186
Nuclear Non-Proliferation Treaty, 186

Office of Democratic Institutions and
    Human Rights (Europe), 106
O'Flaherty, Hugh, 210
OPEC. *See* Organization of Petroleum
    Exporting Countries
Organization for Security and
    Cooperation in Europe (OSCE),
    106

Organization of Petroleum Exporting
    Countries (OPEC), 61, 182, 187

Victim Offender Restorative Program (VORP), 65
violence:
    and aggression, 8–10
    analysis of, 16
    complexity of, 9, 12, 15–16
    costs of, 8
    cultural definitions of, 220–21
    direct vs. structural, 34–35
    in international conflicts, 92–93
    lessons from study of, 220–23
    levels of, 4–5
    micro-macro linkage in, 16
    nature of, 117
    as pervasive, 2, 3
    and power, 7, 76
    as problem-solving, 76, 92
    and social aggression, 8–10
    sources of, 10
    structural, 34–37, 54, 56, 76
    systems/structures, 3–5
    theories of, 18
    web of, 7–8, 17–18, 219
    *See also* specific theories; specific types of violence
Violence Outreach in Communities through Education and Services (VOICES), 96
VOICES. *See* Violence Outreach in Communities through Education and Services
VORP. *See* Victim Offender Restorative Program

Waltz, Kenneth, 171
war culture, 5, 87
    causes, 170–71
    costs, 171
    and Fascism, 178
    identity in, 168
    individual-level analysis of, 173, 179–80

and individual/state, 168
new war, 170
and rape, 77, 81
state-level analysis of, 172, 176–78
systems-level analysis of, 171–75
and youth violence, 55–56
war prevention:
    and development, 188
    and income redistribution, 187
    and integration, 183–84
    and interdependence, 180–83
    and international organizations, 189–90
    and international security, 185–87
    and new social movements, 184–85
weapons, destruction of, 93
white collar crime. *See* corporate violence
WHO. *See* World Health Organization
wife battering. *See* domestic violence
Witty, Cathie, 96
women:
    and consciousness-raising, 202
    elder abuse of, 91
    and equality/inequality, 76, 93, 95, 185
    gender roles of, 168
    incarcerated, 83, 92
    marginalization of, 87, 153
    media on, 53
    participation in violence, 3, 36
    and patriarchal dominance, 39–40, 87, 95, 168, 191
    and peacemaking, 40
    perceptions of, 92, 94, 95
    pregnancy and death, 80–81
    rights, 101, 212
    sexualization of, 79
    *See also* domestic violence; rape; sexual violence
workplace violence, 123–31
    bullying, 130

workplace violence, (*cont'd*)
    injuries, 126
    interventions, 131–35, 136
    random acts, 131
    sexual harassment, 129–30
    statistics, 127–28
    violent employees, 129–30, 133
World Bank, 169, 187
World Health Organization (WHO),
    47–48, 81, 188
World Trade Center attacks. *See*
    September 11 terrorist attacks
World Trade Organization (WTO), 187
WTO. *See* World Trade Organization

Yoder, Kevin, 58
youth violence:
    causes of, 47–55
    community-based programs, 63–65
    death/injury statistics, 47–48, 53, 56
    employment/training programs,
      67–68
    factors in, 49

    family intervention programs, 67
    gangs, 48, 56–60
    and gender, 46
    high-risk youth program, 63
    and home life, 53–54, 78
    intervention/prevention of, 49,
      62–71
    minority males, 54, 60–62
    nature of, 6
    peace education, 68–71
    political, 55–56
    and popular music, 54
    and poverty, 51–52
    and role models, 52–53
    role of media, 53, 54
    school-based programs, 65–66
    in schools, 50–51, 59
    and social cruelty, 50
    and socialization, 59
    structural, 54, 56
    types of, 49

Zimbardo, Philip, 24

CPSIA information can be obtained
at www.ICGtesting.com
Printed in the USA
LVHW111750070822
725304LV00003B/8

9 780896 802858